Using Literature with Young Children

Using Literature with Young Children

Fourth Edition

Betty Coody

Lamar University • Beaumont, Texas

 Wm. C. Brown Publishers

Book Team

Editor *Paul L. Tavenner*
Developmental Editor *Sue Pulvermacher-Alt*
Production Coordinator *Deborah Donner*

 Wm. C. Brown Publishers

President *G. Franklin Lewis*
Vice President, Publisher *Thomas E. Doran*
Vice President, Operations and Production *Beverly Kolz*
National Sales Manager *Virginia S. Moffat*
Group Sales Manager *John Finn*
Associate Executive Editor *Edgar J. Laube*
Senior Marketing Manager *Kathy Law Laube*
Managing Editor, Production *Colleen A. Yonda*
Manager of Visuals and Design *Faye M. Schilling*
Production Editorial Manager *Julie A. Kennedy*
Production Editorial Manager *Ann Fuerste*
Publishing Services Manager *Karen J. Slaght*

WCB Group

President and Chief Executive Officer *Mark C. Falb*
Chairman of the Board *Wm. C. Brown*

Cover design by Benoit & Associates

Cover photo by Peter G. Christie

Library of Congress Catalog Card Number: 90–84416

ISBN 0–697–10086–3

Printed in the United States of America by Wm. C. Brown Publishers, 2460 Kerper Boulevard, Dubuque, IA 52001

10 9 8 7 6 5 4 3 2

To Dr. M. L. McLaughlin, who encouraged me to write

contents

preface

For more than sixteen years, *Using Literature with Young Children* has been remarkably popular with college students who are preparing to teach at the preschool and primary levels. Based on comments and suggestions from those students and their professors, the fourth edition adheres to the dual purpose of its predecessors: to acquaint prospective teachers with some of the best literature available for use with children from one to eight years of age, and to offer a sound methodology in using books to enrich the lives of children.

I believe that children at the prereading and beginning reading stages have special needs in literature. Children are more highly formative at this age than they will ever be again. Their taste in literature is being developed daily, and their attitudes toward reading are being formulated—attitudes that will remain with them throughout life. For these reasons, it is extremely important that young children become involved with the best books that parents and teachers can find. More children's books than ever are being published and the quality of writing and illustration is continually improving. Some four hundred books are reviewed in this fourth edition along with suggestions for using them in creative ways.

Since *Using Literature with Young Children* concentrates solely on literature for preschool and primary children (Grades 1 through 3), it is recommended as a supplementary textbook for courses in early childhood education, as well as courses in children's literature, language arts, and reading. Numerous college teachers, classroom teachers, and students have offered suggestions for improving the book to make it more helpful as a teaching guide. The following new features in the fourth edition reflect their ideas:

1. Some one hundred additional reviews of children's books with suggestions for their use, plus the necessary ordering information.

2. A new chapter that builds a case for viewing the daily newspaper as literature. Suggestions are given for teaching a "Newspaper in the Classroom" unit at the primary level.

3. An expanded chapter on holiday lore includes Hanukkah, St. Patrick's Day, and Cinco de Mayo. These holidays were added at the request of primary teachers who feel the need for more information to use in celebrating them in the classroom.

4. More than forty new black and white photographs with captions that offer additional information and teaching procedures.

5. New line drawings that provide step-by-step directions for constructing materials to accompany the literature program.

6. Extension of the art chapter to include more books that stimulate arts and crafts activities plus a discussion of art appreciation and museum-going.

7. A discussion of the role of parents and grandparents as storytellers and their part in transmitting cultural values to children by means of storytelling.

8. An updated bibliography of related professional books at the end of each chapter.

I am grateful to the people who helped so generously in the preparation of this manuscript. My husband, H. L. Coody, has always been my best friend and support. Now that he is retired, he has been involved in every aspect of this project. The outstanding contributions of Barbara Ellis speak for themselves. As an art teacher at Brooke Elementary School in Austin, Texas, she practices what I preach and improves on it. She is responsible for all the lovely line drawings in the book. Lori Ivins did a splendid job of typing the final manuscript, and she did so while caring for three small children at home. Juanita and Gene Conley, next-door neighbors, made coffee every afternoon and gave me a welcome break from writing and research.

A special appreciation is extended to the reviewers of this fourth edition—Jerry Hill, Central State University; Reba Pinney, Ohio University; Vicki Olson, Augsburg College; Thomas Sherman, Winona State University; and Joanne Bernstein, Brooklyn College. Their insights and suggestions have been invaluable.

I am especially indebted to the graduate students in my foreign studies classes. For the past ten years I have traveled with them throughout Europe and most of our time has been spent in studying literature. I am constantly impressed with the creative ways they use children's literature to enrich the elementary curriculum. Their ideas are reflected throughout the book.

Betty Coody

1

"Read It Again":

Books for Reading Aloud

Research suggests that a person's success in reading depends largely on experiences with literature that take place during the preschool years at home and the first few years of school. Unless wholesome attitudes toward books and reading are developed during the formative years of early childhood, it is extremely unlikely that a child will grow into a reading adult. Such a person may be able to read at a basic, pragmatic level, but the ability to read efficiently for both pleasure and information in all kinds of material has to be built systematically over a period of years. This ability must be nourished by parents and teachers all along the way.

It is ironic that at a time when a book has its greatest impact, the child is almost completely at the mercy of adult choices. Parents, teachers, librarians, and other adults select the books and decide how they will be used. In the process, too many children are forced to exist on an impoverished literary diet. This is not an argument for young children to be given complete freedom of self-selection in literature. It is, on the contrary, a plea for parents and teachers to acquaint themselves with the best in children's books and to use a variety of experiences that will foster a lifelong enjoyment of literature.

More schools nationwide are now turning toward literature-based reading programs as a backlash against the quantifying of reading into hundreds of small, measurable skills. The fragmented reading programs that resulted from so many tedious drills and paper and pencil exercises actually turned children against reading. They were unable to see the main purpose for reading, which is to read for pleasure, information, and survival. But the pendulum has swung back, and the future looks bright indeed for young children and their teachers.

In literature selection, teachers are in a unique and crucial position. They know the children in the classroom as no writer or illustrator can ever know them. It is essential, therefore, that they preview and study children's books, read the reviews of critics, seek out the opinions of librarians, and enroll in literature and reading classes. It is their responsibility, and privilege, to select those books that best fit the needs of the children they teach.

A sound concept of reading readiness and beginning reading should be equated with a rich program of literature that includes reading aloud, storytelling, dramatization, creative writing, art activities, and other book-related experiences that deeply involve children with excellent literature on a day-to-day basis. This book has been designed to assist teachers and parents who are responsible for carrying out such an important task.

Types of Literature for Young Children

Young children begin to look at reading as a necessary and integral part of their lives when respected adults are skillful at sharing good literature with them. Parents and teachers should recognize that reading aloud is the way the prereading child is led into the world of books. Listening to someone read aloud should be considered not only as an indication of reading readiness but also as reading in the fullest sense of the word. The child studies the pictures and follows the story line as the adult unlocks the printed symbols for him or her. Both are engrossed in the reading process.

In selecting books for reading aloud to young children at home or at school, Leland Jacobs has developed a set of criteria to guide adults:

1. The story should have a fresh well-paced plot.
2. It must have unique individuality.
3. It should contain plausible, direct conversation.
4. It must have well-delineated characters.
5. The story must have an authentic outcome.[1]

Moreover, the adult should select books having one main plot, a rousing climax, and a fairly predictable outcome. Other features young children prefer in their literature are action, conflict, heroic characters, and tongue-teasing language. They also want illustrations that are perfectly synchronized with the text.

In choosing books to read aloud to young children, it is necessary to consider the various categories of literature that are recommended for the early childhood library. Since there is seldom enough money to buy

---

1. Leland B. Jacobs, "Children's Experiences in Literature," *Children and the Language Arts,* eds. Virgil E. Herrick and Leland B. Jacobs. (Englewood Cliffs, N.J.: Prentice-Hall, Inc., 1975), p. 194.

Figure 1.1.   Ruth Chambers
wheels one-year-old Chin Betancourt
in a wheelbarrow near Homestead,
Florida, while Chin studies up on
more advanced methods of
transportation (AP Laserphoto),
Photographer Kathy Willens.
(Courtesy of World Wide Photos.)

all the desired books at one time, a satisfactory plan is to develop priority
lists in which certain books are purchased from different classifications
until a varied collection has been acquired. Even a small collection can
be a well-balanced one. Examples of each type of literature found in the
following categories are reviewed at the end of the chapter.

Mother Goose.   The humanism, the fun and nonsense, the high adventure, and the rhythmic language of Mother Goose stories have strong
appeal for each generation of children. These old folk rhymes have been
called the perfect literature for early childhood. As many editions of
Mother Goose as the budget will allow should be provided for the classroom. In addition to books, children enjoy puzzles, art prints, pillows,
figurines, filmstrips, and other materials that depict their favorite Mother
Goose characters (fig. 1.2).

Alphabet Books.   ABC books are used by parents and teachers to
entertain children and to familiarize them with letters of the alphabet
and the sound that each letter represents. ABC books may be illustrated
by means of photographs, realistic paintings, or semiabstract art. Pur-
chasers of ABC books should make certain that each letter of the alphabet

Figure 1.2.   An attractive bulletin board designed to encourage browsing through a supply of Mother Goose books.

is represented by meaningful objects. Only one or two objects should be presented on each page and the letter should stand out in bold relief.

Counting Books.   Counting books are used to present a few basic mathematical concepts and the symbols that represent them. Number books are a necessary part of the early childhood library because they afford the most enjoyable means of acquainting young children with the language of mathematics.

A counting book should have the same high quality artwork that is expected in other kinds of literature for children. Each numeral should have a prominent place on its own page. Shapes and forms used to represent the concept of the numeral should be balanced and spaced on the page to avoid clutter and confusion.

Concept Books.   Concept books are designed to help young children develop the ability to generalize and conceptualize. Abstract ideas such as size, shape, speed, and weight are presented in graphic, artistic form. Teachers usually find it best to read concept books aloud to small groups or to individual children, and to explain and clarify as they go. Concept books must be chosen with care to coincide with the maturity level of the children.

Machines Personified.   Machines personified refers to books in which machines and other inanimate objects are endowed with human qualities by the author and illustrator. The stories are often inspirational in nature, since the plot is built around some staggering, overwhelming task to be accomplished by the machine. Success is always realized and the happy ending leaves the reader or listener with a sense of deep satisfaction.

Animal Stories.   Most animal stories preferred by the youngest children are of the "talking beast tale" variety. These are stories in which the beasts are more human than animal. They work, play, laugh, cry, make foolish mistakes, and perform acts of kindness and wisdom. Children rank them at the top among stories they prefer to have read again and again. James Moffett explains why an animal story like "The Three Billy Goats Gruff" satisfies a young child's desire for novelty and excitement, while at the same time organizes experience in reassuring and resolving ways:

> An ogre tries to eat up anyone who crosses his bridge to graze on the pleasant slopes beyond. Between us and the attainment of our desires lie frightful dangers that we cannot go around. The smallest billy goat encounters the ogre and persuades him to spare his life in favor of eating the larger goat to come. The second billy goat gets by the same way, and the third tears the ogre apart (into a satisfying number of small pieces). The three goats reach and enjoy the pasture. If you're weak and helpless, a child, you can refer the danger to Mother, who, if she cannot cope with it, can refer it to Daddy. *Some* "big person" will come along who is capable of overcoming the forces of evil and ensuring that you get what you have to have without being destroyed in the process. The small are backed up by the mighty, but you may have to make shift with a stratagem of your own. And you have to play on your size, not deny it.[2]

Talking beast tales are, of course, perfect for storytelling as well as for reading aloud and can be told with a minimum of memorization.

Humor and Nonsense Books.   Books from all classifications may be considered humorous books if they make children laugh. One of the basic needs of all children, as well as adults, is the need for change, and a delightful way to enjoy the therapy that comes with change is to read a book made up of humor and nonsense. If children fail to see the humor in a book, it should be reserved for a later date. Perhaps with more maturity they will be able to enjoy the wit intended by the author. Plenty of humorous books are available, guaranteed to make children laugh. There is no need to dwell on a book beyond their understanding (fig. 1.3).

---

2. James Moffett, *A Student-Centered Language Arts Curriculum, Grades K-12: A Handbook for Teachers* (Boston: Houghton Mifflin Co., 1968), pp. 117–18.

Figure 1.3.   Curious George copes with
familiar problems, accomplishes difficult tasks,
and, in general, helps children understand
themselves. (Display Courtesy Lamar University,
Beaumont, Texas.)

Picture Books.   Picture books are those in which the pictures play
such important roles that the text would be incomplete without them.
The favorite picture books of young children are the ones in which the
pictures carry the story so well that even a prereading child can follow
along. The text used in a picture book must be read aloud to beginning
readers, since the readability level is usually about third grade.

The Caldecott Award is presented each year to "the artist of the most
distinguished American picture book for children." The winning book
is selected by a special committee of the Association for Library Service
to Children of the American Library Association. A complete list of the
Caldecott medal books, the artist and publisher of each one, and the year
the award was conferred is presented in Appendix A (fig. 1.4).

Easy-to-Read Books.   Books classified as easy-to-read employ a
controlled vocabulary of frequently used words. Only a few words are
used and they are repeated throughout the text. The print is large and
surrounded by ample white space. Pictures are used to help tell the story,
and the text embodies a great deal of conversation. All these features are
combined to make a book that is entertaining, informational, and, above
all, easy to read. Any child who can read fluently at the primer level should
be able to cope with most of the easy-to-read books (fig. 1.5).

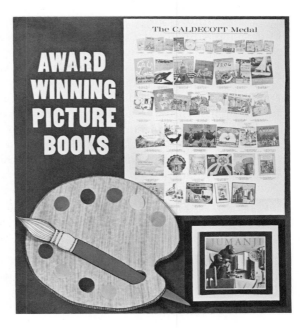

Figure 1.4. A collection of Caldecott books in the classroom is comparable to providing a permanent art gallery for children. Posters and bulletin boards enhance the collection.

So Mother Bear made something

for Little Bear.

"See, Little Bear," she said,

"I have something for my little bear.

Here it is.

Figure 1.5. A typical page from *Little Bear,* written by Else Minarik and illustrated by Maurice Sendak, shows the features that make a book easy to read. (Text and illustration on p. 12 in *Little Bear* by Else Minarik, Pictures by Maurice Sendak. Text copyright © 1957 by Maurice Sendak. By permission of Harper & Row, Publishers, Inc.)

Participation Books.   Just as the name implies, participation books are designed to involve a child in the sensory experiences of looking, feeling, patting, and smelling. They also provide challenging mental tasks of finding visual clues, solving problems, and making choices.

A participation or manipulative book may seem more like a toy or game than a book, and young children are fascinated by them. They also seem to be irresistible to adults who see them on bookstore shelves.

Because of their instant appeal to toddlers, participation books are excellent to use as "first" books to introduce a child to literature. They are best used in a one-to-one situation, with the adult letting the child set a leisurely pace.

Participation books are often used by teachers to lure into books those kindergarten and primary children who have not learned to care for literature. These books are also considered the best material to use with those children who for some reason have developed an aversion to books.

Informational Books.   All children have a need to know, and information books of all types are needed to fulfill this basic curiosity. Hundreds of books are published each year in all areas of art, science, and social studies. There are also reference books, encyclopedias, handbooks, and how-to-do-it books. The problem lies not in a shortage of informational books, but in selecting those of quality.

Authors of informational books for children must be extremely knowledgeable in the particular field and also expert at putting complex concepts and terms into language young children can understand without having it sound watered down or condescending.

Used frequently, in appropriate ways, outstanding informational books have the power to develop in young children a scientific mind and an inquiring outlook on life—an insatiable interest in finding out the how and why of things (figs. 1.6 and 1.7).

The Library Center

A book corner containing a variety of books attractively arranged can well become a calm and quiet oasis in a busy classroom. Some teachers set the book center apart with a small rug. Others screen it off with low bookshelves or with an enticing bulletin board (figs. 1.8 and 1.9). A reading table and comfortable slipcovered chairs should be provided for the center. A child-sized rocking chair is a popular item in the library corner.

Figure 1.6. Informational books are used as the basic ingredient in effective learning centers. The science book featured here is *Life on a Giant Cactus* by Patricia Lauber. Note the sand paper letters in keeping with a desert theme. (Courtesy of Barbara Ellis.)

Figure 1.7. Following a study of mythological creatures, students constructed an eight-foot rendition of Bigfoot. Note fur made of cutout handprints. References were *Bigfoot* by Ian Thorne and *Encyclopedia of Legendary Creatures* by Tom McGovern.

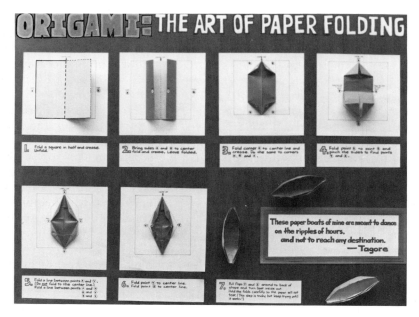

Figure 1.8.   A collection of "how to do it" origami books inspired a bulletin board that combines functional reading with a moving poem. The poem is from *Fireflies* by Rabindranath Tagore. (From *Fireflies* by Rabindranath Tagore, illustrated by Boris Artzybasheff. Copyright © 1928 by Macmillan Publishing Co., Inc., renewed 1956 by Rabindranath Tagore. Reprinted by permission of Macmillan Publishing Co., Inc.)

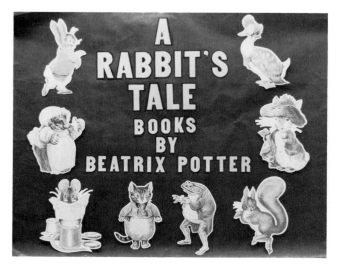

Figure 1.9.   Cardboard cutouts arranged on a bulletin board introduce children to the characters in Beatrix Potter's books. (Courtesy of Barbara Ellis.)

A neat, well-organized library center is always attractive because the books themselves are works of art, but a few green plants, some choice art prints, and a piece of good sculpture that has child appeal will definitely add to its beauty. Any effort that goes into making the classroom library an inviting spot will pay rich dividends in reading achievement and in reading interest (fig. 1.10).

Because the library center should be the quietest and most private area in the classroom, it is wise to locate it out of the line of traffic. On the other hand, such a location can cause a lighting problem. To avoid a gloomy, dreary book corner, provide a table lamp in addition to the traditional classroom lighting if necessary.

It is essential to display many of the books face out. The spine means nothing to a child who cannot yet read, and very little to a beginning reader. Shelves should be wide and deep enough to hold the oversized picture books with their covers showing. Book jackets are designed to invite browsing. If the jacket is hidden or removed, the value of its sales appeal is lost. Some books, of course, are displayed flat on the table, others standing in book racks. Some books should be kept in a cabinet to be brought out on special occasions. This is especially true of holiday books, seasonal books, books with limited appeal, and perhaps books held on reserve for use as bibliotherapy (fig. 1.11).

Figure 1.10.   A collection of figurines makes Beatrix Potter's small books even more appealing to young children.

Figure 1.11.   An attractive, functional library center is the most important feature of the kindergarten and primary classroom. (Courtesy of Barbara Ellis.)

Using an Interest Inventory in Book Selection

To guarantee that books selected for the classroom library center are those that young children want to hear read aloud and to read for themselves, the teacher would be wise to use such aids as recommended lists, personal observation, and informal questioning to determine students' preferences. The following questions constitute an interest inventory to be given orally to individuals or small groups of children:

1. What is the name of your favorite book? Why do you like it?

2. How many books do you own? Where do you keep them?

3. Does someone read aloud to you at home? Who?

4. What kind of stories do you like to hear read aloud?

5. If you could change places with someone, who would it be?

6. What do you like best about reading?

7. What do you like least about reading?

8. What is your favorite television show? Why do you like it?

9. What is your hobby?

10. Do you collect anything? If so, what?

11. How do you feel about reading for fun?

12. Do you own a library card?

13. What are the names of some of the books you have at home?

14. If you were to write your own book, what would it be about? Why?

15. What games or sports do you like?

16. What do you like best about reading class?

17. How would you change the reading class?

18. What do you do when you come to a word you do not know?

19. What is the most important thing that happens in school?

20. What is the next book you plan to read?

These questions should be administered a few at a time and notations made as to the responses. The insights gleaned from the answers should then be used in choosing books for classroom use and for recommending books to parents who request help in book selection.

Children as Librarians

It is advisable to create classroom library committees on a rotating basis so that responsibilities and privileges can be shared in a routine fashion. Children appreciate the library center much more if they have had a hand in planning it, arranging it, and keeping it clean and orderly. It is surprising how well they are able to arrange the books into categories that have meaning for them. They are also quite capable of operating a simple check-out system for books to be taken home. Such a program cannot operate successfully without careful planning and continuous supervision on the teacher's part. The teacher should be aware that attitudes and feelings about books and reading are being developed during the early years of a child's schooling, and that those attitudes and feelings will remain with him or her throughout life.

The Children's Reading Record

The value of a child's own personal reading record has been discovered by many teachers. It is a graphic record of accomplishment and is extremely important because it records independent, self-selected reading, helps to satisfy a child's need for achievement, and encourages sustained silent reading. Such a record is more significant to the student than a similar record kept by the teacher simply because it makes the child responsible for the manipulative activities necessary in keeping the record. Positive reinforcement is gained each time a card is filed.

The reading record chart is made by attaching a series of pockets to poster board, plywood, or bulletin board. When names or numbers are fastened to the pockets, they become personal storage spaces for book

Figure 1.12.   A reading record chart with a Mary
Poppins theme. Book cards are filed in boxes decorated
with houses and storefronts. (Courtesy of Dianne Baker.)

cards. As each library book is completed, the student writes its title,
author, and the date on a small card and files it in his or her special pocket
(fig. 1.12). Enjoyment comes first in reading the book, and second in
watching the card pack grow.

Some criteria helpful to the teacher in constructing a reading record
chart are given below:

1. The chart should be attractive. Since it will remain in view over
   long periods of time, it should also be a beauty spot in the classroom.

2. The chart should contain a caption that promotes books and
   reading. Famous quotations on books and reading from
   Bartlett's *Familiar Quotations* are excellent for captions and
   may also provide a theme for the chart.

3. The chart should be durable. Since it is posted at eye level and
   in constant use by children, it must be well constructed of sturdy
   materials.

4. The chart should be noncompetitive. Each pocket should be
   considered private property with no comparisons made. The only
   competition should be the child's own past record. Since reading

the books and keeping the record are sufficiently pleasurable, tangible rewards are not necessary.

5. The chart should be expandable. Extra pockets need to be prepared in advance so that newcomers to the class can participate in the project without delay.

As to the efficacy of the reading record chart, teachers will at once recognize it as a motivational device to be abandoned when a child no longer needs it, or to be omitted altogether for the child who reads widely in many books, but has no interest in keeping a record of such reading.

An important concomitant value of the student's reading record is its use in parent-teacher conferences to illustrate the child's reading level, interests in reading, and the amount of reading practice taking place.

Reading Aloud

Adjacent to the library center a carpeted area should be set aside for gathering the children together in an intimate story circle. The teacher can then sit at the edge of the circle on a low chair and hold the picture book at the eye level of the child. She or he must, of course, master the art of reading from the side so that the children are able to see the illustrations at all times.

If the story is to be read with feeling and enjoyment, it should be selected and prepared in advance. Obviously, the teacher should choose only those stories she or he enjoys, since boredom with a story will always be transmitted to the listeners. The story should be read in a well-modulated voice that does not overdramatize the conversational parts. Leave something to the imagination of children. The following tips are suggested for teachers who wish to improve their read-aloud sessions.

Tips for Successful Read-Aloud Sessions

Establish a regular schedule for reading aloud. Reading aloud by the teacher should be a routine part of the daily classroom schedule, and children should be able to look forward to an enjoyable experience with literature at approximately the same time each day. To give reading aloud its rightful place in the curriculum, a teacher's lesson plans should indicate the time period for reading aloud, the book to be read, and any planned follow-up activities.

Choose a book with your students in mind. By using interest inventories and daily observation to determine which books are preferred by children, and by supplementing that information with recommended lists for each grade level, a teacher greatly reduces the risk of selecting the wrong book for reading aloud. Generally, nursery, kindergarten, and first grade children prefer picture books that can be completed in one sitting. Reserve continued stories for upper primary children.

Select a book with yourself in mind. Any time you find yourself reading aloud from a book you do not like or one that simply bores you, the children are sure to be as aware of it as you are, and the whole experience will be a disappointment. Since the time for reading aloud always seems to be at a premium, no part of it should be spent on trite and inane books. A really fine book for children is one that appeals to adults as well.

Practice reading the book. A rehearsal smooths out the difficult, sometimes tongue-twisting, language of a book and acquaints the reader with the story's concepts in advance. Familiarity with the story enables the teacher to turn away from the book often for more eye contact with the children; eye contact, of course, is a key ingredient in holding the attention of young listeners.

Create an atmosphere for reading aloud. An area should be set aside for gathering children together in an intimate story circle, or more precisely, a semicircle. The teacher then sits on a low chair at the open end of the semicircle and holds the picture book face out, just slightly above the eye level of the children.

Eliminate undue distractions. The best laid plans amount to little if distractions and interruptions are allowed to interfere with the sanctity of story time. If the story is carefully chosen and well read, even the most active child can be expected to listen attentively throughout. Good listening behavior, however, should always be recognized and reinforced with a compliment.

Read with feeling and expression. A sense of the dramatic is always present in reading aloud, but it should not be overdone. Overdramatization only causes children to concentrate on the reader rather than the story. On the other hand, careful attention to pitch and stress is necessary if the printed dialogue is to sound like conversation. If the teacher enjoys a story and has a good time with it, that feeling will shine through and the children will like it, too.

Discuss unfamiliar words. Of course not every unknown word in a story or book need be analyzed, but the mystery should be taken out of key words that are certain to have a bearing on comprehension. Some teachers prefer to write the new words on the chalkboard at the onset, others define them unobtrusively as the story progresses. In either case, one of the values of reading aloud is the enrichment of children's vocabularies.

Teach the parts of a book. A few minutes of each read-aloud session should be devoted to pointing out the main parts of a book—the jacket, covers, end pages, spine, blurb, and other features until children are completely familiar and comfortable with the terminology. (See p. 22 in this chapter for further information.)

Give opportunity for responses to reading aloud. It is not necessary to discuss every book read in detail, but children usually want to talk about a book they have enjoyed. They like to compare it with other books they know, and perhaps to request a similar one for the next session. A good book may also be followed up with a creative activity, such as cooking, art, creative writing, or dramatization.

Follow-up Discussion

No harm is done to the story if the reader pauses briefly to define a word or point out a comparison, but any lengthy discussion should be reserved until the story is ended. Children readily become accustomed to this routine and are willing to hold most of their questions until the end of the story.

Not every book will be discussed on completion. Some stories are so moving that any comment would be superfluous. But follow-up discussion can be a rich learning experience. It can improve comprehension and heighten the appreciation of a story. The art of asking provocative questions about a piece of literature is an important teaching skill and can be mastered easily with a little practice. In using the questioning method, the teacher should never become so preoccupied with the upcoming question that he or she fails to listen to the responses of children. In fact, most questions should spring naturally from the children's reactions to the book.

Question Types

To illustrate how questions may proceed from surface questions to higher-level ones that call for personal involvement, Peter Spier's book *People* (1980) will serve as an example. It is a factual story about people the world over, their customs, traditions, languages, religions, games, hobbies, and pets. The book is illustrated with numerous fascinating details that lend themselves to class discussion. Only a few questions should be asked at each read-aloud session, but it is important to proceed toward more thought-provoking questions as any book is being considered. As a teacher develops the skill of asking important questions, children learn to react to literature and to give oral expression to those reactions.[3]

Recognition and Recall

How many human beings live on this earth?
Are there any two people exactly alike?
What are the three main religions?

---

3. Written by Betty Coody for *Language Arts Instruction and the Beginning Teacher* by Carl Personke and Dale Johnson. Englewood Cliffs, N.J.: Prentice-Hall, Inc., 1987. Used by permission.

Demonstration of Skill

Show us how "sukatan" is played.
Locate Italy on the globe.
Spell your name with sign language.

Comprehension and Analysis

Why do people live in different kinds of homes?
Why do people have different tastes in art and music?
Why do some people excel at things others could never do?
Why do some people cry at weddings while others smile?

Synthesis

What would the world be like if all people were exactly the same?
What if you were one of the millions of people who cannot read or write?
What would it be like if you could never have any privacy?

Opinion

Why are some people who want to work unable to find a job?
Why do you think some people are rich and powerful while most are not?
Why do you think we still remember people like Benjamin Franklin?

Attitudes and Values

How do you feel when you hear people speaking a language you cannot understand?
Why are most people both wise and foolish?
Why do people everywhere love to play and laugh?
How do you feel about a religion other than your own?

Children Reading to Children

The act of reading aloud has no purpose—no reason for being—unless an audience is present and involved. Providing courteous and interested listeners for fledgling readers is a challenge for teachers of beginning reading. The traditional "reading groups" arrangement allows short periods each day for supervised oral reading, but additional practice in a more informal setting is needed to refine reading skills.

Many teachers have solved the problem of oral reading practice by placing together two children, of similar reading skill, who take turns reading aloud to each other. This plan gives many students an opportunity to read aloud without waiting a long time for a turn. It is a plan well

Figure 1.13.   Pairs of children gather in nooks and crannies around the classroom to take turns reading to each other. (Courtesy Beaumont Independent School District.)

liked by children and thus helps to develop positive attitudes toward books and reading. Its one disadvantage is the potential noise level. With teams reading all over the room, it may sound like the old-fashioned blab school; however, once children learn to read quietly and block out distractions, this small problem is resolved (fig. 1.13).

Another method of giving beginning readers the oral reading practice they need is for them to read daily (or nightly) to younger brothers and sisters at home. The classroom teacher works in close cooperation with the school librarian to compile a collection of easy-to-read books available for young children to check out for home reading.

Approximately once a week both teacher and librarian meet with the children in a "readers' club" format for an appraisal of the read-aloud activity. The children not only share experiences but also recommend books and advise each other in general about how to make the activity more successful. As the program progresses, the primary children become more mature and efficient as readers while their preschool listeners gain a measure of readiness for reading (fig. 1.14).

Figure 1.14. A big brother selects appropriate books to take home from the school library for reading to younger brothers and sisters. (Courtesy Ector County Independent School District, Odessa, Texas.)

Cross-Age Reading

Another ready source of oral readers for young children can be found in upper grade classes in the same school building; older students are asked to read to younger ones. The upper grade teacher cooperates in this project by transforming the language arts class into a reading laboratory arrayed with a smorgasbord of picture books. Students are given time to browse and select books to read to their younger counterparts. Often selections are based on surveys and interviews previously conducted in the kindergarten and primary classrooms (animal stories are found to be perennial favorites).

Once the selections are made, students are given time to practice reading until they have perfected the performance. Visuals may be made to accompany the books. As pairs of readers visit the kindergarten and primary classrooms, they introduce themselves and each book and its author. They also know to gather the children around them in a comfortable arrangement. They learn to show the book's pictures as they read. In a true audience situation, they are challenged to read at their very best.

A follow-up project to the cross-age reading aloud is letter writing by the young listeners. Thank-you notes and letters are very complimentary; the readers are invited back, and suggestions are made for other books to be read. Even poor readers are successful in this project and perhaps for the first time see themselves as efficient readers. In summary,

Figure 1.15. An upper grade student reads aloud to kindergarten children in a cross-age arrangement. (Courtesy Helena Park Elementary School, Nederland, Texas. Photography by Tia Webb.)

young children need to hear fluent reading from quality books; older students need oral reading practice. Both groups grow in the appreciation of fine literature (see fig. 1.15).

The People Who Make a Book

Young children are keenly interested in news and information about the authors and illustrators of their favorite books. A teacher of six-year-olds explained to the children that an author of her acquaintance was writing a story about a horned lizard he had captured. He had put honey on his wife's clothesline to attract a supply of ants for the horned lizard as he studied it in captivity. When the book was finished, he sent the class an autographed copy. Even though it was an informational book of science, the children read it over and over again and frequently requested that it be read aloud at story time.

In addition to the author and illustrator, young children can also understand something about the publisher of a book. The name of the publishing company can be pointed out to them in all the places it normally appears in a book. Occasionally children are interested in the city where

Figure 1.16.   Many teachers like to focus on a
single book and author for a brief time to teach a
mini-unit. From such a project, learnings extend
to other books and authors.

the publishing firm is located. The function of the publisher as manu-
facturer, advertiser, and bookseller is better understood if the class is
given the privilege of selecting a book from a catalogue and then ordering it directly from the publisher. One seven-year-old was heard to
comment, "All of Dr. Seuss's books come from Random House" (fig.
1.16).

The Parts of a Book

Young children are interested in the parts of a book in direct pro-
portion to the teacher's interest in the way a book is put together. The
following parts are those most often discussed and examined in the early
years of school.

The *jacket* is the colorful paper cover that folds around the outside
of the book. It serves as eye appeal to the prospective reader and as protection for the book.

The *flaps* are the parts of the jacket that fold inside the front and back
covers of the book. The front flap contains a brief summary of the book's

contents. Children like calling the summary by its proper name, the "blurb." The black flap usually contains essential information about the author and illustrator and is sometimes called the "continuation of the blurb." (If publishers could see the way boys and girls pore over a picture of their favorite author or illustrator, they would undoubtedly make certain that every back flap contained such photographs.)

The *book cover,* the outside covering of the book, is composed of heavy cardboard covered with paper or cloth. Similar covers can easily be constructed for child-made books by covering cardboard with contact paper.

The *end papers* are those papers pasted in the front and back of a book to cover up the rough edges of the binding. The end papers are often decorated in such a way that they offer a glimpse into the contents of the book. In *Blueberries for Sal,* by Robert McCloskey, the end papers show Sal "helping" her mother can blueberries for the winter. The illustration is said to be an authentic representation of the kitchen in McClosky's boyhood home in Maine. It probably has as much sociocultural content for the young child as any one picture could possess.

The *title page* is the first printed page in a book. It carries the name of the author, illustrator, and publisher. The title page is important to children only if they have been given an understanding of who these three people are and their special roles in the creation of a book.

The *spine* of a book is the part of a book that is visible when the book is shelved. It is the central support or the "backbone" of a book. The spine usually carries the title of the book, last name of the author, and the name of the publisher. A prereading child should not be expected to rely on the spine for selecting a book, since it contains no identifying picture of any kind. The spine is, however, extremely important to the child who can read because most libraries shelve books with only the spine showing.

In conclusion, whether young children gain the maximum benefit from a home or classroom collection will depend almost entirely on the amount of effort expended by parents, teachers, and other significant adults. Reading aloud to young children at home can bring about some of the most memorable family occasions, while routine reading aloud at school has the power to improve attitudes toward reading and toward school in general. E. Paul Torrance has written: "It now seems possible that many things can be learned in creative ways more economically and effectively than by authority."[4] Reading aloud from quality literature is one of the creative ways to teach young children.

---

4. E. Paul Torrance, *Creativity* (Washington, D.C.: The National Education Association, 1963), p. 3.

CHILDREN'S BOOKS FOR READING ALOUD

MOTHER GOOSE BOOKS

Book of Nursery and Mother Goose Rhymes, compiled and illustrated by Marguerite de Angeli. Garden City, N.Y.: Doubleday & Co., Inc., 1953.

> Soft, delicate black and white drawings interspersed with mellow pastel paintings make this fine edition a work of art. Contains 376 of the most popular rhymes.

Mother Goose, compiled and illustrated by Tasha Tudor. New York: Henry Z. Walck, Inc., 1944.

> Quaint, old-fashioned costumes give Tasha Tudor's Mother Goose characters added charm. Contains seventy-seven well-known verses.

The Real Mother Goose, illustrated by Blanche Fisher Wright with introduction by May Hill Arbuthnot. Chicago: Rand McNally & Co., 1944.

> An edition consistently popular with children for more than fifty years. Contains an interesting account of the origins of Mother Goose.

Tail Feathers from Mother Goose, written by Iona and Peter Opie; illustrated by individual artists. Boston: Little, Brown and Company, 1988.

> This volume designated as an "antidote to melancholy" pairs folkloristic rhymes with original paintings by such foremost children's artists as Maurice Sendak, Marc Brown, and Babette Cole. The Opies began collecting early and rare children's literature in 1945 while working on *The Oxford Dictionary of Nursery Rhymes.* The rhymes included in this volume are representative of their scholarly work.

The Tall Book of Mother Goose, compiled and illustrated by Feodor Rojankovsky. New York: Harper & Row, Publishers, 1942.

> Humorous, cartoonlike illustrations and the tall shape of the book make this edition unique among the many versions of Mother Goose.

The Tenggren Mother Goose, compiled and illustrated by Gustaf Tenggren. Boston: Little, Brown & Co., 1940.

> A beautifully illustrated edition with many small pictures sprinkled over every page for young children to find and study.

ALPHABET BOOKS

ABC, An Alphabet Book, photographed by Thomas Matthiesen. New York: Platt & Munk, Publishers, 1966.

> A beautiful photograph in full color of a well-known object represents each letter of the alphabet. An excellent transition from concrete objects to semiabstract art.

The ABC Bunny, by Wanda Gág. New York: Coward-McCann, Inc., 1933.

> Soft black and white drawings illustrate the adventures of a small bunny. Each letter of the alphabet stands out in bright red against a white background. A favorite ABC book of children for many years.

First ABC, by Nancy Larrick; illustrated by René Martin. New York: Platt & Munk, Publishers, 1965.

> Each double page contains one large illustration with a brief, factual story about the picture. Each story is accompanied by the appropriate letter in both upper and lower case. Excellent suggestions for ways to use the book are presented for benefit of parents and teachers.

Hanukkah ABC, by Lillian Abramson; illustrated by Gabe Josephson. New York: Shulsinger Brothers Press, 1968.

> A Hanukkah symbol illustrates each letter of the alphabet. Bold pictures, large print, easy-to-read text, and one letter per page make this volume a fine addition to the alphabet book collection in preschool and primary classrooms.

In a Pumpkin Shell, by Joan Walsh Anglund. New York: Harcourt Brace Jovanovich, Inc., 1960.

> A Mother Goose ABC book in which each nursery rhyme is preceded by a letter of the alphabet and one key word from the verse that begins with the letter shown. Illustrations are rich in detail.

The Marcel Marceau Alphabet Book, by George Mendoza; photographed by Milton H. Green. Garden City, N.Y.: Doubleday & Co., Inc., 1970.

> Marcel Marceau, the world's greatest pantomimist, bends his lithe body into the characterization of a word representing each letter of the alphabet. Superb photographs of Marceau completely surrounded by empty white space. Only the letter of the alphabet is shown in color.

Peter Piper's Alphabet, illustrated by Marcia Brown. New York: Charles Scribner's Sons, 1959.

> Sounds of the alphabet are represented by famous old tongue-twisting nonsense rhymes. The pictures are filled with fun and foolishness to be enjoyed by children and adults alike.

Quentin Blake's ABC, written and illustrated by Quentin Blake. New York: Alfred A. Knopf, 1989.

> Rhyming text and humorous illustrations depict familiar objects for each letter of the alphabet. Each picture contains dozens of details for the young child to discover, and the rhyming phrases are perfect for natural and effortless memorization. Good for both reading readiness and beginning reading.

COUNTING BOOKS

My First Counting Book, by Lilian Moore; illustrated by Garth Williams. New York: Simon & Schuster, 1956.

> A sturdy counting book for beginners. Each number to ten is represented by a familiar plant or animal. Complete review included at the end of the book.

1 is One, by Tasha Tudor. New York: Henry Z. Walck, Inc., 1956.

> A counting book that is also a book of art. Plants and animals, flowers, and fruit decorate the pages in delicate pastel colors or in soft black and white.

Still Another Number Book, by Seymour Chwast and Martin Stephen Moskof. New York: McGraw-Hill Book Co., 1971.

> A number book with a contemporary look. It proceeds from one ship to ten jugglers and then reverses itself to go from ten jugglers down to one ship. Fun for the entire family.

The Twelve Days of Christmas, illustrated by Ilonka Karaz. New York: Harper & Row, Publishers, 1949.

> The ordinal numbers through "twelfth" are reviewed, beginning with the first day of Christmas and a partridge in a pear tree. The gifts accumulate up to the last page where all are shown in sequential order. The book contains sheet music to the old folk song.

The Very Hungry Caterpillar, by Eric Carle. Cleveland, Ohio: Collins, William and World Publishing Company, Inc., 1972.

> A colorful counting book that also teaches the days of the week and the life cycle of a caterpillar. A small hole is cut completely through the book to illustrate how the hungry caterpillar eats through an amazing array of foods. Young children enjoy following the holes to trace the path from egg to butterfly.

Concept Books

The Adventures of Three Colors, by Annette Tison and Talus Taylor. Cleveland, Ohio: World Publishing Co., 1971.

> Explanation of how a rainbow is formed by the division of white light into many colors. As Herbie paints with the three primary colors he has seen in the rainbow, he discovers he can make other colors. Clever overlays show how the primary colors combine to form secondary colors and finally tertiary colors.

Big Ones, Little Ones, by Tana Hoban. New York: William Morrow & Company, 1976.

> A book of black and white photography that shows mature animals and their offspring—creatures large and small. Both zoo animals and domesticated animals are represented.

One Way, written and illustrated by Leonard Shortall. Englewood Cliffs, N.J.: Prentice-Hall, Inc., 1975.

> A picture book designed to help young readers recognize all kinds of traffic signs. Each page is filled with humorous detail. Excellent for reading aloud and discussion with an individual child.

Symbols, written and illustrated by Rolf Myller. New York: Atheneum, 1978.

> A colorful and attractive book designed to show children that a symbol stands for something else and makes possible the quick communication of an idea. Rolf Myller conveys the idea that symbols are everywhere and are a vital part of one's life.

We Read A to Z, by Donald Crews. New York: Harper & Row, Publishers, 1967.

> An alphabet book that teaches concepts and ideas. ("A is for almost. Z is for zigzag.") Each letter of the alphabet is used to introduce a concept; each concept is illustrated with a colorful design. A book that is as fascinating to adults as it is to children.

MACHINES PERSONIFIED

The Little Engine That Could, by Watty Piper. New York: Platt & Munk, Publishers, 1955.

> A favorite story about a little engine with a difficult task to accomplish. "I think I can, I think I can" has helped many a child over a high hurdle.

Little Toot, by Hardie Gramatky. New York: G. P. Putnam's Sons, 1939.

> The story of a mischievous little tugboat who refuses to accept the responsibility of tugboat duties. The other boats have to do his share of the work until Little Toot finally proves his worth by courageous action in a dangerous crisis.

Little Toot on the Thames, by Hardie Gramatky. New York: G. P. Putnam's Sons, 1965.

> A sequel written on the twenty-fifth anniversary of *Little Toot*. Little Toot is accidentally towed to England by a huge tramp steamer and winds up in the Thames River. After many disgraces and successes, Little Toot is escorted back home by the good ship Queen Elizabeth.

Mike Mulligan and His Steam Shovel, written and illustrated by Virginia Lee Burton. Boston: Houghton Mifflin Co., 1939.

> Mary Anne is a steam shovel with personality who digs her way into a deep hole and is unable to get out again. The ending is humorous and satisfying.

ANIMAL STORIES

Curious George, by Hans A. Rey. Boston: Houghton Mifflin Co., 1941.

> This curious little monkey is very much like a child as he explores and examines his environment. His curiosity leads him into trouble, but his friend in the yellow hat always gets him out again. The first in a series of books about Curious George.

Harry the Dirty Dog, by Gene Zion; illustrated by Margaret B. Graham. New York: Harper & Row, Publishers, 1956.

> The story of a dog who gets so dirty that he is unrecognizable and finds that soap and water are important to him after all.

How, Hippo!, written and illustrated by Marcia Brown. New York: Charles Scribner's Sons, 1969.

> An entertaining tale of how a mother hippopotamus teaches her baby hippo to protect himself from enemies by making him learn certain grunts and roars. Beautifully illustrated by a woodcut technique.

The Little Rabbit Who Wanted Red Wings, by Carolyn Sherwin Bailey. New York: Platt & Munk, Publishers, 1951.

> On making a wish at the wishing pond, Little White Rabbit finds he can have long red wings. After losing his friends and family because no one recognizes him, he decides it is better for him to be just a little white rabbit. He promises he will never again wish to be anything but what he really is.

Millions of Cats, by Wanda Gág. New York: Coward-McCann, Inc., 1928.

> Out of the millions of cats, only one is humble and modest, but that one turns out to be the most beautiful and lovable of all. A modern folktale illustrated with black and white drawings.

The Secret Hiding Place, by Rainey Bennett. Cleveland, Ohio: World
Publishing Co., 1960.

> Little Hippo attempts to find his own secret hiding place where he can be
> alone. Eventually, he finds a high cliff that makes a perfect hiding place. He
> is able to get away from the herd of hippos and yet keep them safely in sight.

The Story of Ferdinand, by Munro Leaf; illustrated by Robert Lawson.
New York: The Viking Press, 1936.

> All the other bulls wanted to fight more than anything else. But not Ferdi-
> nand. He just wanted to sit quietly under the cork tree and smell the flowers.
> "His mother saw that he was not lonesome, and because she was an under-
> standing mother, even though she was a cow, she let him just sit there and
> be happy." A gentle satire on bull-fighting and a tongue-in-cheek account of
> a nonconforming individual.

HUMOR AND NONSENSE

Crictor, by Tomi Ungerer. New York: Harper & Row, Publishers, 1968.

> As a birthday gift, Madame Louise Bodot receives a boa constrictor from her
> son who is studying reptiles in Africa. Crictor makes a good pet and rescues
> his mistress from a burglar. Some letters of the alphabet and the numerals
> through eight are reviewed as Crictor coils his body into various shapes for
> the amusement of his friends.

Horton Hatches the Egg, by Dr. Seuss (Theodor Seuss Geisel). New
York: Random House, 1940.

> Dr. Seuss has been called a modern Edward Lear, and Horton is one of his
> most popular characters. An elephant up in a tree is the kind of humor that
> appeals to young children. The story has a happy surprise ending.

Johnny Crow's Garden, written and illustrated by Leslie Brooke. New
York: Frederick Warne and Co., 1903.

> The fun and humor in *Johnny Crow's Garden* and its sequels have proven
> irresistible to children and adults alike for many years. Illustrated with non-
> sensical but highly artistic drawings in black and white.

Rain Makes Applesauce, by Julian Scheer; illustrated by Marvin Bileck.
New York: Holiday House, 1964.

> This is a fanciful, imaginative book of silly talk, the kind of silly talk children
> like to create for themselves. The illustrations are intricate and filled with
> humorous detail. There is one bit of realism on each page. In the lower right
> corner is a sequential story of applesauce from the planting of the seed to
> the cooking and eating of applesauce.

Sylvester and the Magic Pebble, by William Steig. New York: Simon &
Schuster, 1969.

> Sylvester Duncan is a young donkey who lives with his mother and father at
> Acorn Road in Oatsdale. What happens to Sylvester when he finds a magic
> pebble makes for humor and suspense. The illustrations are done in cartoon
> style and form a perfect complement to the droll text.

PICTURE BOOKS

Amigo, by Byrd Baylor Schweitzer; illustrated by Garth Williams. New York: The Macmillan Co., 1963.

> Francisco, a little Mexican boy, wants a pet dog more than anything, but his parents are too poor to feed another mouth. Instead, Francisco decides to tame a prairie dog. At the same time, a prairie dog is making plans to tame himself a boy. How the two finally become fast friends is told in rhythmic verse much like an American folk song.

Cinderella, illustrated by Marcia Brown. New York: Charles Scribner's Sons, 1954.

> The author-artist's delicate illustrations help to make this rags-to-riches story a more delightful folktale than ever. One of our oldest stories of social mobility. A Caldecott Award winner.

Crow Boy, written and illustrated by Taro Yashima. New York: The Viking Press, 1955.

> Chibi, a young Japanese boy, shows how much he values schooling by "leaving his home for school at sunrise, every day for six long years." He is the only one in his class to be honored for perfect attendance. And yet, Chibi is an outsider, never accepted by his peers until an understanding schoolmaster discovers that Chibi can imitate the voices of crows. Chibi finally attains the status he deserves. Beautiful oriental illustrations.

Fables, written and illustrated by Arnold Lobel. New York: Harper & Row, Publishers, 1980.

> This book contains twenty original fables about both wise and foolish animals. It was named the Caldecott winner for 1981.

The Glorious Flight Across the Channel with Louis Bleriot, written and illustrated by Alice and Martin Provensen. New York: The Viking Press, 1983.

> A humorous account of the eccentric Frenchman who invented an automobile searchlight and used the fortune it brought him to build a flying machine—to be more accurate, to build eleven flying machines. After ten crackups, a broken rib, a black eye, and numerous sprains and bruises, Papa climbs into the Bleriot XI and becomes the first person to fly across the English Channel. His wife, five children, dog, cat, and cockatoo cheer him on. Perfect for reading aloud.

The Happy Owls, written and illustrated by Celestino Piatti. New York: Atheneum, 1964.

> The barnyard fowls do nothing but fight and quarrel all day, and they wonder why the owls never seem to fight. On inquiry, the owls explain how they are able to live together in peace. The fowls listen, but understand none of it. They immediately turn back to their quarrelsome ways. The story is illustrated in bold black outlines and bright poster colors. A beautiful book with a subtle message.

The Little Island, written by Golden MacDonald; illustrated by Leonard Weisgard. Garden City, N.Y.: Doubleday & Co., Inc., 1946.

> The little island is shown as having responsibility to the rest of the world in the same way that a person is a necessary part of the society in which he/she lives. A Caldecott Award winner.

Owl Moon, by Jane Yolen; illustrated by John Schoenherr. New York: Philomel Books, 1987.

>A father takes his small daughter into the woods on a snowy winter night to have her hear the cry of the Great Horned Owl. She has been waiting a long time to go owling with Pa. A gentle, poetic story perfect for reading aloud and a good book to help children appreciate the beauties of nature. It also shows an intimate, warm personal relationship between a father and his daughter.

People, written and illustrated by Peter Spier. New York: Doubleday, 1980.

>*People* is a factual story about people the world over, their customs, traditions, languages, religions, games, hobbies, and pets. The book is illustrated with numerous fascinating details that lend themselves to discussion. An excellent selection for both home and school.

Saint George and the Dragon, retold by Margaret Hodges and illustrated by Trina Schart Hyman. Boston: Little, Brown and Company, 1984.

>The classic tale is retold from Edmund Spenser's *Faerie Queene.* It is a story of a monstrous dragon "armed all over with scales of brass fitted so closely that no sword or spear could pierce them." It is a monster story perfectly capable of competing with modern horror books and movies. Should be read aloud to older primary children, but the story is best divided into two or three sessions. Allow time for a discussion of mythological creatures and the larger-than-life heroes who slay them.

Song and Dance Man, by Karen Ackerman; illustrated by Stephen Gammell. New York: Alfred A. Knopf, 1988.

>Grandpa is an old vaudeville man but is still able to take his grandchildren up the attic stairs for a dazzling performance and a look back at the joyous days gone by. Winner of the 1989 Caldecott Award.

Too Many Books, written by Caroline Feller Bauer; illustrated by Diane Patterson. New York: Viking Penguin Inc., 1985.

>"Too many books" is an idea to strike uneasiness in the heart of a reading teacher, but on second glance the humor is understandable. After all, even a dedicated bibliophile has to face the practical problem of where to keep all the books when there is no place left to sit, to walk, and no way to get in the door. The reader is offered a satisfactory solution to the problem and book lovers of all ages will treasure the ending of the story.

EASY-TO-READ BOOKS

Are You My Mother?, by J. D. Eastman. New York: Random House, 1960.

>A very funny book for children who are just beginning to read. A baby bird hatches out and cannot find his mother. He does not even know what she looks like; he mistakes a dog, a cow, a cat, a plane, a boat, and a steam shovel for his mother. Uses only one hundred easy-to-read words.

The Best Nest, by P. D. Eastman. New York: Random House, Inc., 1968.

> Mr. and Mrs. Bird set out in search of a better nest only to discover that the one they left behind is the best nest of all . . . "there 's no nest like an old nest."

Grasshopper on the Road, written and illustrated by Arnold Lobel. New York: Harper & Row, Publishers, 1978.

> Grasshopper sets forth on the road and meets with some unusual characters who find it hard to accept his openhanded philosophy. An excellent example of a quality easy-to-read book.

Little Bear's Visit, by Else Holmelund Minarik; illustrated by Maurice Sendak. New York: Harper & Row, Publishers, 1961.

> A tale of Little Bear's visit to Grandmother and Grandfather Bear who live in a little house in the woods. One of several easy-to-read books about Little Bear, his family, and friends.

PARTICIPATION BOOKS

Brian Wildsmith's Puzzles, written and illustrated by Brian Wildsmith. New York: Franklin Watts, Inc., 1970.

> All the answers to Brian Wildsmith's brainteasing questions can be found in his colorful illustrations. Good humor and beautiful artwork are combined to create an outstanding picture book in which a child can actively participate.

Honeybees, written by Graham Tarrant; illustrated by Tony King. New York: G. P. Putnam's Sons, 1984.

> A "Natural Pop-Ups" book that has the features of a fascinating toy, but at the same time tells an accurate account of honey production from flower to the breakfast table. A third-dimensional beehive opens to reveal bees inside the honeycomb. Enlarged drawings show the perfect geometry of a six-sided cell. Very good for reading aloud to an individual child or a small group of children.

Look Again!, photography by Tana Hoban. New York: The Macmillan Company, 1971.

> A wordless book of photographs featuring small "windows" through which children are given a tantalizing visual clue as to how the total picture will appear on the following page.

Sniff Poems: A Scholastic "Scratch and Sniff" Book, illustrated by James Weil. Englewood Cliffs, N.J.: Scholastic Book Services, 1975.

> A collection of poems on many subjects and by poets whose verses are popular with children. The poems are accompanied by appropriate "scratch and sniff" patches.

Three Jovial Huntsmen, adapted and illustrated by Susan Jeffers. Scarsdale, N.Y.: Bradbury Press, 1973.

> A popular Mother Goose rhyme, but classified here as a participation book because of its illustrations. On each page are featured many small wild creatures carefully hidden by leaves and branches. The animals are always overlooked by the jovial huntsman, but are easily spotted by perceptive young readers.

The Very Hungry Caterpillar, by Eric Carle. Cleveland, Ohio: Collins, William and World Publishing Company, Inc., 1972.

> A colorful counting book that also teaches the days of the week and the life cycle of a caterpillar. A small hole is cut completely through the book to illustrate how the hungry caterpillar eats through an amazing array of foods. Young children enjoy following the holes to trace the path from egg to butterfly.

Zoo City, written and photographed by Stephen Lewis. New York: William Morrow & Company, Inc., 1976.

> Machines, plumbing, cars, and other city fixtures that resemble animals are shown in beautiful black and white photographs, accompanied by pictures of their real-life counterparts. The book is designed with a split-page, puzzle format in which the child matches animals with look-alike objects.

INFORMATIONAL BOOKS

The Amazing Seeds, by Ross E. Hutchins; illustrated with photographs by the author. New York: Dodd, Mead & Co., 1960.

> An excellent resource for parents and teachers, and because of the superb close-up photographs, it is also suitable for young children who have not yet begun to read. Contains directions for making a seed collection.

Cactus in the Desert, by Phyllis S. Busch; illustrated by Harriett Barton. New York: Thomas Y. Crowell, 1979.

> This book is an easy-to-read introduction to the cactus plant—from a tiny pincushion cactus to the giant saguaro. Illustrated in the vivid colors of the desert, it describes how cactus plants are different from other plants in that they are able to live and thrive where it rains only once or twice a year. Other books in the "Let's-Read-and-Find-Out Science Books" Series are:
> *Corn Is Maize; Down Come the Leaves; How a Seed Grows; Mushrooms and Molds; Plants in Winter; Roots Are Food Finders; Seeds by Wind and Water; A Tree Is a Plant; Water Plants; Where Does Your Garden Grow?*

Discovering Plants, by Glenn O. Blough; illustrated by Jeanne Bendick. New York: McGraw-Hill Book Co., 1966.

> The author explains the function of each of a plant's parts. He shows children how to begin the process of scientific observation by using a microscope and magnifying glass.

How to Have Fun Building Sailboats, by editors of "Creative"; illustrated by Harold Henrikson. Chicago: Children's Press, 1974.

> Historical information about boats and sailing technology. Instructions for making sailboats from scrap materials. Very easy to read.

How to Have Fun with a Vegetable Garden, by editors of "Creative"; illustrated by Nancy Inderieden. Chicago: Children's Press, 1974.

> Basic advice for the planting and care of a vegetable garden with particular attention to carrots, peas, radishes, beans, and potatoes.

Kites, written and illustrated by Larry Kettelkamp. New York: William Morrow and Company, 1959.

> Describes the basic types of kites and how to build and fly them for fun or in a tournament. It also tells of kites in other lands and of their practical uses.

Simple Sewing, by Edith Paul and Barbara Zietz; illustrated by
Catherine Scholz and Nancy Sears. New York: Grosset and Dunlap
Publishers, 1969.

> Prepared under the supervision of the Department of Sewing Education of
> the Singer Company for children ages seven and up. How to select and read
> a pattern. How to operate a sewing machine.

Soil, by Richard Cromer; illustrated by Robert J. Lee. Chicago: Follett
Publishing Co., 1967.

> An easy-to-read beginning science book. The vital importance of soil con-
> servation is told in simple terms. Suggestions are given for easy experiments
> with soil and plants.

When an Animal Grows, by Millicent E. Selsam; illustrated by John
Kaufmann. New York: Harper & Row, Publishers, 1966.

> This is a book about the different ways newborn animals grow and are cared
> for by their mothers. The babies compared are a gorilla, a lamb, a duck, and
> a sparrow.

Why People Are Different Colors, by Julian May; illustrated by Symeon
Shimin. New York: Holiday House, 1971.

> The story of how skin colors and hair types have changed as the human body
> has adapted to weather conditions. The overriding concept is that human-
> kind is a simple human species. In the forward the author writes: "An un-
> derstanding of the reasons why people of many colors exist will help us to
> achieve genuine brotherhood among men."

Your Friend, the Tree, by Florence M. White; illustrated by Alan E.
Cober. New York: Alfred A. Knopf, Inc., 1969.

> This book teaches children the many uses of trees and urges them to be good
> to trees. "When a tree is cut down, a new one should always be planted,
> because we cannot live without trees."

BIBLIOGRAPHY

Anderson, William, and Patrick Groff. *A New Look at Children's Literature.* Belmont, Calif.: Wadsworth Publishing Co., Inc., 1972.

Arnstein, Flora J. *Poetry in the Elementary Classroom.* New York: Appleton-
Century-Crofts, 1962.

Cullinan, Bernice E. *Literature and the Child.* 2d ed. New York: Harcourt Brace
Jovanovich, Publishers, 1989.

Cullinan, Bernice, and Carolyn W. Carmichael, eds. *Literature and Young Children.* Urbana, Ill.: National Council of Teachers of English, 1977.

de Regniers, Beatrice Schenk. *Poems Children Will Sit Still For: A Selection for
the Primary Grades.* New York: Scholastic Book Services, 1969.

Georgiou, Constantine. *Children and Their Literature.* Englewood Cliffs, N.J.:
Prentice-Hall, Inc., 1969.

Hearne, Betsy, and Marilyn Kaye. *Celebrating Children's Books.* New York:
Lothrop, Lee & Shepard Books, 1981.

Hollowell, Lillian. *A Book of Children's Literature.* 3d ed. New York: Holt, Rinehart & Winston, Inc., 1966.

Huck, Charlotte S., Susan Hepler, and Janet Hickman. *Children's Literature in
the Elementary School.* 4th ed. New York: Holt, Rinehart & Winston, 1987.

Jacobs, Leland B. "Children's Experiences in Literature." In *Children and the Language Arts,* edited by Virgil E. Herrick and Leland B. Jacobs. Englewood Cliffs, N.J.: Prentice-Hall, Inc., 1975.

Lamme, Linda Leonard, ed. *Learning to Love Literature.* Urbana, Ill.: National Council of Teachers of English, 1981.

Larrick, Nancy. *A Teacher's Guide to Children's Reading.* 5th ed. New York: Bantam Books, 1983.

Lukens, Rebecca J. *A Critical Handbook of Children's Literature.* Glenview, Ill.: Scott, Foresman & Company, 1976. 2d ed., 1982.

Meeker, Alice M. *Enjoying Literature with Children.* New York: The Odyssey Press, 1969.

Moffett, James. *A Student-Centered Language Arts Curriculum, Grades K–12: A Handbook for Teachers.* Boston: Houghton Mifflin Co., 1968.

Nelson, Mary Anne. *A Comparative Anthology of Children's Literature.* New York: Holt, Rinehart & Winston, Inc., 1972.

Norton, Donna. *Through the Eyes of a Child: An Introduction to Children's Literature.* 2d ed. Columbus, Ohio: Merrill Publishing Company, 1987.

Purves, Alan C., and Dianne L. Monson. *Experiencing Children's Literature.* Glenview, Ill.: Scott, Foresman & Company, 1984.

Sadker, Myra Pollack, and David Miller Sadker. *Now Upon a Time: A Contemporary View of Children's Literature.* New York: Harper & Row, Publishers, 1977.

Sebesta, Sam Leaton, and William J. Iverson. *Literature for Thursday's Child.* Chicago: Science Research Associates, Inc., 1975.

Shumsky, Abraham. *Creative Teaching in the Elementary School.* New York: Appleton-Century-Crofts, 1965.

Smith, James A., and Dorothy M. Park. *Word Music and Word Magic: Children's Literature Methods.* Boston: Allyn and Bacon, Inc., 1977.

Stewig, John Warren, and San Leaton Sebesta. *Using Literature in the Elementary Classroom.* Urbana, Ill.: National Council of Teachers of English, 1989.

Sutherland, Zena, and May Hill Arbuthnot. *Children and Books.* 7th ed. Glenview, Ill.: Scott, Foresman & Company, 1986.

Torrance, E. Paul. *Creativity.* Washington, D.C.: The National Education Association, 1963.

Trelease, Jim. *The Read-Aloud Handbook.* New York: Penguin Books, 1982.

Witucke, Virginia. *Poetry in the Elementary School.* Dubuque, Iowa: Wm. C. Brown Company Publishers, 1970.

2

"Once Upon a Time":

Literature for Storytelling

The art of storytelling flourished long before there was a written language to record the tales. Men and women have always gathered to talk over common problems, to ponder on natural phenomena they could not understand, to lavish praise on their heroes, both real and imaginary, to celebrate victories and accomplishments, and to mourn tragic losses.

As people began to travel over longer and longer distances, the stories were carried from one locale to another, changing slightly as storytellers added embellishments to suit their audiences and their own storytelling styles. It is believed that folktales traveled mainly from the Far East to the Middle East and from there to Europe. Finally, the tales were carried from Europe to North and South America.

Today, each country of the world has its own wealth of myths, legends, fables, epics, proverbs, and folktales, and each country's body of folk literature is tantalizingly similar to that found in other countries.

One theory holds that folk literature the world over is basically similar, not only because it was carried from one place to another, but also because people everywhere have always had the same needs and aspirations. They have been concerned with earning a living and providing a comfortable refuge for themselves away from harm and danger. They have struggled to earn love and acceptance from others, and they have worked to accomplish something worthy of respect. People have always searched diligently for knowledge and information. They have managed in various ways to bring an element of romance and beauty into their lives.

It is understandable that these basic tasks of life have been the source and subject of literature down through the ages and doubtless will continue to be so in the future. Several years ago, in her classic book on storytelling, Carolyn Bailey wrote about the significance of folklore on a society:

> The eternal soul of a nation is expressed in its folklore. It is remembered when all else is forgotten. A people may lose fame or even disappear from the face of the earth because of the cruelty of other nations, but its tales remain and are cherished. And they should be cherished by those who tell stories to children, for in them are the ingredients that make for a perfect story. They have all the elements of adventure, entertainment and education.[1]

Out of the abundant riches in folklore available to today's students, folktales remain the favorite of young children. Because these old stories were handed down by word of mouth for so many years, they have become streamlined and stripped of all nonessential elements. Such stark simplicity makes them perfect for storytelling and very appealing to children, who are always anxious to get to the heart of the matter.

One criterion for excellence in children's stories is that they should appeal to adults as well as children. Folktales measure up. Their uncanny power to entertain and enchant people of all ages has caused them to survive thousands of years. "To believe in magic wands, gingerbread houses, talking scarecrows, glass slippers, wishing caps, elves, and trolls is to enter a make-believe world which spans both nations and generations."[2]

Although entertainment was the basic intent of the folktales, a broader viewpoint would also acknowledge the high moral value and warm humanism to be found in them. The imagery created when a folktale is well told has the power to touch the deepest of human feelings and emotions. In a vicarious way it serves to allay fears, to fulfill ambitions, and to provide love. It strengthens, renews, and leaves the listener ready to resume the struggles and stresses of everyday living.

According to Arbuthnot, the old folktales are unsurpassed as a means of showing children the world the way it is and the way it ought to be:

> Stories such as "Cinderella," "Three Little Pigs," "Three Billy Goats Gruff," and "Snow White" dramatize the stormy conflict of good and evil. And they reiterate the old verities that kindness and goodness will triumph over evil if they are backed by wisdom, wit, and courage. These

---

1. Carolyn S. Bailey, *The Story-Telling Hour* (New York: Dodd, Mead & Co., 1934), p. 49.
2. Carole Mosley Kirkton, "Once Upon a Time . . . Folk Tales and Storytelling," *Elementary English* 48 (1971): 1024.

basic truths we should like built into the depths of the child's consciousness; they are the folk tales' great contribution to the child's social consciousness.[3]

The renowned poet and storyteller Padraic Column also has great faith in the value of folk literature. He feels that the voice of a good storyteller has the ability to heighten the impact of a tale and make it remembered long after the telling: "The human voice, when it can really charge itself with what is in a poem or a story, more powerfully than any other agency, can put into our deeper consciousness those lasting patterns which belong to the deeper consciousness of the race."[4]

Marcia Brown, an author-illustrator who has won the Caldecott Award three times and was a runner-up six times, has turned again and again to folk literature for inspiration. She tells us that the folktales are deeply true to life and explains why they are needed by today's children:

> The heritage of childhood is the sense of life bequeathed to it by the folk wisdom of the ages . . . fairy tales are revelations of sober everyday fact. They are the abiding dreams and realities of the human soul.
>
> This very day some rogue has by his quick wit opened a new world to his master and helped him win the princess of his heart, to whom he is entitled by sensibilities if not by birth.
>
> Today a staunch soldier, through circumstances not of his own making, goes through terrible trials, but remains steadfast in his devotion to his ideal.
>
> Tonight somewhere Cinderella, through the magic of kindness, has been enchanted into greatest beauty; tonight Cinderella goes to her ball to meet her prince.[5]

More and more, modern educators are beginning to view the systematic study of folk literature as a necessary component of the young child's curriculum. It is now believed that high school and college students can more easily acquire an adequate understanding and appreciation of the great literature introduced at those levels if they have had the advantage of hearing folktales in early childhood. This philosophy is bringing about a revival of interest in the heritage of poetry and story:

> For without some ability for making ourselves at home in the world of thought, imagination, intuition, a boy or a girl will never be able to understand all that is summed up in art and philosophy, will never have

---

3. May Hill Arbuthnot, *Children and Books,* 4th ed. (Glenview, Ill.: Scott, Foresman & Company, 1972), p. 20.

4. Padraic Colum, *Story Telling New and Old* (New York: The Macmillan Co., 1968), p. 21.

5. Helen W. Painter, "Marcia Brown: A Study in Versatility," *Elementary English* 43 (1966): 855.

any deep feeling for religion, and will not be able to get anything out of the reading of history; in short, unless they are somewhat at home in that world, they will live without any fineness in their lives.[6]

Telling Folktales to Children

Even though early storytellers created their stories with adults in mind and told them mainly to audiences of men and women, we know that the children had a way of listening in. As has always been the case, they took from the adult stories those parts that held meaning and interest for them and simply ignored (or promptly forgot) the rest. When adults realize that even young children are equipped with the amazing ability to discard those things that are irrelevant, they will never again be guilty of "watering down" literature before presenting it to them. On the contrary, oral interpretation of literature should lead children to greater depths of understanding:

> The storyteller must have respect for the child's mind and the child's conception of the world, knowing it for a complete mind and a complete conception. If a storyteller have that respect he need not be childish in his language in telling stories to children. If the action be clear and the sentences clear one can use a mature language. Strange words, out-of-the-way words do not bewilder children if there be order in the action and in the sentences.[7]

It may seem paradoxical to discuss the ancient art of storytelling as a modern teaching procedure, but, nevertheless, it would be difficult to find any teaching practice in the modern curriculum that is more effective or one that is more favored by children.

According to Dewey Chambers, the teacher who tells stories as a pedagogical technique is employing an educational procedure that has been used by some of the world's greatest teachers: "Jesus used it, as did Plato, Confucius, and other great philosophers and teachers. It is an instructional technique that did not belong only in the past. It has relevance to today's teacher, as well. The modern teacher who employs this technique as a teaching tool is using an ancient method that is as modern as tomorrow."[8]

In the past few years, both pre-service and in-service programs for teachers have emphasized the importance of storytelling as a means of elevating literature to its rightful place in the early childhood curriculum. However, many teachers have yet to be converted to the art of storytelling as a basic teaching procedure, and to folk literature as an open sesame to the world of reading.

---

6. Colum, op. cit., p. 22.
7. Colum, op. cit., p. 13.
8. Dewey W. Chambers, *Literature for Children: Storytelling and Creative Drama* (Dubuque, Iowa: Wm. C. Brown Co. Publishers, 1970), p. 43.

The Storyteller

Once a commitment is made to the efficacy of storytelling, it is possible for any teacher, aide, librarian, parent, or other interested adult to become an effective teller of tales to young children.

Each potential storyteller has a lifetime of experiences from which to draw, and, with practice, can become quite skillful at using life's experiences to enrich and enliven stories. "So, making a good storyteller is like making a good forest or garden or home or person. It is a way of life, in which a channel is opened through which may pour all the background, experiences, awareness, skill, artistry, which you can possess and can develop."[9]

Ruth Sawyer feels that the most successful storytellers are those who are able to enjoy nature, to see beauty in everyday experiences:

> To be a good storyteller one must be gloriously alive. It is not possible to kindle fresh fires from burned-out embers. I have noticed that the best of traditional storytellers whom I have heard have been those who live close to the heart of things—to the earth, the sea, wind and weather. They have been those who knew solitude, silence. They reach constantly for understanding. They have come to know the power of the spoken word.[10]

If the storytelling venture is to be of maximum worth to children, a great deal of time, energy, and effort are demanded of the teacher. Hours must be spent in studying children's literature; in seeking the right stories; in learning, preparing, and practicing each story for telling; in setting the stage for storytelling; and in providing appropriate follow-up activities to the stories. An apathetic teacher will never be an effective storyteller.

Many of the great storytellers have felt compelled to warn the beginner that storytelling takes effort. Marie Shedlock writes:

> . . . I maintain that capacity for work, and even drudgery, is among the essentials of storytelling. Personally, I know of nothing more interesting than watching the story grow gradually from mere outline into a dramatic whole. It is the same pleasure, I imagine, which is felt over the gradual development of a beautiful design on a loom. I do not mean machine-made work, which has to be done under adverse conditions in a certain time and which is similar to thousands of other pieces of work; but that work upon which we can bestow unlimited time and concentrated thought.[11]

---

9. Ruth Tooze, *Storytelling* (Englewood Cliffs, N.J.: Prentice-Hall, Inc., 1959), pp. 28–29.

10. Ruth Sawyer, *The Way of the Storyteller* (New York: The Viking Press, 1962), p. 29.

11. Marie L. Shedlock, *The Art of the Story-Teller* (New York: Dover Publications, Inc., 1951), p. 28.

Selecting the Story

In choosing a story to tell in nursery school, kindergarten, or the primary grades, the teacher might keep in mind the following questions to ensure that time spent in selecting, preparing, and telling the story will be worth the effort expended.

1. Is the story interesting and entertaining to you, the storyteller?
2. Does the story fit your personality, style, and talents?
3. Will the story appeal to the interests of the children for whom it is intended?
4. Is the story appropriate to the age and ability level of the children?
5. Is the story brief enough for young listeners, with a minimum of characters and events?
6. Is there ample dialogue and action in the story?
7. Are there few lengthy descriptive passages and can they be easily condensed?
8. Will the story be relatively easy to prepare?
9. Will the story add variety and contrast to the storyteller's repertoire of stories?
10. Is it a story that would be better told than read aloud?

Of course, these are not the only features to consider in the selection of a story, but if the storyteller is able to give an affirmative answer to the questions listed, the story being considered has a much better chance of meeting the needs and interests of children than another story chosen at random.

There is no guarantee of success in storytelling. Careful planning and preparation can only reduce the risks. Storytelling is as highly personal as any of the other arts. A story may have instant appeal for one group and leave another completely unmoved. When a story does fail to captivate a group, the storyteller would be wise to analyze the situation and find out why. Constant evaluation and appraisal are necessary measures for perfecting the art of storytelling.

It would be impossible to enumerate the benefits that accrue to young children when a story is well chosen and well told. Some of the most obvious values of effective storytelling are:

1. It introduces the child to some of the finest literature available.
2. It acquaints the child with an array of cultures from around the world.
3. It brings to the child many characters with whom he or she can identify.

4. It creates a wholesome relationship between a child and an adult.

5. It helps the child to better understand life, to establish worthy goals and purposes for her- or himself.

6. It whets the appetite for further literary experiences and creates an interest in reading.

7. It enriches and enlarges the vocabulary.

8. It improves listening and comprehension skills.

9. It stimulates creative writing and other creative activities.

10. It provides the child with valuable information and knowledge.

Preparing the Story

To memorize a story for telling verbatim is usually a mistake. In the first place such a procedure is entirely too time consuming, and a dearth of stories would inevitably be the result for most teachers. Second, a memorized story lacks the warmth, naturalness, and spontaneity needed to give it life and breath. And finally, when a story has been memorized word for word, there is always the danger that forgotten lines may throw the storyteller off course and spoil the story completely.

A more practical and realistic plan is recommended by many experienced storytellers. It calls for memorizing only certain passages from a story and for learning the rest by scenes or "pictures" as they appear in the story. Since this plan has a great deal of merit for the novice storyteller, it will be more fully discussed on the following pages.

Because the opening or introduction to a story should be presented as close to perfect as possible to capture the interest and imagination of children, memorization or near-memorization of this part is justifiable.

A typical folktale's introduction is disarmingly brief and simple, and yet it usually presents the characters, the time, the place, and perhaps a hint of the conflict to be resolved. One of the favorite tales from the Grimm Brothers, "The Fisherman and His Wife," opens in this way:

> There was once a fisherman and his wife. They lived together in a vinegar jug close by the sea, and the fisherman went there every day and fished: and he fished and he fished.[12]

Characteristic of the old folktales is a regularly recurring phrase or verse. As far as children are concerned, this repetition is one of the most appealing features in literature. The young listeners expect (and deserve) to hear a story's refrain repeated accurately each time, and for this

---

12. Jacob and Wilhelm Grimm, *Tales from Grimm,* translated and illustrated by Wanda Gág (New York: Coward-McCann, Inc., 1936), p. 149.

reason it should also be memorized. Actually, it is the easiest part of a story to learn. The same rhythm that enchants children virtually sings its way into the storyteller's memory. Listen to the rhythm of the refrain in "The Fisherman and His Wife":

> Manye, Manye, Timpie Tee,
> Fishye, Fishye in the sea,
> Ilsebill my wilful wife
> Does not want my way of life.[13]

Many storytellers maintain that a well-told conclusion is so vital to the success of a story that it should also be committed to memory. Many an otherwise good story has been ruined because the storyteller strung out the conclusion or allowed it to taper off to nothing. A good ending to a folktale comes immediately after the climax. It is brief, concise, emphatic, and conclusive. "Snip, Snap, Snout. This tale's told out."[14]

The following outline is an informal way of making notations about the scenes of a story.[15] Key clues can help in learning the story and also in reviewing it for retelling.

The Three Billy Goats Gruff

   I. Introduction

      "Once upon a time there were three billy goats who were to go up to the hillside to make themselves fat, and the name of all three was 'Gruff'."

  II. Development

     A. Troll under the bridge

     B. Youngest goat's crossing

        1. Goats' refrain: "Trip, trop! trip, trop!"

        2. Troll's refrains: "Who's that tripping over my bridge?" "Now, I'm coming to gobble you up!"

     C. Second goat's crossing

 III. Climax

     A. Third goat's crossing

     B. Destruction of troll

 IV. Conclusion

     A. Goats reach the hillside "Snip, Snap, Snout. This tale's told out."

---

13. Ibid., p. 151.

14. Marcia Brown, *The Three Billy Goats Gruff* (New York: Harcourt Brace Jovanovich, Inc., 1957).

15. Ibid.

Once the scenes of a story are clearly in mind, the storyteller needs to practice telling it several times, paying special attention to the introduction, climax, conclusion, and rhythmic refrain. Oral rehearsals should be repeated until the story is completely mastered.

Creating a Climate

To give children a better opportunity for effective looking and listening, the teacher will want to set the stage for storytelling. A low chair or stool for the storyteller is placed in the most advantageous spot in the classroom. It then becomes the focal point for the storytelling circle.

If aids or related objects are to be used with the story, a small desk or table to hold them may be placed beside the chair. All such items should be assembled and arranged, in the order they are to be presented, before the children are seated. Once the storyteller's station has been established and realia are in place, the children may then come to the area and seat themselves in a semicircle around the storyteller.

Various methods of providing seating for children in uncarpeted classrooms have proven successful. Some teachers prefer to have the children bring chairs to the circle. Others provide an area rug that is reserved solely for storytelling and reading aloud. Still other teachers have obtained inexpensive cushions on which the children can comfortably sit cross-legged. If cushions are used, they may be stored in a large box or basket that the children have decorated with bright poster paint. Alternatives to cushions might include carpet samples, bath towels, foam rubber squares, or mats made by stitching several thicknesses of cloth together.

More and more kindergarten and primary classrooms are being carpeted, and floor space is being utilized to give children some sorely needed leg room. Many newer classes are being designed and built with a "story well"—a sunken, carpeted circle lined with soft benches for snug, intimate seating. The story well is an updated version of the primitive "story ring" composed of logs and arranged around an open campfire.

Many seating arrangements are possible. A teacher may wish to experiment with more than one type. In any case, the seating of the children should add to the ceremonial ritual of the storytelling period. The established routine of preparing for a story in a special way offers young children a certain kind of security. It also conjures up the feeling that magic and excitement are just around the corner. Once the mood is created, the storyteller's task is one of pure delight (fig. 2.1).

Figure 2.1. A third dimensional display
prepared by a student teacher was used in the
elementary classroom to promote a popular
book. (Courtesy Lamar University.)

Setting a Time

There is probably no "best" time of the day to tell stories in the classroom. Some teachers prefer to use storytelling at various intervals during the day to give children a break from tedious mental tasks. This is a sound plan, since there is evidence that they are able to take up their work again, rested, refreshed, and with a renewed interest that allows them to accomplish more.

Story time is used by other teachers as a way to calm children and settle them down when they arrive in the classroom. A "decompression chamber" is the way one teacher refers to the early morning story circle, a place where children are able to put aside some of the anxieties they bring with them to school.

Story time is used by many kindergarten teachers as a means of calling children from their work at interest centers when it is time for planning, for directed activities, or for evaluation. (One teacher claps two small wooden blocks together to summon children, just the way oriental storytellers have done for centuries.) For the most part, children do not like having to leave the interest centers, and storytelling serves to soften what could amount to an unhappy transition for many of them.

One plan that should be carefully considered by all teachers of young children is the practice of telling a story just before children leave for home. The satisfying experience of sharing a good story with other children and with the teacher is a nearly foolproof way to ensure that each child leaves with a positive feeling about school. Such an attitude is reflected to parents when the child relates the activities of the school day. Thus, storytelling becomes a way of improving home–school relations in which the child becomes the beneficiary in the long run.

Barriers to Good Storytelling

Certain limitations and problems exist in the practice of telling stories to young children. However, they are difficulties that can be predicted, anticipated, and subsequently resolved. Many master storytellers have issued warnings to those who are novices in the art, with the hope that their years of trial-and-error experiences can be of assistance to the beginner. Some of their most helpful suggestions are as follows:

1. Avoid using moralizing stories with strong didactic overtones. Such stories only serve to offend the sensibilities of children and leave them with a feeling of having been "preached to" by one who lured them into the situation on the promise of entertainment.

2. Overacting, making too many gestures, and talking down to children are flaws that can cause a story to fall short or fail completely. Storytellers should remain true to their art and refuse to engage in practices that turn it into a tortured performance. Children can see that kind of production any hour of the day on television. Storytelling is, and must remain, an experience of higher quality.

3. There should be no attempt to analyze every story told. Interested children will ask questions, and discussions should take place in a natural way. The storyteller may wish to ask leading, provocative questions, which is quite acceptable, but this part of the storytelling session should be informal and spontaneous. Ultimately, each child should have the freedom of interpreting the literature in his or her own way.

4. Listeners should not be *required* to retell a story or to react to it in other ways. Children frequently choose to write about a story they have enjoyed, to interpret it in painting, or to act it out. Of course, this privilege should always be extended, but experiences with literature are too personal and individualized to demand the same kind of feedback from all the children in a group.

5. Distracting influences should not be consistently tolerated by the storyteller. If a story is worth telling, it deserves a respectful, interested, attentive audience. Many stories have been spoiled for all the listeners because a few children were allowed to wander in and out of the listening group, to play with distracting objects, or to make irrelevant, extraneous comments. Effective listening can be taught and storytelling is a reliable means of doing it.

Using Visual Aids

Purists in the field of storytelling often criticize the use of aids to enhance a story and view them only as distracting elements. On the other hand, teachers who make a practice of telling stories frequently to the same children over the span of a school year recognize the need for variety in the routine of storytelling.

In most cases, teachers of older elementary students rely solely on the story itself and the human voice to carry it forward, whereas teachers of younger children make frequent use of the flannelboard, pocket chart, flip chart, pictures, records, puppets, cutouts, and related objects to illustrate and dramatize a story. Paul Anderson defends the use of graphic devices to hold the attention of younger children (fig. 2.2):

> When Hans Christian Andersen entertained the children of Denmark with his stories, he used to cut out silhouettes in order to make his characters more vivid. In ancient China the storyteller would cast shadows to illustrate the characters in his tales of magic and ancient ways. The modern movie cartoon favorites use a combination of silhouette figures and movement to hold attention. In the modern classroom, the flannelboard provides the storyteller with the means of achieving similar types of movement, magic and characterization.[16]

It would seem plausible that, by using aids as a motivating introduction to a story or as a graphic follow-up activity to a story, the two viewpoints could be reconciled. Visual aids could serve their purpose of making the story more interesting and understandable, while the story itself could be presented completely unadorned and true to the ancient style of storytelling.

Once the flannelboard or pocket chart has been used to illustrate a story, it should be left in place for a few days as an interest center for the children. A great deal of oral language is stimulated as children manipulate the cutouts and tell their own versions of the story.

Paper and pellon cutouts for the flannelboard or pocket chart may be conveniently stored in file folders labeled with the title of the story.[17]

16. Paul S. Anderson, *Language Skills in Elementary Education* (New York: The Macmillan Co., 1964), p. 299.

17. Pellon is a fabric used in sewing to stiffen collars and cuffs.

Figure 2.2.   A white tablecloth draped over an inflated balloon creates a facsimile of "Gus the Friendly Ghost." (Courtesy Lamar University.)

If the cue card or outline used in learning the story is filed along with the visuals, it becomes a simple matter for the teacher or aide to retrieve and review the story for presentation at a later date. Fortunately for the storyteller, children request the same stories over and over again.

By adding a few stories each year to a story file, a teacher accumulates a good supply. On hand will be stories for telling on all holidays and special occasions, along with many other stories to make a routine school day not so routine.

The following story invites listener participation. Each time the storyteller pauses, the children should join in and repeat the refrain, "Cheese, peas, and chocolate pudding."[18]

Cheese, Peas, and Chocolate Pudding

There was once a little boy who ate cheese, peas, and chocolate pudding. Cheese, peas, and chocolate pudding. Cheese, peas, and chocolate pudding. Every day the same old thing: cheese, peas, and chocolate pudding.

---

18. Betty Van Witsen, "Cheese, Peas, and Chocolate Pudding," *Believe and Make-Believe*, edited by Lucy Sprague Mitchell and Irma Simonton Black. (New York: Bank Street College of Education, 1956); pp. 31–34. Copyright © 1956 by Bank Street College of Education. Used with permission of the College.

For breakfast, he would have some cheese. Any kind. Cream cheese, American cheese, Swiss cheese, Dutch cheese, Italian cheese, blue cheese, green cheese, yellow cheese, brick cheese. Even Liederkrantz. Just cheese for breakfast.

For lunch he ate peas. Green peas or yellow peas. Frozen peas, canned peas, dried peas, split peas, black-eyed peas. No potatoes, though; just peas for lunch.

And for supper he would have cheese *and* peas. And chocolate pudding. Cheese, peas, and chocolate pudding. Cheese, peas, and chocolate pudding. Every day the same old thing: cheese, peas, and chocolate pudding.

Once his mother brought a lamb chop for him. She cooked it in a little frying pan on the stove, and she put some salt on it, and gave it to the little boy on a blue dish. The boy looked at it. He smelled it (it did smell delicious!). He even touched it. But—

"Is this cheese?" he asked.

"It's a lamb chop, darling," said his mother. The boy shook his head.

"Cheese!" he said. So his mother ate the lamb chop herself, and the boy had some cottage cheese.

One day his big brother was chewing a raw carrot. It sounded so good, the little boy reached his hand out for a bite.

"Sure!" said his brother, "Here!" The little boy *almost* put the carrot into his mouth, but at the last minute he remembered, and said, "Is this peas?"

"No, it's a carrot," said his brother.

"Peas," said the little boy firmly, handing the carrot back.

Once his daddy was eating a big dish of raspberry pudding. It looked so shiny red and cool, the little boy came over and held his mouth open.

"Want a taste?" asked his daddy. The little boy looked and looked at the raspberry pudding. He almost looked if off the dish.

"But, is it chocolate pudding?" he asked.

"No, it's raspberry pudding," said Daddy. So the little boy frowned and backed away.

"Chocolate pudding!" he said.

His grandma bought him an ice cream cone. The little boy just shook his head.

His aunt and uncle invited him for a fried chicken dinner. Everybody ate fried chicken and fried chicken and more fried chicken. Except the little boy. And you know what he ate.

Cheese, peas, and chocolate pudding. Cheese, peas, and chocolate pudding. Every day the same old thing: cheese, peas, and chocolate pudding.

But one day—ah, one day a very funny thing happened. The little boy was playing puppy. He lay on the floor and growled and barked and rolled over. He crept to the table where his big brother was having lunch.

"Arf-arf!" he barked.

"Good doggie!" said his brother, patting his head. The little boy lay down on his back on the floor, and barked again.

But at that minute, his big brother dropped a piece of *something*.

Something dropped into the little boy's mouth. He sat up in surprise.

Because *something* was on his tongue. And *something* was warm and juicy and delicious!

And it didn't taste like cheese. And it did *not* taste like peas. And it certainly wasn't chocolate pudding.

The little boy chewed slowly. Each chew tasted better. He swallowed *something*.

"That's not cheese," he said.

"No, it's not," said his brother.

"And it isn't peas."

"No, not peas," said his brother.

"It couldn't be chocolate pudding."

"No, it certainly is not chocolate pudding," smiled his brother.

"It's hamburger."

The little boy thought hard. "I like hamburger," he said.

So ever after that, the little boy ate cheese, peas, chocolate pudding, and hamburger.

Until he was your age, of course. When he was your age, he ate everything.

The following is a popular story that lends itself to flannelboard presentation. It may be used at various seasons by showing the head as made of a jack-o-lantern, a valentine, a shamrock, or an Easter egg. The children think a teacher is very ingenious to be able to make their favorite story fit the season at hand.[19]

Queer Company

A little woman lived all alone in a little old house in the woods. One Halloween she sat in the corner, and as she sat, she spun.

> Still she sat and
> Still she spun and
> Still she wished for company.
> Then she saw her door open a little way, and in came
> A pair of big, big feet
> And sat down by the fireside.
> "That is very strange," thought the old woman, but—
> Still she sat and
> Still she spun and
> Still she wished for company.
>
> Then in came
> A pair of small, small legs,
> And sat down on the big, big feet.
> "Now that is very strange." thought the old woman, but—
> Still she sat and

19. Paul S. Anderson, "Queer Company," *Flannelboard Stories for the Primary Grades* (Minneapolis, Minn.: T. S. Denison & Co., Inc., 1962) pp. 30–31. Copyright © 1962 by T. S. Denison & Co., Inc. Reprinted by permission of the publisher.

Still she spun and
Still she wished for company.
Then in came
A wee, wee waist,
And sat right down on the small, small legs.
"Now that is very strange," thought the old woman, but—
Still she sat and
Still she spun and
Still she wished for company.
Then in came
A pair of broad, broad shoulders,
And sat down on the wee, wee waist.
But—
Still she sat and
Still she spun and
Still she wished for company.
Then in through the door came
A pair of long, long arms,
And sat down on the broad, broad shoulders.
"Now that is very strange," thought the little old woman,
but—
Still she sat and
Still she spun and
Still she wished for company.
Then in came
A pair of fat, fat hands,
And sat down on the long, long arms
But—
Still she sat and
Still she spun and
Still she wished for company.
Then in came
A round, round head,
And sat down on top of all
That sat by the fireside.
The little old woman stopped her spinning and asked
"Where did you get such big feet?"
"By much tramping, by much tramping." said Somebody.
"Where did you get such small, small legs?"
"By much running, by much running," said Somebody.
"Where did you get such a wee, wee waist?"
"Nobody knows, nobody knows," said Somebody.
"Where did you get such broad, broad shoulders?"
"From carrying brooms," said Somebody.
"Where did you get such long, long arms?"

"Swinging the scythe, swinging the scythe," said Somebody.
"Where did you get such fat, fat hands?"
"By working, by working," said Somebody.
"How did you get a huge, huge head?"
"Of a pumpkin I made it," said Somebody.
Then said the little old woman,
"What did you come for?"
"YOU!" said Somebody.

The ancient art of storytelling remains as effective today as it ever was. It is an art form that can easily compete with television, movies, and recordings. In the midst of visual and auditory bombardment vying for attention, the child wants and needs to hear stories told by a storyteller who commands a quiet confidence.

Teachers of young children have a responsibility for sharing with them the great stories of the past, but they also should show them how modern writers are creating tales that mirror our culture, tales that will eventually take their place alongside the classics. This generation is producing its own hero stories, legends, myths, and proverbs—folklore that will find its way into the mainstream of literature, to be read and told, pondered over, and wondered about in ages to come.

CHILDREN'S BOOKS FOR STORYTELLING

Andersen's Fairy Tales, translated and adapted by Katherine Folliot; illustrated by Paul Durand. New York: Derrydale Books, 1988.
> Some of the best-loved stories of all time were created by Hans Christian Andersen. Six of his most popular stories are presented in this volume: "The Shepherdess and the Chimney Sweep," "The Princess and Pea," "The Ugly Duckling," "The Little Tin Soldier," "Thumbelina," and "The Emperor's New Clothes." Large, colorful watercolor illustrations make it suitable for reading aloud to groups of children and a fine selection for the library center in the classroom.

Andersen's Fairy Tales, written by Hans Christian Andersen; illustrated by Troy Howell. Stamford, Conn.: Longmeadow Press, 1988.
> The thirty-eight stories in this classic book were originally published in the first quarter of this century. Andersen's first stories were retellings of folktales told to him as a child, but as he grew in confidence as a storyteller, he created his own stories. He is now recognized as a master of the literary fairy tale. His stories touch every reader and listener and are consistently appreciated from one generation to the next.

Bring Back the Deer, written by Jeffrey Prusski; illustrated by Neil Waldman. San Diego, Calif.: Harcourt Brace Jovanovich, 1988.
> The language of this story is sparse and rhythmic, typical of an ancient Indian folktale. The illustrations show plants and animals of the forest in a style reminiscent of Indian pertroglyphs.

Favorite Stories for the Children's Hour, edited by Carolyn Sherwin
Bailey, and Clara M. Lewis. New York: Platt & Munk, Publishers, 1965.

> An anthology of favorite folktales, fables, and legends. The collection is made
> up of some of the most popular stories from the hundreds written and retold
> by Carolyn Bailey.

Grimm's Fairy Tales, written by the Brothers Grimm and illustrated
by Allen Atkinson. New York: Simon & Schuster, 1982.

> The two German scholars began collecting folktales in the early 1800s. They
> listened to German storytellers and transcribed the tales they heard. It is
> believed that they tried to keep the tales in their most simple and original
> form. This volume contains thirty-five of the best-known and popular stories.
> Since the stories were handed down in the oral tradition, they are ideal for
> storytelling or reading aloud. This is a beautifully bound and illustrated edi-
> tion.

Ming Lo Moves the Mountain, written and illustrated by Arnold Lobel.
New York: Greenwillow Books, 1982.

> Ming Lo's wife loves her house, but not the mountain that stands beside it.
> She persuades Ming Lo to move the mountain. All the futile methods he uses
> to move it make for a delightful, hilarious folktale. Adults and children alike
> will appreciate the story's outcome. A valuable resource for both story-
> telling and reading aloud.

Shadow, translated and illustrated by Marcia Brown. New York:
Charles Scribner's Sons, 1982.

> The poet Blaise Cendrars talked with shamans and African storytellers to verify
> the dancing image of Shadow. Marcia Brown translated her story from the
> French and illustrated it with black cutout figures against bright back-
> grounds to create a beautiful picture book. She tells us, "The eerie, shifting
> image of Shadow appears where there is light and fire and a storyteller to
> bring it to life." A Caldecott Award book.

Stories for Little Children, by Pearl S. Buck. New York: The John Day
Co., Inc., 1940.

> These short stories are episodes in the lives of five young children as they
> strive to understand such phenomena as daylight, darkness, and the seasons
> of the year.

Stories to Tell Boys and Girls, compiled and edited by Al Bryant.
Grand Rapids, Mich.: Zonderman Publishing House, 1952.

> These stories were collected and arranged for the purpose of satisfying spir-
> itual and moral needs of children. Each story is intended to teach a realistic
> lesson from life.

The Story of Jumping Mouse, retold and illustrated by John Steptoe.
New York: Lothrop, Lee & Shepard Books, 1984.

> John Steptoe's interpretation of a moral tale that originated among the Plains
> Indians of North America. A small humble mouse yearns to journey to far-off
> places. On his wanderings he donates his gift of sight to a blind buffalo and
> his sense of smell to an old wolf who can no longer find his way. Magic frog
> rewards the unselfish behavior of the mouse with a special gift that allows
> him to live in the far-off land forever.

A Treasury of Irish Myths, Legend, and Folklore, edited by William Butler Yeats. New York: Crown Publishers, Inc., 1986.

> An ample collection of fairy tales and folktales of the Irish peasantry selected and edited by Ireland's master poet, the Nobel Prize laureate, William Butler Yeats. It was first published in 1888 and has become the most popular anthology of Irish folklore ever published. The tales run the gamut from dancing fairies to witches, sorcerers, leprechauns, devils, giants, and ghosts. It is beyond the readability level of most young children but is an indispensable storytelling aid to the classroom teacher at all levels from primary through high school. An excellent sourcebook to accompany the St. Patrick's Day unit.

The World's Great Stories: 55 Legends That Live Forever, written by Louis Untermeyer; illustrated by Mae Gerhard. Philadelphia, PA.: J. B. Lippincott, Co., 1964.

> "The Trojan Horse," "Daedalus and Icarus," "Romulus and Remus," and other stories loved by children have been rewritten by Louis Untermeyer to update the language and images for modern readers.

BIBLIOGRAPHY

Anderson, Paul S. *Flannelboard Stories for the Primary Grades.* Minneapolis Minn.: T. S. Denison & Co., Inc., 1962.

————. *Language Skills in Elementary Education.* New York: The Macmillan Co., 1964.

Bailey, Carolyn S. *The Story-Telling Hour.* New York: Dodd, Mead & Co., 1934.

Briggs, Nancy E., and Joseph A. Wagner. *Children's Literature Through Story Telling & Drama.* 2d ed. Dubuque, Iowa: Wm. C. Brown Company Publishers, 1979.

Brown, Marcia. *The Three Billy Goats Gruff.* New York: Harcourt Brace Jovanovich, Inc., 1957.

Cameron, Eleanor. *The Green and Burning Tree.* Boston: Little, Brown & Co., 1969.

Chambers, Dewey W. *Literature for Children: Storytelling and Creative Drama.* Dubuque, Iowa: Wm. C. Brown Company Publishers, 1970.

Colum, Padraic. *Story Telling New and Old.* New York: The Macmillan Co., 1968.

Coody, Betty, and David Nelson. *Teaching Elementary Language Arts: A Literature Approach.* Belmont, Calif.: Wadsworth Publishing Company, 1982.

Grimm, Jacob, and Wilhelm Grimm. Translated and illustrated by Wanda Gág. New York: Coward-McCann, Inc., 1936.

Hopkins, Lee Bennett. *The Best of Book Bonanza.* New York: Holt, Rinehart and Winston, 1980.

Kirkton, Carole Mosley. "Once Upon a Time . . . Folk Tales and Storytelling." *Elementary English* 48 (1971): 1024.

Mitchell, Lucy Sprague, and Irma Simonton Black, eds. *Believe and Make-Believe,* New York: Bank Street College of Education, 1956.

Moore, Vardine. *Pre-School Hour.* New York: The Scarecrow Press, Inc., 1966.

Painter, Helen W. "Marcia Brown: A Study in Versatility." *Elementary English* 43 (1966): 855.

Sawyer, Ruth. *The Way of the Storyteller.* New York: The Viking Press, 1962.

Shedd, Charlie, and Martha Shedd. *Tell Me a Story.* Garden City, N.Y.: Doubleday & Co., 1984.

Shedlock, Marie L. *The Art of the Story-Teller.* New York: Dover Publications, Inc., 1951.

Sutherland, Zena, and May Hill Arbuthnot. *Children and Books.* 5th ed. Glenview, Ill.: Scott, Foresman & Company, 1977.

Tooze, Ruth. *Storytelling.* Englewood, Cliffs, N.J.: Prentice-Hall, Inc., 1959.

Ziskind, Sylvia. *Telling Stories to Children.* New York: The H. W. Wilson Company, 1976.

3

"Let's Act It Out":

Literature for Dramatization

The use of dramatization as an educational procedure is unsurpassed as a means of helping children interpret and understand literature. Such dramatization might be defined as play-making jointly planned and executed by the children and their teacher. No written script is involved; no lines are memorized. Few, if any, properties or costumes are required. In spite of this lack of structure, or perhaps because of it, young children take their roles quite seriously. They imitate characters and act out scenes with a freedom of imagination to rival the greatest of professional actors.

Scholars in the fields of anthropology and psychology tell us that imitation is primal in men and women. Paintings, sculpture, music, dance, drama, and literature handed down to us from the past all testify that humans have long had within them an innate urge to imitate. People not only have imitated other people, but also animals, plants, and natural phenomena. Through such imitation humans have attempted to understand others. Above all, they have sought to understand themselves and their own purpose in life.

Most teachers recognize that young children need to act out their fantasies in wholesome ways, and thus provide many opportunities for them to do so. Rudolph and Cohen explain the importance of fantasizing in which children are able to imitate or act out what (at least for the moment) they would like to be:

> The world of make-believe has an almost real quality for children and they can pretend within a wide range of possible behavior. They can wish themselves anything they like, and play that it becomes a reality. They can pretend to be glib and powerful and authoritative, even if they really are only little children with very little power indeed. They can pretend that they are angry tigers, growling dogs, and fierce lions, even if in reality they are gentle and well-mannered boys and girls. They can try on for size the feeling of being a mother, a father, a street cleaner,

or a truck driver. They can go back to babyhood or forward to adulthood, they can frighten others or be the thing they are themselves afraid of. This inner life of children we call their fantasy life and it represents an integral part of children's efforts to comprehend themselves and the world around them.[1]

Informal creative drama usually begins with a literature experience. No matter whether the teacher chooses to read aloud one of the popular contemporary stories, tell a favorite old folktale, recite an appealing poem, or sing a Mother Goose rhyme, the children involved should be afforded an opportunity to give personal expression to the literature. Dramatization is the most natural and childlike means of expression.

Because there is no better way to make literature come alive for children, a well-balanced literature program should include all forms of dramatization that are suitable for young children—dramatic play, pantomime, creative dramatics, puppetry, and Readers Theatre.

Dramatic Play

Dramatic play is the acting out of life roles and situations. It is unstructured, and for the most part, unsupervised. Ordinarily, there are no costumes, no prescribed dialogue, and no audience. A child simply "plays like" she or he is a mother or father, a police officer, a bear, a horse, or perhaps a character from literature.

Although dramatic play is frequently enjoyed by children at all levels in the primary grades, it probably reaches its peak in nursery school and kindergarten. Interest centers (sometimes called learning centers, and more recently, "involvement" centers) are used at those levels, mainly to enrich the quality of dramatic play. Tantalizing materials and equipment are arranged for easy accessibility in separate areas around the classroom. Child-sized tables are filled with objects that encourage curiosity, manipulation, and "play like."

Some teachers provide a small store front that can be easily converted into a grocery store, post office, bank, shoe store, hamburger stand, ice cream parlor, beauty or barber shop, flower shop, drugstore, or any other establishment the children happen to be interested in at the moment. To accompany the various occupations and professions inspired by the store front, a series of "prop" boxes may be supplied. A box might contain, for example, a nurse's cap, a stethoscope, and a hot water bottle, or a chef's hat, an apron, and a pancake turner. Only a few properties are needed. The main ingredient will be the child's imagination. It is generally agreed, however, that children learn more from dramatic play when a trained, interested adult knows how to spark and nourish it.

---

1. Marguerita Rudolph and Dorothy H. Cohen, *Kindergarten, A Year of Learning* (New York: Appleton-Century-Crofts, 1964), p. 58.

A careful observation of children at work in interest centers will quickly reveal the fact that they re-create and reenact past experiences through play. Their past experiences include meaningful encounters with literature. In the housekeeping center children may be acting out the adventures of Papa Small, Mama Small, and the Small Smalls. In the building block area, other children may be working on a snug harbor for Little Toot or an airport for Loopy. A new chair for Peter and another for Baby Bear may be under construction in the woodworking corner. This kind of healthy fantasizing about characters goes on day after day wherever and whenever it is allowed to flourish. Thus dramatic play and literature are inextricably bound together, and both are an integral part of the early childhood curriculum.

Pantomime

Pantomime is the ancient art of telling a story with bodily movements only—without benefit of dialogue. Records show that pantomime was present in primitive societies, expressing itself in war dances, animal mimicry rites, and in rituals of sacrifice. Later, it became popular to act out the lives of saints in mime fashion; eventually masks, properties, and music were added to pantomime as an art form.

Pantomime has a place in today's classroom as an excellent means of studying literature. Children learn to understand and appreciate literature as they silently interpret it in pantomime form, while other children gain similar understandings by watching the performance.

Many children have had little or no experience with pantomime, but the teacher needs only to illustrate the procedure by acting out, in mime fashion, a familiar piece of action or characterization from literature.

Robert Whitehead writes about children's interest in mimesis and the teacher's part in encouraging it:

> Children find pantomime activities to be genuine fun, and literature comes alive as children give lifelike reenactments of situations and characters from books and stories. This is especially true if the teacher is willing to demonstrate techniques through her own pantomimes, and if she shows sincerity and empathy with the children in their interpretations of characters and scenes.[2]

Children may choose to pantomime only one scene from a story or poem, or they may wish to reenact an entire piece of literature as the teacher reads it aloud part by part. It should be kept in mind that pantomime is based solely on movement. Each gesture or motion should be clear-cut, purposeful, distinct, and realistic, so that the audience will have no difficulty in determining the character and the specific action.

---

2. Robert Whitehead, *Children's Literature: Strategies of Teaching* (Englewood Cliffs, N.J.: Prentice-Hall, Inc., 1968), p. 169.

For this reason, stories and poems selected for pantomime should be thoroughly familiar to the audience. The effort it takes to make wise literary selections and to promote effective pantomime skills will pay dividends as children begin to show a keener interest in literature.

Creative Dramatics

Although creative dramatics is informal, with no printed script or memorized lines, it is still more formal and structured than dramatic play. It is the making of a play, usually based on literature, by a group of children working under the guidance of a teacher or an aide. The play is designed to be presented before an audience of peers.

In creative dramatics, the dialogue is extemporaneous, but the children decide in advance which scenes will be reenacted. They assign parts, prepare simple properties and costumes, and finally present the play, all in a brief period of time. Again, Robert Whitehead has done an excellent job of delineating the teacher's role during this period of highly creative endeavor by children:

> Through all of this the teacher serves in a supportive role, helping the children to visualize the scenes and characters, serving as a source of properties, and helping with room arrangement and staging. Once the play is in progress, the teacher melts into the background, coming forward only if the continuity of the play falters, or acting as a prompter if a bit of dialogue is momentarily displaced. When the informal dramatization is over, the teacher leads the class in an analysis of the production.[3]

The teacher's guidance is needed to help children see that not every detail of a story need be dramatized. Some time must be spent in helping them to isolate the main events, to arrange them in sequential order, and to prepare them for dramatization. All this must be done in such a way that the plot and theme of the story remain identifiable to a youthful audience. Many children, both performers and viewers, have been disappointed with the results of a dramatization simply because not enough supportive assistance was given by the teacher during the early stages of planning the production.

If the literature is to pave the way for dramatization, it should be recognized that some books have more theatrical potential than others. Any dramatization experience will be more successful if the literature contains lively action and strong characterization. The following is a brief list of popular contemporary books that lend themselves well to creative dramatics:

Drummer Hoff by Barbara Emberley
The Happy Lion by Louise Fatio

---

3. Ibid., p. 178.

Anatole and the Cat by Eve Titus
The Bears on Hemlock Mountain by Alice Dalgliesh
Finders Keepers by Will Lipkind and Nicolas Mordinoff
Jeanne-Marie Counts Her Sheep by Françoise
Little Tim and the Brave Sea Captain by Edward Ardizzone
Mr. Penny by Marie Hall Ets
Play With Me by Marie Hall Ets
Seven Diving Ducks by Margaret Friskey
Henry-Fisherman by Marcia Brown
May I Bring a Friend? by Beatrice Schenk de Reginers

Puppetry

No one knows for sure where or when the art of puppetry originated, but it is known that the little actors were popular long before the time of Christ. Ancient tombs and burial grounds in all parts of the world have revealed carved figures, jointed in various ways to permit movement by hand.

The word "puppet" means "doll," but a puppet is actually much more than a doll. It is a constructed figure, moved by human effort for the purpose of entertaining or teaching an audience. A puppet is an extension of the human being who operates it. Bil Baird, one of the world's most famous puppeteers, describes the relationship between a puppet and its creator:

> . . . He is the result of the concept, the animation, and the design of some of us fallible creatures. We make either good puppets or bad ones, and although the puppets do succeed to some extent in filtering out the egos of their creators, some of our foibles seem to come through.[4]

Professional puppeteers look on their puppets not as toys, but as mechanical actors operated by human endeavor. They consider the most important feature of any puppet to be its "humanized" movement. Shari Lewis, the popular puppeteer of television fame, discusses the loss of human quality in those puppets operated electronically by remote control:

> . . . They are astounding and quite lifelike, but in my opinion, lack the spontaneity, charm, warmth, and humanity that can be found only when the puppeteer is in direct contact with his alter ego.[5]

A puppet may represent a person, an animal, a machine, or an abstraction, but no matter what form it takes, the art of puppetry is an ancient and effective way in which humans express themselves and

---

4. Bil Baird, *The Art of the Puppet* (New York: The Macmillan Co., 1965), p. 223.
5. Shari Lewis, *Making Easy Puppets* (New York: E. P. Dutton & Co., Inc., 1967), p. 13.

communicate with others. Before the advent of television, it was a popular form of home entertainment. Fortunately, in homes where television has not been allowed to assume so important a role, children and their parents still have time for such activities as storytelling, reading aloud, and puppetry.

By the same token, in classrooms that have not become overmechanized, puppetry is still used to dramatize events in history, to illustrate ways of life in other cultures, to encourage acceptable social behavior, to emphasize desirable health practices, to stimulate creative activities, to promote literature, and simply to entertain children.

Puppetry is widely used as an educational practice during early childhood because teachers recognize the value of a puppet to help young children with personal development (fig. 3.1). It is nothing short of miraculous the way some children are able to express thoughts, ideas, and feelings through the mouth of a puppet with a fluency they could never achieve otherwise.

Edward Mattil is one who sees the puppet as having therapeutic value for children who need to gain confidence in themselves:

> . . . There is probably no greater thrill or sense of satisfaction than that which comes to the teacher, who through planning and effort, finds his pupils unfolding and revealing qualities that had lain dormant. Often these very qualities are not evident because the child lacks confidence in himself or is unable to communicate his thoughts and feelings for lack of the right medium.[6]

Figure 3.1.   An appealing puppet encourages a young child to extend and refine oral language skills. (Courtesy of Michael Coody.)

6. Edward L. Mattil, *Meaning in Crafts* (Englewood Cliffs, N.J.: Prentice-Hall, Inc., 1971), p. 91.

Teachers who use puppets on a regular basis, just as they do other curriculum materials, vouch for their effectiveness as a means of developing self-confidence in shy children. Through the voice and gestures of the puppet, a child is able to say what he or she would like to say in real life situations, but does not in fear of disapproval or outright reprisal.

Through puppetry, the child controls the puppet, and in so doing, controls the environment. He or she can be as superior to the puppet as he or she wishes to be. It will do exactly as commanded. In this way a child is able to express hidden or suppressed emotions to a nonpunishing audience. Release of this type is very important to healthy personality development.

Mattil makes an interesting statement regarding the benefits of classroom puppetry on the development of children. He sees puppets as a way to offset the limitations of the fragmented curriculum that is evident today in so many classrooms:

> In addition to the satisfaction of making a puppet, the child should have the opportunity to project even more of himself in the experience through performing. It is in this phase that children are able to express freely and openly some of the things which are difficult to express in the classroom. This is not to suggest that puppets are a catharsis; instead, they become a tool for easier and more open expression. The range of ideas and emotions are almost limitless in a puppet play in which children are encouraged to give full play to their imaginations and their fantasies. The play or show culminates the activity, thus eliminating the fragmented or partial experience, so commonplace in education.[7]

Puppetry and Children's Literature

Young children seem to have an instinctive urge to imitate what they see and hear. Acting out a concept is a way of demonstrating to themselves and others that they understand. A good story told or read often needs to be imitated or acted out, and puppetry is a natural vehicle for this kind of drama.

Stories that can be readily adapted to puppet plays for and by young children are quite plentiful. The old folktales with their humanism, their lively plots, and realistic themes are undoubtedly the best sources of material for puppetry. Economy of events and characters in the tales make puppet construction and staging relatively simple. The repetition and rhythmic language offer added appeal. Imagine Henny Penny, Cocky Locky and Ducky Lucky moving across the stage as stick puppets, shouting to all, "The sky is falling! The sky is falling! I must go and tell the king!"

---

7. Ibid., p. 103.

In selecting stories to tell and read aloud, teachers should keep in mind that children like lively dialogue, much action, a conflict to be resolved, heroes that *do* things, a rousing climax, and a satisfactory ending. Of course, these qualities are distinguishing characteristics of folktales, and thus set them apart as ideal for puppet dramatization. The following list suggests some of the stories considered best for puppetry at the kindergarten and primary levels:

"The Three Little Pigs"
"The Three Billy Goats Gruff"
"The Three Bears"
"The Three Little Kittens"
"Jack and the Beanstalk"
"Henny Penny"
"The Pancake"
"The Little Red Hen and the Grain of Wheat"
"Bremen Town Musicians"
"Mr. and Mrs. Vinegar"
"Little Red Riding Hood"
"Cinderella"
"Rumpelstiltskin"
"The Old Woman and Her Pig"
"Hansel and Gretel"
"The Wolf and the Seven Little Kids"

Puppet Types

Once the children have chosen a favorite tale to be dramatized, the next step is to decide which type of puppet will best represent the story characters. It is imperative that the teacher and the aide know many puppet types and how to make them. Materials for constructing various kinds of puppets should be easily accessible so that children can make the puppets and hold an impromptu performance while interest in the story is at its peak.

Realism can be ignored in the art of puppet making. Exaggeration, imagination, and whimsy always make for better puppetry than does any attempt to duplicate nature. When children are provided with many interesting materials, and freedom to use them in fresh and original ways, they can create puppets that will bring pleasure both to themselves and to their audience.

An endless variety of puppets may be constructed from the four classic puppet types:

1. The hand puppet. This type, as the name implies, is made to fit over the hand of the puppeteer. The head of the puppet is usually moved by the puppeteer's index finger, and the arms are

moved by the third finger and thumb. Some of the hand puppets are the easiest of all types to construct and manipulate.

2. The rod puppet. This type of puppet is controlled by one or more rigid rods to which the puppet is attached. In staging, the rod is usually hidden from view, and the puppet appears to move through space unassisted. Rod puppets are easily adaptable for use with children of all ages.

3. The shadow puppet. This type of puppet has been extremely popular in almost every culture. Early shadow puppets were made from the hides of animals. Figures were cut from the hide and fastened to a thin wire. When the figure was moved about between a bright light and a tightly stretched screen, a shadow or silhouette was seen by the audience. Modern children are able to produce very effective shadow puppet shows by means of the overhead projector and figures cut from black paper.

4. The marionette. This basic type of puppet is a jointed figure whose parts are manipulated by strings. Of all the puppet types, marionettes are the most difficult puppets to construct and to operate. For the most part marionettes are too intricate for young children to manage, even though they enjoy watching marionette performances staged by adults or older students. Because marionettes are better left to upper-grade students, they will not be given further consideration in this discussion of puppetry for young children. Directions for making a variety of puppets from the other three classic types are given on the following pages.

Puppet Construction

Paper Sack Puppets.   A paper sack puppet is made by painting the face of a person or an animal on the folded end of a closed paper bag (fig. 3.2). The mouth of the face should be divided with the upper lip on the bottom of the paper bag and the lower lip on the bag itself. When the hand is placed inside the bag with fingers inside the flap, the puppet will open and close its mouth as the hand is opened and closed. Hair, ears, clothing, and other features may be made by gluing on bits of cloth, colored construction paper, costume jewelry, artificial flowers, or buttons and braid.

A puppet stage may consist of a chair or sofa, a table turned on its side, a doorway draped with a sheet, a chart rack, or a large cardboard carton.

Rubber Ball Puppets.   The head of this type of puppet is made by cutting a hole inside a hollow rubber ball large enough for the puppeteer's index finger. Facial features are added to the ball with paint or with felt pieces glued on. The body of the puppet is made by draping a handkerchief over the hand. Rubber bands twisted around the third finger and thumb will hold the handkerchief securely in place and provide the puppet with two flexible arms (fig. 3.3).

A styrofoam ball may be used instead of a rubber ball to form a puppet head. It will be necessary to hollow out a depression in the foam large enough for the index finger to be inserted. Colored thumb tacks make suitable features for the styrofoam ball puppet.

Sock Puppets.   A sock puppet is made by inserting an oval cardboard approximately five inches by three inches into the foot of the sock as an innersole. The cardboard should extend from the toe to the heel of the sock. The cardboard is then folded across the center, forming the upper and lower jaws of the puppet. When the puppeteer's hand is placed inside the sock with fingers above the top fold of the cardboard and thumb below the bottom fold, the puppet's mouth will open and close as the thumb and fingers are brought together. Features may be made with brads and scraps of colored paper or felt (fig. 3.4).

Box Puppets.   Box puppets are made by taping two small, deep boxes together with the openings of both boxes facing the puppeteer. A face is painted on the bottom of the two boxes with the mouth divided between the two. The upper half of the mouth goes on one box, and the lower half on the other. When the puppeteer's fingers are placed in the upper box and the thumb in the lower box, the puppet's mouth will open and close as the thumb and fingers are brought together (fig. 3.5).

Fruit and Vegetable Puppets.   Puppets may be made from oranges, apples, pears, potatoes, carrots, and turnips by impaling the fruit or vegetable on a stick. (Children usually need help with this step.) Features for the puppet may be made of thumb tacks, brads, push pins, gold stars, and paper reinforcements.

The body of the fruit or vegetable puppet is made by inserting the stick through a small hole in the center of a handkerchief used to cover the puppeteer's hand (fig. 3.6). Fruit and vegetable puppets are, of course, perishable, but they will last for several days.

Cylinder Puppets.   A cylinder puppet may be made by using a three-inch section cut from a paper towel tube. Hair, eyes, ears, nose, mouth, and clothing may be cut from felt or colored paper and glued in place on the cylinder. The puppet will move when the puppeteer's index and third fingers are placed inside the cylinder and bent forward (fig. 3.7).

Figure 3.3.   Rubber ball puppet.

Figure 3.2.   Sack puppet.

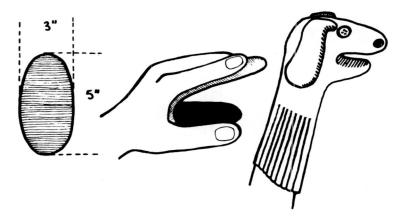

Figure 3.4.   Sock puppet.

Figure 3.5.   Box puppet.

Figure 3.6.   Vegetable puppets.

Figure 3.7.   Cylinder puppets.

Figure 3.8.   Stick puppet.

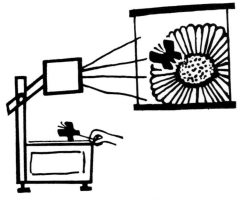

Figure 3.9.   Shadow puppet.

Figure 3.10.   Humanette puppet.

Figure 3.11.   Mask puppet.

Stick Puppets.   The easiest of all puppets to construct and operate are the stick puppets. Pictures of people, animals, machines, furniture, and toys are cut from magazines. The shapes are glued on thin cardboard and cut out a second time. The stiffened shape is then taped to a stick or plastic drinking straw. The puppeteer grasps the stick and moves the puppet back and forth behind a screen (fig. 3.8). The audience sees only the body of the puppet above the screened area.

The artwork of children may also be used to make very effective stick puppets.

Shadow Puppets.   Shadow puppets for the overhead projector may be made by cutting silhouettes of storybook characters from black paper and taping them to a thin, stiff wire. By holding the wires, the puppeteer is able to move the shapes across the glass surface of the overhead projector without his or her hands being visible to the audience. The black paper blocks out the light and causes large images to appear on the screen (fig. 3.9).

Backgrounds for this type of shadow puppet can be made by drawing scenes on transparencies with colored felt point pens. Colored acetate can also be used effectively.

Humanette Puppets.   The humanette is a variation of the comical puppets used years ago to entertain vaudeville audiences. The humanette is a large cardboard cutout in the shape of a person, animal, plant, or machine. It is usually painted with tempera paints.

Openings are cut in the cardboard to allow the puppeteer's face and arms to come through (fig. 3.10). A finished humanette will fit children of all sizes and may be used over and over to give all the children an opportunity to dramatize various character parts. No stage is needed.

Mask Puppets.   Masks are made and worn by people to disguise, to transform, and to protect themselves. Children in the primary classroom usually make and wear masks to entertain themselves and others, yet they also can appreciate the fact that some people wear them for very serious reasons.

There is probably no exhibit easier to assemble than a display of masks, and none that provides more implications for cultural understanding. The ways in which masks are worn for protection by miners, firefighters, skiers, welders, divers, motorcyclists, chemists, surgeons, and various other people make a fascinating study for young children.

Practically any character from children's literature may be depicted by means of a simple, child-made mask. The easiest of all is made by stretching a nylon stocking over a wire coat hanger that has been slightly bent to form a face shape. Features are made by gluing felt, jewelry, buttons, or paper to the nylon. The puppeteer holds the mask in front of his or her face by grasping the hook of the coat hanger (fig. 3.11).

Milk Carton Puppets.   One of the easiest papier-mâché puppets to make has a large milk carton as its base (see fig. 3.12). The top is cut from the carton, and an inflated balloon is inserted. The balloon is covered with layers of paper strips dipped in paste. When dry, the balloon is popped, leaving a firm structure to be painted with tempera paint and turned into any storybook character. A drawstring slipcover forms the clothing or "fur." The milk carton puppet is large, and the full length of a child's arm may be used to manipulate it. This type of puppet is excellent for a large audience because it can be seen easily at a distance (figs. 3.13 and 3.14).

MILK CARTON PUPPETS

CUT EVENLY ALONG TOP EDGE OF CARTON.

PLACE INFLATED BALLOON SO THAT IT RESTS SOLIDLY ON THE CARTON'S CUT EDGE AND SECURE WITH MASKING TAPE.

APPLY 3 SOLID LAYERS OF PAPIER-MÂCHÉ STRIPS TO BALLOON AND CARTON TOP AND LET DRY. WHEN PASTE IS DRY, POP THE BALLOON AND CUT THE BOTTOM FROM THE CARTON.

APPLY FEATURES TO THE HEADS BY PAINTING FLAT FACES OR BUILDING DIMENSIONAL FEATURES WITH PAPIER-MÂCHÉ OVER CARDBOARD.

CONSTRUCT A TUBE "SKIRT"(WITH A DRAW-STRING AT ONE END) TO FIT OVER THE CARTON. THE STRING CINCHES AT THE NECK AND TIES IN A BOW.

Figure 3.12.   Milk carton puppets.

Figure 3.13. These puppets show the versatility of papier-mâché over an inflated balloon. Much larger than traditional puppets, they project farther and are well-suited to a large audience.

Figure 3.14. Young children are very fond of folk tales and any folk tale character can be replicated by means of papier-mâché over an inflated balloon. This group represents "Little Red Riding Hood." For directions in making puppets, see Figure 3.12. (Courtesy of Carol Van Fleet.)

Puppetry for Instructional Purposes

Puppets should never be used for preachy didactism, and children should not feel that when the teacher brings out a puppet they are in for a heavy dose of reprimand and guilt. On the contrary, puppetry is an excellent way to motivate effort and also to reward it. It lightens the load of tedious mental tasks that are a part of every school day, and it has a remarkable ability to facilitate communication. It should at all times remain lighthearted and enjoyable. The following activities are suggested as ways to use puppetry for curriculum enrichment:

- To make oral assignments
- To direct practice exercises
- To administer oral tests
- To present information
- To make announcements
- To emphasize health practices
- To stimulate conversation
- To foster self-expression
- To introduce book characters
- To review books
- To develop cultural awareness
- To read poetry
- To direct choral speaking
- To interview students
- To personify environmental problems
- To teach library skills
- To present riddles (or answers)
- To prepare for a field trip
- To inspire creative writing
- To break the ice and get acquainted
- To consider family relationships
- To direct practice in phonics
- To lead sing-alongs
- To present holiday characters
- To give oral directions for cooking
- To narrate material for an experience chart
- To dramatize myths and legends

Readers Theatre

"Readers Theatre" is a rather new name for the ancient practice of interpreting a piece of literature by means of oral reading. Because it is done by several individuals reading the dialogue of various characters, it is sometimes called "group reading." Roy A. Beck writes "Since one reader usually reads several parts, he merely *suggests* each character vocally, he does not characterize as an actor does. In oral interpretation, emphasis is placed on the literature, and *the readers communicate with the audience through the literature.*"[8]

There are no hard and fast rules in Readers Theatre, and experimentation has always been one of its attractions. However, one of its distinguishing features is that the performance is usually carried out without benefit of stage properties, costumes, or lighting (fig. 3.15). If these traditional theater accoutrements are used, they are kept to a bare minimum. The emphasis is on the literature.

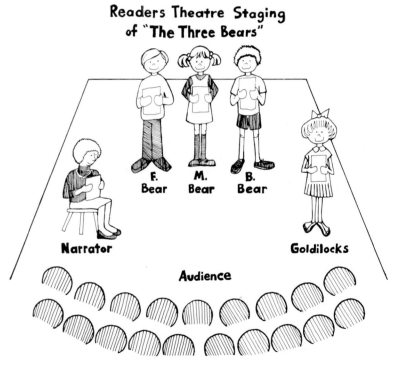

Readers Theatre Staging of "The Three Bears"

F. Bear   M. Bear   B. Bear

Narrator

Goldilocks

Audience

Figure 3.15.   No stage is necessary. Readers are arranged as shown in the front of the classroom. The narrator is seated on a low stool and faces both audience and readers. The audience is seated in a semicircle directly in front of the readers. (Drawing courtesy of Barbara Ellis.)

We ordinarily think of Readers Theatre as a performance by adults for other adults, or as a group reading by older students for their peers. Such is not the case. The fun of oral interpretation need not be reserved for grownups. As a matter of fact, Readers Theatre has become a highly successful creative art form for young children who have learned to read well.

In staging a Readers Theatre performance for a primary classroom, the teacher is the most likely candidate for the role of narrator. It is the narrator who bridges the space between readers and listeners, who simplifies descriptive passages, and generally sets the mood for the reading. The children who are to read either sit or stand before the audience, holding the manuscripts in a natural and relaxed fashion.

The reading is done in a similar relaxed manner, naturally and without undue dramatization. The reader never attempts to become the character, but merely implies the character. Attention should be drawn to the literature rather than to the reader, and this can be accomplished only if each reader is thoroughly prepared, knows the material well enough to read it smoothly, and continues to concentrate on the meaning of the passages being read.

In a successful classroom production of Readers Theatre, both the children who are readers and the children who are listeners reap many benefits. For promoting excellent literature, it has the same value as storytelling. It obviously strengthens both reading and listening skills. It offers the satisfying sensation of performing before an audience. The most important function of Readers Theatre, however, is the sheer enjoyment it provides—the chance it gives children to have good fun with literature.

The following suggestions may prove helpful in the selection of literature for Readers Theatre productions in the primary classroom:

1. The characters should have distinguishing features and personalities.

2. The language should be rich, rhythmic, and colorful.

3. The selection should provoke laughter and surprise, wonder and imagination.

4. There should be a good story line with an element of conflict and suspense.

5. The material should be easy to read and should have a great deal of dialogue.

6. Selected materials should require a minimum of rewriting.

7. Remember that almost any material suitable for storytelling is also good for readers theatre: ''The Three Bears,'' ''The Three

Little Pigs," "The Three Billy Goats Gruff," "Henny Penny," "The Little Red Hen," and the "Bremen Town Musicians."

8. Inexpensive paperback books may be purchased in the necessary numbers (one book per character and an additional one for the narrator) and kept on file to be used with various groups of students.

Only the simplest form of story, one that is brief and filled with dialogue, is naturally suited for Readers Theatre at the primary level. Other stories must be adapted by the teacher. Adaptation consists mainly of rewriting the material to condense and simplify it, deleting extraneous material, adding needed information to clarify, and rearranging material for more effective oral communication.

It should be acknowledged here that some teachers are bothered by literature "adaptation" and by any attempt to lower its readability level. There is no need for concern. Readers Theatre adaptations are not intended to dilute literature, but simply to make it more "oral" in nature. It is reassuring to know that an effective Readers Theatre production will usually send children scurrying to ferret out the original version.

Preparing the Scripts

Once a story is selected for Readers Theatre, it should be rewritten as a script, typed, and duplicated—one copy for each character. A character's part is marked throughout with a pastel-colored liner and then stapled into a folder of the same color. It should then be labeled with the character's title. The next character's part is underlined with another color and stapled into its own folder and so on. Folders are stacked together and fastened with a rubber band. When an ample number of plays have been prepared they should be stored in a "Readers Theatre" box for easy access by the students.

Preparing a set of easy-to-read scripts is a time-consuming task for a teacher, but fortunately it is material that can be used for years to come. Readers Theatre is an activity thoroughly enjoyed by students and one of the most effective procedures available for building oral reading skills.

CHILDREN'S BOOKS FOR DRAMATIZATION

A, B, C: Go!, edited by Margaret E. Martignoni. New York: The Crowell-Collier Publishing Co., 1962.
This collection of poems and stories for children is one of the "Collier's Junior Classics," a series of literature samplers. The volume is well illustrated with most of the art coming from the original works. It contains a total of 380 poems and stories by outstanding authors and poets.

Anatole and the Cat, by Eve Titus; illustrated by Paul Galdone. New York: Whittlesey House, 1957.

> Anatole, the Cheese Taster, is the most honored and respected mouse in all of France. He also turns out to be the bravest by figuring out a way to do something that other mice had been talking about for thousands of years— a way to bell the cat!

The Bears on Hemlock Mountain, by Alice Dalgliesh; illustrated by Helen Sewell. New York: Charles Scribner's Sons, 1952.

> Darkness overtakes Jonathan on Hemlock Mountain, where he was sent to borrow a large iron cooking pot from his Aunt Emma. When two bears block his path, Jonathan takes refuge under the big iron pot and stays there until help comes. Young readers are always amused and impressed by Jonathan's ingenuity.

Children's Literature for Dramatization: An Anthology, edited by Geraldine Brain Siks. New York: Harper & Row, Publishers, 1964.

> A collection of fifty-six stories and eighty-two poems chosen by the editor for their dramatic content. Many of the selections have been adapted for dramatic presentation. All the stories and poems were dramatized by children before being included in the collection.

Chimney Corner Stories, edited by Veronica S. Hutchinson and illustrated by Lois Lenski. New York: Minton, Balch & Co., 1925.

> This fine old collection contains sixteen of the world's most loved tales. It includes "The Three Billy Goats Gruff," "The Three Pigs," "The Pancake," "Henny Penny," and "The Little Red Hen and the Grain of Wheat."

Drummer Hoff, by Barbara Emberley; illustrated by Ed Emberley. Englewood Cliffs, N.J.: Prentice-Hall, Inc., 1967.

> This is an adaptation of an old folk rhyme in which many people bring parts to assemble a cannon. Events accumulate until the cannon is finally fired— "Drummer Hoff fired it off." The rhyme ends abruptly as the cannon is fired. The last picture leaves the reader with a feeling of peace.

The Family Treasury of Children's Stories, Book I, edited by Pauline Rush Evans and illustrated by Donald Sibley. Garden City, N.Y.: Doubleday & Co., Inc., 1956.

> This book is a mammoth collection of some of the finest poems and stories that have ever been written for children. It begins with Mother Goose rhymes and the simplest stories for very young listeners.

Finders Keepers, written and illustrated by William Lipkind and Nicolas Mordvinoff. New York: Harcourt Brace Jovanovich, Inc., 1951.

> This is a story of two dogs who live together in peace and friendship until they find a bone. They ask all passersby to decide which of the two deserves to keep the bone. The ridiculous answers they get leave them no wiser. When they are forced to fight for the bone, they decide to share it.

The First Book of Indians, by Benjamin Brewster; illustrated by Ursula Koering. New York: Franklin Watts, Inc., 1950.

> Benjamin Brewster, the author of this book, has been interested in Indians for many years. The book is authentic, factual, and filled with accurate drawings and diagrams.

The Happy Lion, by Louise Fatio; illustrated by Roger Duvoisin. New York: Whittlesey House, 1954.

> Everyone loves the happy lion so long as he is in the zoo surrounded by a moat, but when he escapes the zoo and strolls down the street, people behave differently. All in all he finds it best to be back in the zoo on the other side of the moat where people love him again.

Henry-Fisherman, written and illustrated by Marcia Brown. New York: Charles Scribner's Sons, 1949.

> Henry, a young boy living on an island in the Caribbean, wants more than anything to be a fisherman. When his father finally invites Henry to go out in the boat with him, exciting adventures ensue. This is a beautiful picture book that captures the beauty of a Caribbean island harbor "as safe as heaven itself."

Jeanne-Marie Counts Her Sheep, written and illustrated by Françoise. New York: Charles Scribner's Sons, 1951.

> Jeanne-Marie makes elaborate plans for all the things she will buy when her sheep Patapon has lambs. As she imagines more and more lambs, Jeanne-Marie's list of wanted items grows. Eventually Patapon has one little lamb and there is just enough wool to knit Jeanne-Marie a pair of new socks. The story is illustrated with bright, posterlike pictures.

Little Tim and the Brave Sea Captain, written and illustrated by Edward Ardizzone. New York: Henry Z. Walck, Inc., 1955.

> Tim, a small boy who wants more than anything to be a sailor, stows away on an ocean steamer. He is forced to face storms, hard work, and other perils of being a sailor. Tim proves to be courageous and hardworking. He endears himself to the other sailors and especially to the captain, who finally sees Tim safely home again.

May I Bring a Friend?, written by Beatrice Schenk de Regniers and illustrated by Beni Montresor. New York: Atheneum, 1965.

> A young boy brings all his animal friends with him when he is invited to have tea with the king and queen. The animals return the hospitality by entertaining the king and queen with a tea at the city zoo. It is a delightfully humorous story told in verse form. It includes an informal presentation of the days of the week.

Mr. Penny, written and illustrated by Marie Hall Ets. New York: The Viking Press, 1935.

> Mr. Penny's large family of lazy farm animals keep him working long hours at the factory to keep them supplied with food. Finally, they have remorse and begin working together to make a fine garden for Mr. Penny. The garden provides funds for a new house, and Mr. Penny and his animals turn out to be "the happiest family in Wuddle."

Nora Kramer's Storybook, edited by Nora Kramer and illustrated by Beth and Joe Krush. New York: Gilbert Press, Inc., 1955.

> This book is an ample collection of stories and verse selected from contemporary literature. The material was chosen especially for children of ages three and four. Such writers as Kate Seredy, David McCord, and Munro Leaf are represented.

Once Upon A Time, edited by Rose Dobbs. New York: Random House, 1950.

>This is a collection of twenty old tales that have been favorites for story-telling over many years. Included are "The Half-Chick," "The Pine Tree," and "Clever Elsie." Many of the stories have been retold by the editor. They are very easy to prepare for storytelling.

Play with Me, written and illustrated by Marie Hall Ets. New York: The Viking Press, 1955.

>A girl tries to capture small animals for companionship. None of them will play with her. Finally, she sits very still and waits for them to come to her. An excellent book to show that pets need kindness, gentleness, and care.

Seven Diving Ducks, written by Margaret Friskey; illustrated by Jean Morey. New York: Children's Press, 1965.

>One little duckling in a family of seven is afraid to swim and dive. Father Duck is about to send him to live with the chickens, when something happens that helps the timid little duck to be able to swim and dive as well as the others.

BIBLIOGRAPHY

Ackley, Edith Flack, *Marionettes.* Philadelphia, Pa.: J. B. Lippincott Co., 1929.

Ando, Tsuruo. *Bunraku, The Puppet Theatre.* New York: Walker-Weatherhill, 1970.

Arnott, Peter D. *Plays Without People.* Bloomington: Indiana University Press, 1964.

Baird, Bil. *The Art of the Puppet.* New York: The Macmillan Co., 1965.

Batchelder, Marjorie. *The Puppet Theatre Handbook.* New York: Harper & Row, Publishers, 1947.

Batchelder, Marjorie, and Virginia Lee Comer. *Puppets and Plays,* New York: Harper & Row, Publishers, 1956.

Beck, Roy A. *Group Reading: Readers Theatre,* Skokie, Illinois: National Textbook Company, 1969.

Brooks, Keith, Eugene Bahn, and LaMont Okey. *The Communicative Act of Oral Interpretation.* 2d ed. Boston: Allyn and Bacon, Inc., 1976.

Coger, Leslie Iren, and Melvin R. White. *Readers Theatre Handbook.* Glenview, Ill.: Scott, Foresman & Company, 1967.

Currell, David. *Learning with Puppets.* Boston: Plays, Inc., 1980.

Egoff, Shelia, G. T. Stubbs, and L. F. Ashley. *Only Connect: Readings on Children's Literature.* New York: Oxford University Press, 1969.

Emberly, Ed. *Punch and Judy.* Boston: Little, Brown & Co., 1965.

Hanford, Robert Ten Eyck. *Puppets and Puppeteering*. New York: Sterling Publishing Company, Inc., 1981.

Hunt, Kari, and Bernice Wells Carlson. *Masks and Mask Makers*. New York: Abingdon Press, 1961.

Johnson, Edna, et al. *Anthology of Children's Literature*. 5th edition. Boston: Houghton Mifflin Co., 1987.

Krider, Margaret. "Puppet Theatre in the Classroom." *School Arts,* December 1980, pp. 54, 55.

Larson, Martha L. "Readers Theatre: New Vitality for Oral Reading." *The Reading Teacher* (1976): 359–360.

Lewis, Roger. *Puppets and Marionettes*. New York: Alfred A. Knopf, Inc., 1952.

Lewis, Shari. *Making Easy Puppets*. New York: E. P. Dutton & Co., Inc., 1967.

Long, Beverly Whitaker, Lee Hudson, and Phillis Jeffrey. *Group Performance of Literature*. Englewood Cliffs, N.J.: Prentice-Hall, Inc., 1977.

Lukens, Rebecca J. *A Critical Handbook of Children's Literature*. 4th ed. Glenview, IL: Scott, Foresman & Company, 1990.

Mattil, Edward L. *Meaning in Crafts*. Englewood Cliffs, N.J.: Prentice-Hall, Inc., 1971.

McNeil, Jacqueline. "Shadows that Light Up the Classroom." *Teacher,* January 1981, pp. 43, 44.

McRuliffe, June C. "The Child and Puppets: A Belief and a Project." *School Arts,* December 1980, pp. 48–49.

Ratliff, Gerald Lee. "Puppetry and Communication Skills." *School Arts,* December 1980, pp. 46–48.

Rudolph, Marguerita, and Dorothy H. Cohen. *Kindergarten, A Year of Learning*. New York: Appleton-Century-Crofts, 1964.

Scott, A. C. *The Puppet Theatre of Japan*. Rutland, Vt.: Charles E. Tuttle Co., 1963.

Siks, Geraldine Brain. *Children's Literature for Dramatization: An Anthology*. New York: Harper & Row, Publishers, 1964.

Whitehead, Robert. *Children's Literature: Strategies of Teaching*. Englewood Cliffs, N.J.: Prentice-Hall, Inc., 1968.

"Say Me a Poem":

Poetry Activities for Young Children

Young children need poetry the way they need fresh air and sunshine, to lift and nourish the spirit. To deprive them of quality poetry is to keep from them one of life's important treasures.

Because so many poems written for young children are of inferior quality, it is important for teachers to make a thorough study of poems written by outstanding, well-known poets who have a reputation for writing the kind of verses children want to hear. The teacher who is completely familiar and at ease with such a body of fine poetry is then in a position to share it with young children and to use it as a measuring stick in selecting other poetry for them.

Some very dependable names to consider when deciding on poetry for young children are: David McCord, Eve Merriam, Langston Hughes, Walter de la Mare, Aileen Fisher, Rowena Bennett, Myra Cohn Livingston, Vachel Lindsay, and Marchette Chute. There are many others, of course, but the above list would provide a good beginning for the teacher who is hesitant about selecting poetry to use in kindergarten and primary grades.

An important factor to consider in the acquisition of anthologies and books by a single poet is variety. A well-balanced poetry collection for young children will include Mother Goose and nonsense rhymes, humorous poetry, light poetry, and serious poetry. The classroom teacher should then take care that all four types of poetry are included in the reading-aloud repertoire.

Suggestions for Reading Poetry Aloud

1. Read the poem several times to become more familiar and comfortable with it.

2. Look up the meaning of all words that are not understood in context. It may be important to the meaning of the poem that a word origin or definition be checked. Be sure to study the pronunciation of individual words.

3. Look at the poem through the eyes of the poet to better understand what the poem is trying to say. Such understanding may then be translated into the spoken interpretation.

4. Notice the punctuation marks in the poem. Where is the best place to pause? To drop the voice? To raise the voice?

5. Read the poem aloud at a comfortable pace. Vary the rate as needed. Slow down to build suspense, to suggest slow movement, or to give an opportunity for the reader to react. Speed up to simulate action or suggest movement.

6. Vary the tone, pitch, or volume; voice dynamics is important to the reading of a poem. If the poem mentions a clock ticking or alludes to people shouting, for example, use the appropriate cadence or intonation.

7. Tape-record yourself reading the poem and evaluate your performance.

8. Listen to the poet or to professional actors read the poem. Cues for reading may then be taken from the performance of the actor or poet.

9. Allow time for children to respond to the poetry reading. Repeat poems on request.

10. Plan follow-up activities to some of the poems—activities such as choral speaking, dramatization, art activities, and creative writing.

Criteria for Selecting Poetry

Rhythmic language.   A poem chosen for presentation to young children should contain words and phrases that are melodious and harmonious to the ear. A really beautiful poem stays with the listener and repeats itself over and over. It is the lilting language that gives poetry such a unique quality and sets it apart from other literature. No matter what virtues a poem may hold, if the language is not rhythmic and melodic, it is a poor selection for young children.

Emotional appeal.   A poem should elicit an emotional response from its listeners—sadness, delight, introspection, empathy, anger. A well-chosen poem, effectively presented, will cause children to *feel* something, to be lifted beyond themselves for a moment. No poem should be presented to children that leaves the teacher completely unmoved. The simple lack of enthusiasm will cause the poem to fail.

Familiar themes.   Children enjoy poems that relate to their own experiences, poems about the everyday life going on around them. Studies of poetry preferences have revealed that their favorite poems focus on well-known animals, people, and places.

Although preschool and primary children will accept a certain amount of serious poetry if it is effectively presented, they genuinely prefer poems that contain fun and humor, and they are especially fond of poems that tell a story (a five-year-old of my acquaintance carries around the hardback version of Shel Silverstein's *Where the Sidewalk Ends,* begging any adult in sight to read the poems to her).

Sensory appeal.   The content of a poem that stimulates the senses of touch, taste, smell, sight, and sound makes a poem liked by young children. The need for sensory appeal is so strong that any poem which lacks that elusive quality is almost certain to be disliked by children. Children do not have to understand every nuance of a poem to be moved by its imagery, to feel that "here is something great that touches and moves me."

When poems are selected for their rhythmic language, emotional and sensory appeal, and familiar subjects, they have the power to improve the taste and appreciation of children. The daily sharing of such poetry in the early childhood classroom begins a lifelong fondness for poetry of many kinds.

Art and Poetry in Partnership

To help a beginning teacher plan and carry out a mini-unit based on poetry, this classroom-tested art activity is described in detail; it is intended as a model for a variety of poetry experiences that involve art as a follow-up activity:

While the twenty-four kindergarten children were out of the classroom with an aide, their teacher set up the room for an art and literature activity. She covered four tables with newspapers and placed different kinds of art material on each one as follows:

Table A—Smocks*, white art paper, colored chalk, and scissors.
Table B—Smocks, white art paper, mixed tempera paint in rack, and
    scissors.

---

*Smocks are made out of men's discarded shirts from which collars and cuffs have been removed. The child wears the shirt backward with one button fastened at the neck.

Table C—Construction paper in assorted colors, felt markers, hole punch, and scissors.

Table D—Thin paper plates, crayons, string, and scissors (these were to be cut in spiral shape for mobiles).

Once the tables were in readiness, the teacher attached a large sheet of white craft paper, approximately three yards, to the bulletin board as a background for a frieze. A coffee can of mixed wheat (wallpaper) paste and several wide brushes were placed on a desk near the bulletin board.

When the children returned to the classroom, they seated themselves in a story circle around the teacher. At this time she read to them the following poem by Shel Silverstein:

> Boa Constrictor[1]
> Oh, I'm being eaten
> By a boa constrictor,
> A boa constrictor,
> A boa constrictor,
> I'm being eaten by a boa constrictor,
> And I don't like it—one bit.
> Well, what do you know?
> It's nibblin' my toe.
> Oh, Gee,
> It's up to my knee.
> Oh my,
> It's up to my thigh.
> Oh, fiddle,
> It's up to my middle.
> Oh, heck,
> It's up to my neck.
> Oh, dread,
> It's upmmmmmmmmmmmmffffffffff. . . .

Ample time was provided for the children to react to the poem—to discuss it, to act it out, and to play around with the rollicking language. Most of them committed the poem to memory just by repeating it a few times.

As a corollary to "Boa Constrictor," the teacher read *Crictor* by Tomi Ungerer and followed the reading with a series of discussion questions (see chapter 1 for question types). Some of the adjectives used by the children to describe Crictor were *curvy, wiggly, slithery, long, coiled, colorful, beautiful,* and *graceful*—descriptive terms that were to carry over into their artwork.

---

1. "Boa Constrictor" (text only) from *Where the Sidewalk Ends*. The Poems and Drawings of Shel Silverstein. Copyright © 1974 by Shel Silverstein. By permission of Harper & Row, Publishers, Inc.

While the class as a whole was still seated together, the teacher divided the children into four groups and gave them instructions in making a frieze (see chapter 6 for a discussion on frieze construction). She was careful to point out the need for large shapes; boa constrictors versus worms was the analogy used to convey the idea.

Both the aide and the teacher assisted and generally supervised various aspects of the project as the children worked at the four tables to create "Critor's Cousins," boa constrictors of all sizes, shapes, and colors. As each boa was completed, the child immediately pasted it on the background (reserving space for the teacher-made caption) and returned to create another one.

After forty-five minutes of work, the teacher called time, and each group became responsible for cleaning up its own table and storing away materials. From reading aloud to washing up consumed approximately seventy minutes. The entire class reassembled to review the project, to summarize the learnings, and best of all to enjoy its own handiwork. The poem was repeated a few more times for emphasis. It was obvious that the artwork had given the children an added appreciation of both the poem and the book.

Not every poem or story, of course, will elicit such an extensive follow-up project, but many will. It may seem to be a great deal of trouble and effort to carry out such a lesson, but the learnings that accrue are well worth the time consumed. The curriculum areas involved in the reading aloud, the follow-up discussion, and the art activity were as follows:

- Language development—Vocabulary was extended by new words from both the poem and the book, by discussion following the reading, and by conversation during the art activity.

- Literature appreciation—Shel Silverstein and Tomi Ungerer were introduced to the children as poet and author along with the memorable book characters of Crictor and Madame Godot.

- Art experience—Four kinds of art media were made available for experimentation and exploration. The finished product was a satisfying outcome of a group project.

- Crafts activity—Both the paper-plate mobiles and the completed frieze were in the handicraft genre.

- Environmental awareness—A greater respect for harmless reptiles (as opposed to complete disdain) was stressed during the project.

- Drama and speech—The acting out of Shel Silverstein's poem "Boa Constrictor" was dramatic and the repetition of the poem became a kind of impromptu choral speaking.

This series of photographs shows the processes involved in making a classroom frieze based on stories and poems. (Courtesy Sam Houston Elementary School, Port Arthur, Texas.)

Other poems suitable for art projects similar to the one described above are "Alligators All Around" by Maurice Sendak, "Snowman" by Shel Silverstein, "Macavity: The Mystery Cat" by T. S. Eliot, "The Snake" by Karla Kuskin, and "Crows" by David McCord.

Books that may be read aloud at one sitting and lend themselves well to frieze making are *Burt Dow: Deep Water Man* by Robert McCloskey, *Mushrooms in the Rain* by Mirra Ginsburg, *The Very Hungry Caterpillar* by Eric Carle, *Make Way for Ducklings* by Robert McCloskey, *Mr. Popper's Penguins* by Richard and Florence Atwater, *Millions of Cats* by Wanda Gág, and *Two Hundred Rabbits* by Lonzo Anderson and Adrienne Adams.

CHILDREN'S BOOKS FOR POETRY ACTIVITIES

The Bat Poet, by Randall Jarrell; illustrated by Maurice Sendak. New York: Macmillan, 1967.

> The story of a little brown bat who couldn't sleep days and thus began to see the world differently. It is both a delightful animal fantasy and a commentary on the writing of poetry. Randall Jarrell's poems are as unusual and creative as the story itself.

The Book of a Thousand Poems: A Family Treasury, collected by J. Murray Macbain. New York: Peter Bedrick Books, 1983.

> A collection of poems for very young children by poets ranging from William Blake and Henry Wadsworth Longfellow to Emily Dickinson and Robert Louis Stevenson. The poems are arranged by topics such as the seasons, nursery rhymes, and lullabies and cradle songs. The anthologist suggests many practical ways the collection may be used in the classroom and at home.

The Complete Nonsense Book, by Edward Lear. New York: Dodd, Mead & Company, 1912.

> This version is said to be the only complete and authorized edition of Edward Lear's nonsense rhymes accompanied by his own equally nonsensical drawings. In addition to Lear's famous limericks, this book also includes "The Owl and the Pussy Cat" and other nonsense songs and stories.

Dogs and Dragons, Trees and Dreams, written by Karla Kuskin. New York: Harper and Row Publishers, Inc., 1980.

> In this book, Karla Kuskin gathered together some of her favorite poems written for children between 1958 and 1975. Contains her notes on poetry writing and appreciation.

Don't You Turn Back: Poems by Langston Hughes, selected by Lee Bennet Hopkins and illustrated by Ann Grifalconi. New York: Alfred A. Knopf, 1969.

> Most of the poems in this collection were written while Langston Hughes was traveling around the world as a merchant seaman. They portray many rich cultures; the bold woodcuts are a perfect accompaniment to the poems. There is an introduction by Arna Bontemps.

Faces and Places: Poems for You, selected by Lee Bennett Hopkins
and Misha Arenstein and illustrated by Lisl Weil. New York: Scholastic
Book Services, 1971.

> A selection of fifty-two popular poems for children of all ages. A large number
> of poets are represented from both the past and present.

Favorite Poems by Dorothy Aldis, by Dorothy Aldis. New York:
Putnam, 1970.

> After the death of Dorothy Aldis, her publisher compiled some of her most
> popular poems. The poems center on everyday experiences and family re-
> lationships.

Hailstones and Halibut Bones, by Mary O'Neill; illustrated by
Leonard Weisgard. Garden City, N.Y.: Doubleday & Company, 1961.

> A very popular book of color poems that can be used at all grade levels, not
> only for reading aloud, but as a springboard for many activities such as art,
> creative writing, and dramatization. Twelve colors are vividly described in
> rhyming verse that names familiar objects, feelings, and concepts. Beauti-
> fully illustrated by Leonard Weisgard.

Hey, Bug! and Other Poems About Little Things, selected by
Elizabeth M. Itse and illustrated by Susan Carlton Smith. New York:
American Heritage, 1972.

> These poems feature beetles, mice, snails, and other small creatures that fas-
> cinate young children. Some of the poets represented are David McCord,
> Aileen Fisher, Elizabeth Coatsworth, Hilda Conkling, and Hilaire Belloc. Il-
> lustrated with scientifically accurate botanical drawings.

The New Kid on the Block, by Jack Prelutsky; illustrated by James
Stevenson. New York: Greenwillow Books, 1984.

> A collection of humorous poems for young children by one of their favorite
> poets. Poems in this collection involve such unlikely topics as jellyfish stew,
> a boneless chicken, and gloppy gloppers. The book includes not only an
> index to titles, but also a helpful index to first lines.

No Way of Knowing: Dallas Poems, written by Myra Cohn Livingston.
New York: Atheneum, 1980.

> A series of poems based on the author's experiences in the black community
> of Dallas, Texas, from 1952 to 1964. These poems capture the rich speech
> patterns of a people who made lasting contributions to our culture.

Out Loud, by Eve Merriam; illustrated by Harriet Sherman. New York:
Atheneum, 1973.

> This unusual collection of modern poems about everyday objects and ex-
> periences emphasizes sound. The illustrations, line drawings, and titles give
> it a unique visual appeal to younger readers.

Oxford Book of Poetry for Children, compiled by Edward Blishen and
illustrated by Brian Wildsmith. New York: Franklin Watts, Inc., 1963.

> The anthologist sets out to compile a collection that would introduce young
> children to poetry and help them make the leap from nursery rhymes to
> more serious verse. It is an excellent anthology that contains all kinds of
> poetry. Brian Wildsmith's paintings help set the mood for the poems.

Peacock Pie, by Walter de la Mare. Chicago: E. M. Hale and Company, 1932.

> An example of the many fine books of poetry available that feature the work of a single poet. The eighty-two poems are classified as to boys and girls, people and places, witches and fairies, and so on. Illustrated with black line drawings.

Peter Piper's Alphabet, written and illustrated by Marcia Brown. New York: Scribner, 1979.

> Sounds of the alphabet are represented by famous old tongue-twister nursery rhymes. The pictures are filled with fun and foolishness to be enjoyed by children and adults alike.

Poems, written by Rachel Field. New York: Macmillan, 1957.

> Primary grade children will instantly recognize the delightful imagery found in Rachel Field's poems. Her book includes selections from *The Pointed People* (1924) and *Taxis and Toadstools* (1926). Familiar poems such as "Skyscrapers," "Taxis," "City Rain," and "Snow in the City" are contained in this collection. Many of the poems are known by teachers because of their frequent inclusion in language arts textbooks and poetry anthologies.

Poems Children Will Sit Still For: A Selection for the Primary Grades, compiled by Beatrice Schenk de Regniers, Eva Moore, and Mary Michaels White. New York: Scholastic Book Services, 1969.

> Each of the 106 poems has been selected on the basis of the individual preferences of several well-known poets. The poems are grouped into categories such as fun, rhythm, numbers, and letters. For many of the poems, suggestions are offered for reading aloud, audience participation, and class discussion.

Poems Make Pictures, Pictures Make Poems, written by Giose Rimanelli and Paul Pimsleur. New York: Pantheon, 1971.

> A marvelous picture book collection of simple poems arranged as visual puzzles. Words in the shape of objects such as an umbrella, a whale, and rain splattering on a house help to create the poetic image.

The Random House Book of Poetry for Children, selected by Jack Prelutsky and illustrated by Arnold Lobel. New York: Random House, 1983.

> In his work with children, Jack Prelutsky finds that children prefer poems that evoke laughter and surprise, that paint pictures and bring pleasure in language. At the request of teachers and librarians, he compiled 572 poems that fulfill these criteria. Each page is filled with short poems by some of the most popular poets ever to write for children. Moreover, each page contains four or five of Arnold Lobel's appealing illustrations.

See My Lovely Poison Ivy: And Other Poems About Witches, Ghosts, and Things, written by Lilian Moore; illustrated by Diane Dawson. New York: Atheneum, 1975.

> A poetry anthology on a variety-of-subjects that children enjoy is created by Lilian Moore's special talent. Children in the primary grades will enjoy these poems at Halloween time.

Side by Side: Poems to Read Together, collected by Lee Bennett
Hopkins and illustrated by Hilary Knight. New York: Simon &
Schuster, 1988.

> This is a collection of familiar poems selected for sharing one to one with a
> young child, hence the title "side by side." Poets included range from Edward
> Lear, Robert Louis Stevenson, and Kate Greenaway to David McCord, Aileen
> Fisher, and Eve Merriam. Watercolor illustrations contain fascinating details
> to discuss with the young listener.

Sing a Song of Popcorn, poems selected by Beatrice Schenk de
Regniers, et al. and illustrated by nine Caldecott Medal artists. New
York: Scholastic Inc., 1988.

> A collection of 128 poems gleaned from the work of renowned poets who
> include Shel Silverstein, Robert Louis Stevenson, Emily Dickinson, Edward
> Lear, Ogden Nash, and A. A. Milne. The poems range from pure nonsense to
> serious themes, from ancient to modern poems, and include a diversity of
> cultures and locales. A fine book for the school library and also for the class-
> room book collection. Suitable for all ages.

Something Special, written by Beatrice Schenk de Regniers; illustrated
by Irene Hass. New York: Harcourt Brace Jovanovich, 1958.

> A collection of original poems for children in the primary grades, including
> the popular "Keep a Poem in Your Pocket."

Time for Poetry, 3rd general edition, edited by May Hill Arbuthnot
and Shelton L. Root, Jr., and illustrated by Arthur Paul, Glenview, Ill.:
Scott, Foresman, 1968.

> With over seven hundred poems by poets ranging from Mother Goose to T. S.
> Eliot, this is probably the most comprehensive anthology of children's poetry
> available for the language arts classroom. Though somewhat dated, it con-
> tains many popular traditional and modern poems. The conclusion of the
> book contains some excellent suggestions for a classroom poetry program,
> and useful teaching notes are presented along with the individual poems.

The Way Things Are and Other Poems, written by Myra Cohn
Livingston; illustrated by Jenni Oliver. New York: Atheneum, 1974.

> Simple poems written from the perspective of a child are presented by a
> well-known poet. Not only has this talented writer edited children's poetry
> anthologies (*Listen Children, Listen* and *A Tune Beyond Us*), Myra Cohn
> Livingston makes it clear that she understands the poetry preferences of
> younger children.

Where the Sidewalk Ends, written and illustrated by Shel Silverstein.
New York: Harper & Row, 1974.

> Children of all ages enjoy the humorous poetry of Shel Silverstein. His poems
> tells stories of amusing animals and people who find themselves in the kind
> of absurd situations very familiar to children.

You Read to Me, I'll Read to You, written by John Ciardi; illustrated by Edward Gorey. Philadelphia: Lippincott, 1962.

> Every other poem in this collection uses only a basic first-grade vocabulary. On the opposite page is a poem suitable for an adult to read to a child. For additional contrast, the poems are printed in two colors—one for the child and one for the adult.

•
BIBLIOGRAPHY

Arnstein, Flora. *Poetry in the Elementary Classroom.* New York: Appleton-Century-Crofts, 1962.

Boyd, Gertrude A. *Teaching Poetry in the Elementary School.* Columbus: Charles E. Merrill, 1973.

Gray, Stephanie. *Teaching Poetry Today.* Portland, Main: J. Weston Walch, Publishers, 1976.

Hopkins, Lee Bennett. *Pass the Poetry Please!* New York: Citation Press, 1972.

Larrick, Nancy, ed. *Somebody Turned on a Tap in These Kids: Poetry and Young People Today.* New York: Dell, 1972.

Painter, Helen W. *Poetry and Children,* Newark, Del.: International Reading Association, 1970.

Smith, James A., and Dorothy M. Park. *Word Music and Word Magic.* Boston: Allyn and Bacon, 1977.

Stewig, John Warren. *Read to Write: Using Children's Literature as a Springboard to Writing.* New York: Hawthorne Books, 1975.

Witucke, Virginia. *Literature for Children: Poetry in the Elementary School.* Dubuque, Iowa: Wm. C. Brown Company Publishers, 1970.

5

"Talk Written Down— and More":

Books and the Language Experience

That children should read life before they read books is a belief held by most teachers concerned with reading readiness and beginning reading. The skills of communication—oral language, listening, reading, and writing—begin in the home long before a child enters school. Moreover, a child's success in school may well depend on the quality and quantity of experiences that have been encountered earlier. Only out of a reservoir of experiences is a fledgling reader able to bring meaning to the printed page. Unfortunately, many children have a limited backlog of experiences. The school is obligated to make up the deficit.

Numerous studies have shown the correlation between enriched learning experiences and success in reading. Conversely, the same studies serve to point up the relationship between a dearth of experiences and failure in reading. After studying the school records and interviewing the parents of 106 first graders, Almy concluded that there is a positive relationship between success in reading and such experiences as being read to, looking at books and magazines, and an interest in words found on labels and signs.[1]

Lamoreaux and Lee maintain that readiness for reading depends on an accumulation of rich background experiences over a period of time:

> Our only means of understanding, of interpreting what we see and hear and feel, is through our own experience, real and vicarious. When a child's background of experience is so limited that he can find in it

---

1. Millie Corrine Almy, "Children's Experiences Prior to First Grade and Success in Beginning Reading," *Contributions to Education, No. 954* (New York: Bureau of Publications, Teachers College, Columbia University, 1949), p. 111.

no basis for interpreting the material he reads, it will have no more meaning for him than highly technical material in an unfamiliar field would for us.[2]

Esther Milner's study, completed a few years later, corroborated their opinion.[3] She compared the achievement of children from middle-class homes with that of children from lower-class homes and found that the child from a middle-class home had a definite verbal advantage and was therefore better equipped for reading. She attributed the differential to experiences provided in the middle-class home.

Many writers have been concerned with providing compensatory experiences in the classroom for those students who lack the necessary generalizations and understandings to bring meaning to the printed page. Harris describes the need for teachers to provide vicarious experiences in the classroom for such students:

> If a child has never seen a horse, and if his teacher finds it inconvenient to take him to a farm, a photograph or drawing will substitute for the actual experience. A geography teacher usually cannot take his class on a surveying trip to Colorado, but a good map will tell the students more about the state's geography than a thousand words. It may not be practical to dismantle a jet engine in a classroom, but drawings and diagrams are more effective substitutes than a fat and wordy textbook.[4]

Trauger stresses that all teachers should know ways to seek out interesting concrete materials of various kinds to help students enlarge and enrich their accumulation of experiences:

> A teacher's search for audiovisual possibilities may correct the prevalent inclination to talk too much and too abstractly. Language arts classes tend to be overwordy—a tendency prompted by the nature of the subject. Use of graphic materials reduces abstractness and excessive talk.[5]

Strickland also strongly emphasizes the need for all kinds of learning experiences with audiovisual aids, to be supplied by the school in a planned and routine fashion:

> Firsthand and vicarious experiences are both essential to language development. Field trips, experimentation, and various types of indi-

2. Lillian A. Lamoreaux and Dorris May Lee, *Learning to Read Through Experience* (New York: Appleton-Century-Crofts, 1943), p. 5.

3. Esther Milner, "A Study of the Relationship Between Reading Readiness in Grade One School Children and Patterns of Parent-Child Interactions," *Child Development* 22 (1951):95–112.

4. Ben M. Harris, *Supervisory Behavior in Education* (Englewood Cliffs, N.J.: Prentice-Hall, Inc., 1963), p. 303.

5. Wilma K. Trauger, *Language Arts in Elementary Schools* (New York: McGraw-Hill Book Co., 1963), p. 8.

vidual exploration are used where they prove valuable. Reading and audiovisual materials supply vicarious experiences.[6]

The National Council of Teachers of English has long urged teachers to meet the diverse needs of students by providing them with interesting, challenging experiences that demand involvement and participation:

> Planning individual and group projects and making contacts with resource persons are challenging experiences through which young people gain competence in observing, thinking, speaking, listening, reading, and writing. Such planning is one means of individualizing goals, procedures, materials, and evaluation. Sharing the results of individual and small group projects can socialize individual talent and achievement.[7]

Bernard records the psychological bases for drawing on a child's own experiences to teach him or her the various language skills:

> Meaning always has reference to the individual and it is derived from his own experiences. The pupil must touch, feel, taste, see, hear, and manipulate objects in his environment in order to understand them. As he shifts from the world of objects to the realm of words, which represent objects and situations, he must make the transition in progressive steps. Meanings, to a great extent, actually constitute the environment of the individual—especially his psychological environment.[8]

John Dewey was concerned with the *quality* of the experiences provided children and consistently emphasized the need for "carry over" value in the experiences offered: "The more definitely and sincerely it is held that education is a development within, by, and for experience, the more important it is that there shall be clear conceptions of what experience is."[9] Dewey held that each experience should be of the quality to bring forth other fruitful experiences in the future (fig. 5.1).

Burton and his collaborators see, as did Dewey, the importance of quality in the experiences planned and arranged for children and advocate activities that would lead to inquiry and problem solving:

> The teacher must respect and keep alive the poking of little children from which knowledge results. Inquisitiveness, asking others, must be encouraged and stimulated until it becomes the ability to find out things

6. Ruth G. Strickland, *The Language Arts in the Elementary School* (New York: D.C. Heath and Co., 1963), p. 61.

7. National Council of Teachers of English, *The English Language Arts* (New York: Appleton-Century-Crofts, 1952), p. 257.

8. Harold W. Bernard, *Psychology of Learning and Teaching* (New York: McGraw-Hill Book Co., 1954), p. 34.

9. John Dewey, *Experience and Education* (New York: The Macmillan Co., 1938), p. 17.

Figure 5.1.   An example of a child's creative art work enhanced by her first efforts at creative writing. (Courtesy of Beaumont Independent School District, Beaumont, Texas.)

for oneself, ability to "think up" new hypotheses to be followed. The school must lead "curiosity" over into vital problem solving and more critical inquiry which constitutes thinking.[10]

Even a brief survey of the literature reveals a consensus among child development specialists, curriculum planners, and language authorities that young children need stimulating work centers, rich play activities, ample space, movable furniture, good classroom libraries, and quantities of raw materials for work. Great strides have been made in implementing the results of studies and of using the knowledge such studies have contributed to the area of early childhood education.

Experience Charts

Learning to read through experience is based on the premise that a reader recognizes printed symbols and endows them with meaning. Meaning comes from within the reader rather than from the reading ma-

---

10. William H. Burton, Roland B. Kimball, and Richard L. Wigg, *Education for Effective Thinking* (New York: Appleton-Century-Crofts, 1960), p. 339.

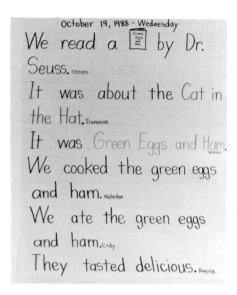

Figure 5.2. An example of a literature-based chart in which each member of the group contributed a sentence.

terial. A dramatic episode in the life of Helen Keller describes her sudden discovery that printed words are representations of oral language:

> We walked down the path to the well-house, attracted by the fragrance of the honeysuckle with which it was covered. Someone was drawing water and my teacher placed my hand under the spout. As the cool stream gushed over one hand she spelled into the other the word *water,* first slowly, then rapidly. I stood still, my whole attention fixed upon the motions of her fingers. Suddenly I felt a misty consciousness as of something forgotten—a thrill of returning thought; and somehow the mystery of language was revealed to me. I knew then that "W-A-T-E-R" meant the wonderful cool something that was flowing over my hand. That living word awakened my soul, gave it light, hope, joy, set it free![11]

Something akin to that experience of Helen Keller's happens to young children who are permitted to observe their own experiences recorded in print and then read back to them.

The experience chart is the most effective means by which to help a child conceptualize what reading is—speech written down—and more. It also captures an experience in permanent form and provides highly interesting reading material for the classroom (fig. 5.2).

11. Helen Keller, *The Story of My Life* (Garden City, N.Y.: Doubleday & Co., Inc., 1920), pp. 23–24.

Figure 5.3.   Here a kindergarten teacher has recorded a segment of the discussion that followed the reading of *Make Way for Ducklings* by Robert McCloskey.

Figure 5.4.   A typical example of a language-experience chart in which a child's language is recorded by the teacher and used as the child's own reading material. (Courtesy of Lamar University.)

If the experience has been a shared one, the teacher and children can usually produce the chart story cooperatively, with the teacher serving as secretary or recorder to get the children's ideas down on paper (fig. 5.3). If the experience has been a personal one, the teacher may wish to help the child compose an individual chart story (fig. 5.4). In either case, the chart is a joint enterprise growing out of an experience that is happening at the present time, has happened in the recent past, or is to take place in the near future. In other words, the teacher does not compose a chart for children in their absence, present it to them for reading, and then perhaps store it for use with a new group of students. Such a chart might have a worthy purpose, but it would be a misnomer to label it an *experience* chart.

Composing the Experience Chart

When an experience has been interesting enough to stimulate discussion by the children, the teacher should be prepared to record key comments and ideas on chart paper, trying to write the chart sentences in the child's own language. Any radical departure from a child's original contribution is apt to cause him or her to be skeptical of the entire process. If the teacher feels the need to make a change in the content or structure of a child's contribution, the change should be carefully explained to the child and made only on his or her approval. No honest effort of a child to express himself or herself in art, in writing, or in oral language should be altered by the "touch of the master's hand" to the point it is no longer the child's creation.

Sources of Experiences

Many experiences suitable for chart making are spontaneous classroom situations, and a perceptive teacher is continually alert to the value of such windfalls. But teaching cannot depend on serendipity, and it becomes necessary to plan and initiate experiences on a routine basis. Any teacher who knows well the interests and abilities of the children, and their readiness for a particular activity, can become skillful at creating happenings guaranteed to give them something to think about, talk about, read and write about.

Systematic analysis and evaluation of experiences are necessary if objectives of the experience approach are to be attained. This includes making careful notes of the conversation and comments made by children during a happening. It may also include the use of tape recordings, Polaroid snapshots, and other methods of recording reactions.

A teacher aide is invaluable in the task of recording an experience, and with supervision and practice, can learn to observe, record, and retrieve the most important elements of the experience. The teacher, of course, is occupied during this time as a catalyst in making significant things happen, in asking leading questions, and in clarifying concepts. Graphic records produced by such a team effort not only provide a means of appraisal but are also raw material for chart making.

Books and the Language Experience

Children's literature is a ubiquitous source of rich language experience for children. Books are always ready and available when other experience sources, such as a field trip or resource person, are impractical at the moment. Books obviously do not substitute for real life experiences, but they add to the richness of a firsthand experience, and they can also provide some of the vicarious experiences necessary in a child's life.

When children have been introduced to such interesting and entertaining books as *The Five Chinese Brothers, Where the Wild Things Are, The Crows of Pear Blossom,* or *Many Moons,* the natural outcome is lively discussion. And from the flow of oral language, reading charts are developed. Effective uses of such literature charts over a period of time help young children to develop positive attitudes toward books and reading.

Authors, librarians, illustrators of children's books, teachers of literature, book sellers, storytellers, and other bibliophiles make excellent resource people for the classroom, not only because they recognize children as consumers of their product, but also because most of them genuinely like to talk about books—especially to such avid fans as young children. Charts may be developed in planning the visit, in recording the interaction between the visitor and children, and in a follow-up summary of the visit. Other language experiences to be gleaned from literature might include the purchase of a needed book, the arrival of a shipment of paperbacks, a comparative study of two popular books, construction of a literature bulletin board, a study of illustrations, and a reorganization of the classroom collection.

The following brief list offers additional possibilities for rich language activities:

Resource persons	Cooking
Field trips	Celebrations and holidays
Creative dramatics	"Show and tell"
Storytelling	Outdoor play
Puppetry	Films and film strips
Creative writing	Slides and transparencies
Experiments	Pictures and art prints
Work sessions	Advertisements
Dramatic play	Travel posters
Discussions and conversations	Objects and models
Art activities	Pets and animals

Chart Making

If language-experience charts are to be employed as an integral part of the reading and reading readiness programs, both the teacher and aide must be able to make them quickly, efficiently, and fluently. Tedious and laborious efforts are certain to cause a loss of interest among the children who are observing and participating in the chart's development. At the same time, the finished chart should be attractive, well balanced, and above all, legible. Only with much practice on the spot in the classroom can the skill of chart making be fully attained.

Since language experience charts are to serve as a transition between oral language and reading, they should resemble as closely as possible the printed page. The writing should be done in manuscript form with black ink on white paper. Chart papers range from newsprint to the more expensive lined tagboard. The purpose and intended uses of the chart determine the degree of permanency desired. A chart that proves to be better than average may always be transferred to a better-quality paper. Materials needed for chart making include:

Chart tablets
    24″ × 16″ (easel style)
    24″ × 32″ (full length)
Sentence strips and rolls
Pocket chart
Chart paper
Primary typewriter
Felt point pens
Waterbase pens for children's use
Crayons
Pictures
Scissors and paste
Manuscript alphabet guide

The want ad section and stock market page of the daily newspaper make excellent material for practicing manuscript writing. If the paper is turned crosswise, the columns provide lines and spaces of the correct size for writing.

Illustrating the Chart

Any chart that is to be used several times with a group of children deserves to be illustrated either by the children or by the teacher. Appropriate illustrations, such as pictures in books, add color and emphasis to the printed material and make it much more appealing and understandable to children (figs. 5.5 and 5.6). However, no chart should become cluttered with pictures. Illustrations are meant to enhance the writing and not detract from it. The following list offers sources of materials to use in illustrating charts:

Paintings and drawings made by the students
Paintings and drawings made by the teacher or aide
Art prints
Magazine pictures
Photographs
Rebus drawings
Book jackets
Travel folders

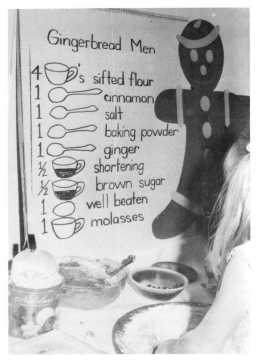

Figures 5.5. and 5.6.   Rebus pictures make a recipe chart easy to read and follow. Reviewing the recipe chart can help children to see that writing is a way of recording information for future reference.

Worn-out picture books
Illustrations from workbooks
Old readiness books
Illustrations from sales catalogues, stamp books, and seed catalogues

Using the Chart

Although the language experience approach is seldom used as the sole method of teaching reading, it is considered by most reading specialists to be an excellent vehicle for personalizing the reading program.

Authorities hesitate to recommend the experience approach as a total program for fear that the systematic teaching of reading skills might be neglected. Heilman is one of the writers in the field of reading who has reservations about using the language experience chart as a total program. He believes that the method should be a supplement to other materials designed to teach reading skills:

> Most teachers prefer to use the experience chart as a supplement to basals and other materials. This permits certain of the weaknesses to be

minimized. The basic readers provide drill on sight vocabulary and control over the introduction of new words. The use of experience charts add flexibility and interest to the program.[12]

Perhaps it would be risky to use experience charts as a total method, but it certainly is a misconception to assume that charts do *not* teach reading skills. A well-made reading chart, arising out of a significant experience, makes reading personal and relevant: It also strengthens and reinforces the skills of reading. Both teacher-made and commercial reading materials have a place in the classroom.

The greatest strength of the experience chart is its appeal for children. Because of the ego involvement inherent in formulating a chart, children are immediately attracted to it. It is not difficult to understand why. Charts employ the names of the children, and the names of their friends, relatives, and acquaintances. They make use of the names of plants, animals, machines, toys, buildings, cities, foods, holidays, celebrations, and other words of high appeal to children. They also use an abundance of service words needed to tie the more colorful and interesting words together. In fact, an experience chart is one of the most palatable ways to give children the necessary multiple exposures to service words.

If the experience chart is to be considered a springboard for skill activities, as well as a means of creating interest in reading, teachers and aides need to know a variety of chart types. The following list offers some of the major initial uses of a chart:

To illustrate how speech can be recorded in print
Review an experience
Present new information
Provide oral and silent reading practice
Form a base for discussion
Enlarge and enrich vocabulary
Give directions
List criteria
State hypotheses
Record a happening
Summarize learnings
Initiate a project
Celebrate an occasion
Reinforce skills
Promote creative writing
Provide reference material
Evaluate an activity
Dramatize a book or an event

---

12. Arthur W. Heilman, *Principles and Practices of Teaching Reading,* 4th ed. (Columbus, Ohio: Charles E. Merrill Publishers, 1976), p. 211.

Follow-up uses for charts are as numerous as the teacher's imagination and ingenuity will allow. Some of the more obvious uses of a chart that has served its initial purpose are given below:

1. The chart can be cut into sentences and reassembled to give practice in sequence.

2. The chart can provide practice on the word attack skills—phonetic analysis, context clues, and structural analysis.

3. The chart can be used to review capitalization, punctuation, and sentence structure.

4. Several charts can be bound together to make an oversized book of stories for the reading table.

5. Chart stories can be transcribed on the primary typewriter to make small booklets for the reading table.

6. Charts and booklets can be exchanged with other classes to provide more practice in silent reading.

7. Dated charts can be sent home for children to read to parents.

8. Some charts can be cut up to make dictionary boxes and word games.

Creative Writing and the Language Experience

As children experience the joy of seeing their own thoughts and ideas recorded in print, they soon feel the need to do some of their own writing. It is a short step from the dictated story to one that a child writes for her- or himself. In watching the teacher record their speech, the children have learned something about letter formation, spelling, sentence structure, punctuation, and other elements of writing. With a great deal of help and encouragement, they are able to use the mechanics of writing to express their own thoughts and feelings (fig. 5.7).

Writing is creative when a child gives an honest and sincere response to the world around him or her, and then is able to capture that response in writing. Essential mechanics of writing are necessary tools for recording responses, but rules and technique are never more important than the expression itself. In beginning writing, the emphasis must always be on freedom of expression.

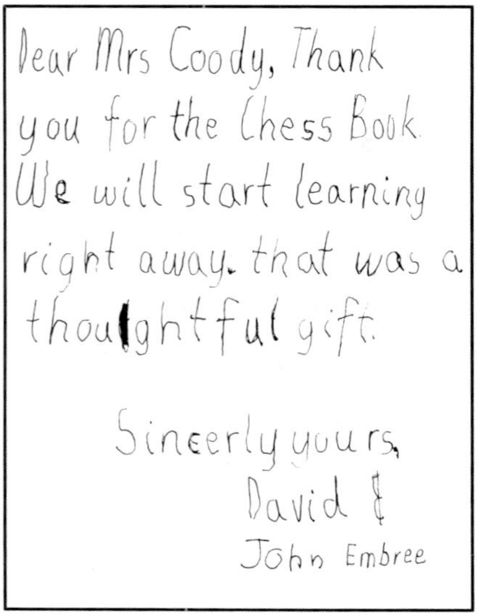

Dear Mrs Coody, Thank
you for the Chess Book.
We will start learning
right away. that was a
thoughtful gift.

Sincerly yours,
David &
John Embree

Figure 5.7. The gift of a book provides incentive for both reading and writing practice. (Courtesy of Sue Embree.)

Years ago, Alvina Burrows and her colleagues conducted exhaustive experiments in which they attempted to release free expression from children while cultivating the skill necessary for writing with correctness and ease. They arrived at the following conclusion, which might well serve as a guide for today's teachers of language arts:

> We know that if a child is to be an effective, poised personality, he must have an awareness and an appreciation of his own power. Such self-knowledge comes only through frequent opportunity to experiment and to fumble along the lines of his desire until out of his effort he fashions something which in his eyes is good. That the product is often crude and clumsy does not matter. The important thing is that the child, out of himself and working in his own way, has produced a thing of which he can approve.[13]

The Teacher of Creative Writing

An inspiring teacher is the key to creative writing. It is the teacher's responsibility to maintain a relaxed and accepting environment, to provide many ideas and topics for writing, to give needed help with composition, and to make wise use of the finished products. Above all, the teacher must be encouraging. Nothing squelches the urge to write like

---

13. Alvina Treut Burrows et al., *They All Want to Write* (Englewood Cliffs, N.J.: Prentice-Hall, Inc., 1952), pp. 1–2.

Figure 5.8.   When free expression in art and writing is permitted and encouraged, a child's honest emotions can be revealed in wholesome ways.

a disapproving teacher. A harshly critical word at a crucial moment can cause a child to become overly cautious and less creative in future attempts. An understanding teacher realizes that the young writer's ideas are fragile and vulnerable and respects them accordingly.

Maintaining an environment where creativity can flourish and giving children many opportunities for self-expression are vital to creative writing (fig. 5.8). These two practices alone, however, are not the sole answer. Creative writing must be systematically and routinely taught. Petty and Bowen give a convincing argument that creative writing be taught much like the other creative arts:

> We say that it really *can* be taught—just as the other creative arts are—but it must be *taught*. While it is true that some painters, musicians, or dancers are innately talented and have received little teaching, the majority of persons engaged in these arts, professionally or simply for enjoyment, have received instruction—they have been *taught*.[14]

Teachers who are successful in the teaching of creative writing seem to have certain characteristics in common. They are sensitive to their students' needs and interests. They are tolerant of their students' awkwardness, and more generous in the appraisal of their efforts. They genuinely appreciate and respect the language of children with its straightforward frankness.

---

14. Walter T. Petty and Mary E. Bowen, *Slithery Snakes and Other Aids to Children's Writing* (New York: Appleton-Century-Crofts, 1967), pp. 4–5.

Lowenfeld and Brittain have found that whatever teachers do in stimulating creativeness greatly depends on three factors: their own personalities, of which their own creativeness, degree of sensitivity, and flexible relationships to environment are an important part; the ability to put themselves into the place of others; the understanding and knowledge of the needs of those whom they are teaching.[15]

Herbert Kohl, the author of *36 Children,* is a staunch advocate of creative writing in the classroom as a means of improving the self-image of students. He believes that if children are encouraged by teachers to discover themselves in the classroom, they will not need to resort to self-discovery on the streets and through drugs. After many attempts to free children of the self-doubt that inhibits expression, Kohl wrote:

> It is absurd that young people fear their own writing and are ashamed of their own voices. We have to encourage them to listen to themselves and each other, and to take the time to discover who they are for themselves. If teachers respect the voices of the young, and nurture them instead of tearing them down or trying to develop ones for students, then perhaps school will be less oppressive and alienating to the young.[16]

Fortunately, very young children have not become so self-conscious about expressing themselves and, for the most part, are anxious to write. They see writing as a fascinating extension of their own speech. Once they have attained the rudimentary skills of writing, have something to say and a reason for saying it, they write willingly and freely.

Literature and Creative Writing

As in the case of experience chart making, stimulating experiences with children's literature are among the best sources of input for creative writing. They provide the inspiration and raw material for letters, stories, poems, plays, and reports.

Literature read aloud to children in the classroom brings forth all manner of creative expression. If the teacher reads "The Elephant's Child" from Kipling's *Just So Stories,* some children may immediately make drawings and paintings of the bicolored python rock snake. Moreover, they are often stimulated to create excellent "why" stories of their own.

If the teacher shares unrhymed poetry with the children, they may want to try their hand at it—even if only a line or two. Their poems may be transferred to newsprint to be used as reading charts and, eventually, taken home for parents to enjoy.

---

15. Viktor Lowenfeld and W. Lambert Brittain, *Creative and Mental Growth,* 4th ed. (New York: The Macmillan Co., 1964), p. 11.

16. Herbert Kohl, "Writing Their Way to Self-Acceptance," *Grade Teacher* 87 (1969): 9–11.

Animal stories read aloud by the teacher or aide trigger memories of all kinds of experiences children have had with pets and animals, and original stories are often the result. Such stories make excellent reading material if they are illustrated, bound together, and placed on the library table. Such books as *The Cow Who Fell in the Canal, Harry the Dirty Dog,* and *Five-O'Clock Charlie* show animals in humorous situations and give children a starting point for their own stories about wise and foolish animals.

The correlation between literature and creative activities is endless. The teacher only needs to know ways of bringing the two together. Listed below are a dozen double-purpose activities for the promotion of both literature and creative writing:

1. Writing personal reactions to books that are read aloud by the teacher or aide at story time. Bind reactions together into a book for the library table.

2. Making new book jackets for favorite books. Use any art process desired to decorate the jacket and then write a blurb that will advertise the book. Write a continuation of the blurb containing a biographical sketch of the author.

3. Compiling a scrapbook of brief book reviews written by children. Let it serve as a source of information to young browsers.

4. Writing a set of provocative questions about books that have circulated in the class. The questions are then compiled into a literary quiz program for the class.

5. Writing letters to the librarian requesting purchase of books that follow interests of class members. Such books might include information on hobbies, collections, sports, or pets. Explain why such books are needed.

6. Writing comparative essays in which one book is compared to another. Other comparisons might include authors, illustrators, or book characters.

7. Writing additional adventures to a book that is made up of episodes such as *Hitty: Her First Hundred Years, Homer Price, My Father's Dragon, Pippi Longstocking,* or *Amelia Bedelia.*

8. Writing a letter to parents explaining why a certain book is wanted as a Christmas or birthday gift.

9. Writing a letter to a classmate recommending a certain book. Justify the recommendation with valid arguments for the book's merit.

10. Writing an essay explaining why a certain book deserved to win the Caldecott Award.

11. Writing a new ending to an old favorite such as *The Pied Piper of Hamelin, Miss Hickory,* or *Down, Down the Mountain.*

12. Writing an imaginary letter to a well-known book character, or an imaginary conversation between two characters.

Books Made by Children

One of the most effective ways to give children a high regard for books and the people who make books is to help them create some of their own. No one expects child-made books to have the literary quality of professional ones, but these one-of-a-kind books do have great appeal for the children who make them, and that, of course, is the main thing.

Subject matter for student-made books might include original poems, plays, stories, reports, essays, and riddles; collections of post cards, stamps, cutout pictures, photographs, art prints, travel folders, and cartoons. There are endless possibilities. Almost anything a child is interested in can be organized and preserved in a handsome book.

The binding of student-made books does not have to be a complicated affair. In fact, for young children, the simplest form of binding is best, one they can have a hand in making.

Large pages of white or brown butcher paper, stapled together with open edges to the back and folded edges out, make fine scrapbooks. Colored construction paper stapled together also gives a satisfactory surface for pasting student work. Tagboard cut to size and fastened together with rings makes a sturdy book. For a book that looks more like a book, cardboard backs may be covered with cloth or paper and fastened together with string. (See fig. 5.9.)

As an occasional departure from the more traditional ones, children enjoy making books in unusual shapes and sizes. Three of the most popular books of the "exotic" type are shape books, accordion books, and scrolls.

The accordion or zigzag book is made by folding a long strip of heavy paper back and forth in a "Japanese fan" pattern. Shelf paper or wrapping paper is about the right weight, and if the folds are creased and reinforced with masking tape, the book will stand alone. A heavier cover may be glued to the ends for added durability and attractiveness. Students may write and paint directly on the pages, or if preferred, both writing and illustrations can be pasted in place. The title of the book and the name of the author should be printed on the front cover to complete the book.

Bookbinding

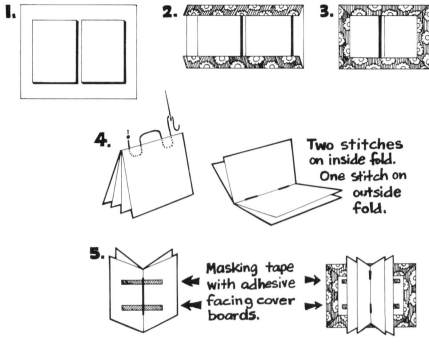

Figure 5.9.   Bookbinding.

Shape books are small booklets made by cutting two matching shapes from tagboard and then stapling several pages of lined notebook paper between them. When the notebook paper has been trimmed to conform to the shape of the covers, the booklets are ready for students to fill with short stories suggested by the shape of each one. In lieu of writing, kindergarten children may paste small, appropriate pictures in the booklets. Shape booklets may be made in the form of a snowball, valentine, shamrock, Easter egg, Jack-o-lantern, Christmas tree, or other subjects of interest to children.

The first step in making a scroll is to fill a long strip of paper with writing and illustrations that tell a good story. Writing and painting should be done directly on the scroll paper. The ends of the paper are then fastened to two sticks so that the strip may be rolled from one end to the other as the reader goes through the story section by section in left to right progression.

Whole Language

There is a current movement in early childhood education toward the "whole language" approach and away from isolated language exercises. The movement advocates an integrated language arts program that allows children to live and work in a rich language environment throughout the school day, and which, ideally, is continued by parents at home. The fragmented curriculum characterized by workbooks, skill sheets, and textbooks has been replaced by children's creative writing, reading-aloud and storytelling sessions, dramatization and puppetry, chart making, art activities, science–social studies projects, and other child-centered experiences that call for communication in a natural childlike way. It is the kind of curriculum that children would develop for themselves if they were given the opportunity to do so.

The idea of the integrated curriculum is by no means a new one. Many teachers have been convinced of its effectiveness all along and have not wavered from the belief that children learn to read by reading, to write by writing, to speak by speaking. In their classrooms, children's talk is treasured, written down, and read back; children learn to write and to discuss books at the same time they are learning to read them. Listening skills are developed and refined as the teacher reads aloud and as children read to each other. The language arts are inextricably bound together, and in the whole language approach children are led to appreciate that interrelatedness.

Library books (trade books) are the basic feature of the whole language curriculum. Stories created by outstanding writers for children and illustrated by skillful, talented artists are used consistently to stimulate reading, writing, listening, and speaking. Teachers need to know how to judge the quality of books they plan to use as language models for children. They must also be able to select specific books to initiate the desired language situations in the classroom.

It has been found that teachers who have not learned to appreciate children's literature and are not really familiar with many children's books have a tendency to rely more heavily than their counterparts on workbooks and worksheets. Children's books are tools of the teaching trade and, therefore, must be studied routinely along with other professional literature.

CHILDREN'S BOOKS FOR LANGUAGE EXPERIENCES

All About Eggs and How They Change Into Animals, written by Millicent Selsam; illustrated by Helen Ludwig. New York: William R. Scott, Inc., 1952.

> A science book of factual information that is interesting enough to hold the attention of young children and simple enough for them to understand. The story of eggs begins with the most familiar of all, the egg of a hen. It ends with a description and an illustration of the egg that grows inside a human mother.

The Cow Who Fell in the Canal, written by Phyllis Krasilovsky; illustrated by Peter Spier. Garden City, N.Y.: Doubleday & Co., Inc., 1957.

> Hendrika, a faithful milk cow, lives on a farm in Holland, but she is bored with eating and eating and eating. One day she falls into the canal and onto a raft. The raft floats downstream to a city. There Hendrika sees so many interesting sights that she stores up enough memories to keep her entertained the rest of her life on the farm.

Down, Down the Mountain, written and illustrated by Ellis Credle. New York: Thomas Nelson and Sons, 1934.

> Hetty and Hank, who live in a little log cabin in the Blue Ridge Mountains, want new shoes to wear to church on Sunday. Their granny tells them to plant turnip seeds and trade the turnips for shoes. This plan brings many adventures to Hetty and Hank. Eventually they take their fine big turnips down to the town at the foot of the mountain.

Five O'Clock Charlie, written by Marguerite Henry; illustrated by Wesley Dennis. New York: Rand McNally & Co., 1962.

> Based on a true incident, as are all of Marguerite Henry's horse stories, *Five O'Clock Charlie* is the story of an endearing old work horse who refuses to accept retirement with its life of ease—and boredom. Charlie finds a way "to make his loneliness vanish like a fog when the sun comes out." Most horse stories are too difficult for young readers. This one is an exception.

Hitty: Her First Hundred Years, written by Rachel Field; illustrated by Dorothy Lathrop. New York: The Macmillan Co., 1930.

> Hitty, a small antique wooden doll carved from mountain ash wood, writes her memoirs over a period of a hundred years. Hitty's thrilling adventures take her across the United States and to foreign countries. The story was actually inspired by a doll the author and illustrator purchased years ago from an antique shop in New York City.

Homer Price, written and illustrated by Robert McCloskey. New York: The Viking Press, 1943.

> Six tales of riotous laughter are built around the escapades of a typical adolescent boy. All the characters with whom Homer Price has dealings are memorable and very much like our own neighbors. The book is extremely popular with both boys and girls.

Just So Stories, written and illustrated by Rudyard Kipling. Garden City, N.Y.: Doubleday & Co., Inc., 1907.

> These long popular "why" stories tell how the various animals came to be. Similar to ancient folktales, each story is pure fun and nonsense balanced with the right amount of realism. The stories are excellent for the teacher or aide to read aloud because of the rich vocabulary and rhythmic style. For smooth reading, the stories should be practiced in advance.

Many Moons, written by James Thurber; illustrated by Louis Slobodkin. New York: Harcourt Brace Jovanovich, Inc., 1943.

> The story of how a little princess named Lenore asks for the moon and gets it. When all the Royal Wise Men have tried and failed to capture the elusive moon, Lenore and her friend, the Court Jester, devise a plan that works. A delightful fantasy for eight- and nine-year-olds.

Miss Hickory, written by Carolyn Sherwin Bailey; illustrated by Ruth Gannett. New York: The Viking Press, 1946.

> Miss Hickory is a doll made from an applewood twig with a hickory nut head. She lives in a corncob house under a lilac bush. This story of fantasy tells how Miss Hickory lives among neighbors like Crow, Bull Frog, Ground Hog, and Squirrel. The surprise ending to the book teaches a subtle lesson on hope and immortality.

My Father's Dragon, written by Ruth Stiles Gannett; illustrated by Ruth Chrisman Gannett. New York: Random House, 1948.

> A young boy rescues the baby dragon from his tormentors by outwitting the wild animals who are using the dragon as a ferryboat to cross the river. A humorous adventure story of danger and daring. Chapter titles such as "My Father Meets a Lion" and "My Father Meets a Gorilla" appeal to young readers and listeners.

Pelle's New Suit, written and illustrated by Elsa Beskow. New York: Harper & Row, Publishers, 1929.

> In this realistic story from Sweden, a small boy earns his new suit by raising his own sheep. After shearing the sheep, Pelle takes the wool to be carded, spun into yarn, woven into cloth, dyed, and sewn into a suit. It is a simplified, entertaining story of how woolen cloth is made. Beautiful illustrations make it easy for young children to follow the sequential steps.

Pippi Longstocking, written by Astrid Lindgren; illustrated by Louis S. Glanzman. New York: The Viking Press, 1950.

> Pippi Longstocking is one of the most hilarious characters in children's literature. She is a little orphan girl who lives alone except for her pets and has the privilege of doing exactly as she pleases. She keeps telling everyone, "Don't worry about me. I'll come out on top." Indeed she does. Young readers envy her carefree existence.

BIBLIOGRAPHY

Allen, R. Van. *Language Experiences in Communication*. Boston: Houghton Mifflin Company, 1976.

Almy, Millie Corine. "Children's Experiences Prior to First Grade and Success in Beginning Reading." *Contributions to Education,* No. 954. New York: Bureau of Publications, Teachers College, Columbia University, 1949.

Applegate, Mauree. *Easy in English*. New York: Harper & Row, Publishers, 1960.

———. *Freeing Children to Write*. New York: Harper & Row, Publishers, 1963.

Bernard, Harold W. *Psychology of Learning and Teaching*. New York: McGraw-Hill Book Co., 1954.

Burrows, Alvina Treut, June D. Ferebee, Doris C. Jackson, and Dorothy O. Saunders. *They All Want to Write*. New York: Prentice-Hall, Inc., 1952.

Burton, William H., Roland B. Kimball, and Richard L. Wigg. *Education for Effective Thinking*. New York: Appleton-Century-Crofts, 1960.

Corcoran, Gertrude B. *Language Experience for Nursery and Kindergarten Years*. Itasca, Ill.: F. E. Peacock Publishers, 1976.

Frost, Joe L. *Early Childhood Education Rediscovered*. New York: Holt, Rinehart & Winston, Inc., 1968.

Graves, Donald H. *Writing: Teachers and Children at Work*. Portsmouth, N.H.: Heinemann Educational Books, 1983.

Hall, Mary Anne. *Teaching Reading as a Language Experience*. Columbus, Ohio: Charles E. Merrill Publishers, 1970.

Harris, Ben M. *Supervisory Behavior in Education*. Englewood Cliffs, N.J.: Prentice-Hall, Inc., 1963.

Heilman, Arthur W. *Principles and Practices of Teaching Reading*. 4th ed., Columbus, Ohio: Charles E. Merrill Publishers, 1972.

Herrick, Virgil E., and Marcella Nerbovig. *Using Experience Charts with Children*. Columbus, Ohio: Charles E. Merrill Publishers, 1964.

Hoskisson, Kenneth. *Language Arts: Content and Strategies*. Columbus, Ohio: Merrill Publishing Co., 1987.

Keller, Helen. *The Story of My Life*. Garden City: Doubleday & Co., 1920.

Koch, Kenneth. *Wishes, Lies, and Dreams: Teaching Children to Write Poetry*. New York: Vintage Books Chelsea House Publishers, 1970.

Kohl, Herbert. *36 Children*. New York: The New American Library, 1967.

———. "Writing Their Way to Self-Acceptance." *Grade Teacher* 87 (1969): 8–10.

Lamoreaux, Lillian A., and Dorris May Lee. *Learning to Read Through Experience*. New York: Appleton-Century-Crofts, 1943.

Lee, Dorris May, and R. V. Allen. *Learning to Read Through Experience*. New York: Appleton-Century-Crofts, 1963.

Lowenfeld, Viktor, and W. Lambert Brittain. *Creative and Mental Growth*. 4th ed. New York: The Macmillan Co., 1964.

Milner, Esther. "A Study of the Relationship Between Reading Readiness in Grade One School Children and Patterns of Parent-Child Interaction." *Child Development* 22 (1951):95–112.

National Council of Teachers of English. *The English Language Arts.* New York: Appleton-Century-Crofts, 1952.

Pappas, Christine C., Barbara Z. Kiefer, and Linda S. Levstik. *An Integrated Language Perspective in the Elementary School.* New York: Longman, 1990.

Petty, Walter T., and Mary E. Bowen. *Slithery Snakes and Other Aids to Children's Writing.* New York: Appleton-Century-Crofts, 1967.

Petty, Walter T., Dorothy C. Petty, Richard Salzer, and Marjorie Becking. *Experiences in Language.* 5th ed. Boston: Allyn and Bacon, 1989.

Ross, Elinor P., and Betty D. Roe. *An Introduction to Teaching the Language Arts.* Chicago: Holt, Rinehart and Winston, Inc., 1990.

Stauffer, Russell G. *The Language Experience Approach to the Teaching of Reading.* New York: Harper & Row, Publishers, 1970.

Stewig, John Warren. *Read to Write: Using Children's Literature as a Springboard to Writing.* New York: Hawthorn Books, Inc., 1975.

Strickland, Ruth G. *The Language Arts in the Elementary School.* New York: D. C. Heath and Co., 1963.

Temple, Charles, and Jean Wallace Gillett. *Language Arts: Learning Processes and Teaching Practices.* 2d ed. Glenview, Ill.: Scott, Foresman & Company, 1989.

Trauger, Wilma K. *Language Arts in Elementary Schools.* New York: McGraw-Hill Co., 1963.

Weiss, Harvey. *How to Make Your Own Books.* New York: Thomas Y. Crowell Company, 1974.

6

"Every Young Child is an Artist":

Books That Stimulate Art Projects

Art expression as an extension of oral language and writing is a very effective means by which children can communicate their feelings and ideas to others and, at the same time, experience the profound sense of release that accompanies creative effort. As Nancy Larrick writes, "Creative activities turn dormant buds into blossoms. Any child or adult expands as he realizes that he is expressing himself in his own way. His attitudes and behavior are influenced by his new sense of individuality."[1]

An art program designed for young children should have as its basic purpose the eliciting of free expression from those children. Each activity and experience should be seen as a means of releasing the creative urge in wholesome and childlike ways. By nature, all young children have such a creative urge. They are imaginative, inventive, eager, and original until they have lived long enough to learn clichés and stereotypes that stifle the creative impulse. This reality of "diminishing creativity" makes the art curriculum for young children all the more important.

> . . . all humans have some creative potential whose release produces a measure of satisfaction. Therefore, a curriculum designed to encourage creativeness holds value for all students, not merely the creatively gifted minority.[2]

1. Nancy Larrick, *A Teacher's Guide to Children's Books* (Columbus, Ohio: Charles E. Merrill Publishers, 1963), p. 147.
2. John Curtis Gowan, George D. Demos, and E. Paul Torrance, *Creativity: Its Educational Implications* (New York: John Wiley & Sons, Inc., 1967), p. 205.

Modern education is at last directing its attention toward providing creative opportunity in every area of education, preschool through college. Research findings have brought about this emphasis by making known the importance of the creative personality to our society. Burton and Heffernan write in the introduction to their handbook on creativity:

> The development of personality is desirable in and for itself. Meanings, attitudes, and appreciations are distinctly enhanced through efforts at creative expression. Creative self-expression is a normal characteristic of desirable living. The person whose response is original, inventive, and atypical is extremely important socially, because progress takes place through constructive variations from the accepted, the conventional, and the routine.[3]

Because the expression or the process itself is more important to young children than the finished product, teachers should not be unduly concerned with the *results* of a child's efforts in art. A young child expresses what he or she *feels about things,* which may mean large splotches of color applied in a purely abstract arrangement. This kind of painting is, of course, a more honest and sincere form of expression than he or she will be able to duplicate later on. For this reason, it should be appreciated, enjoyed, and encouraged by adults who are significant to the child.

For teachers who are interested in promoting creativity in young children, Wilson and Robeck developed three basic themes to guide them. Those themes are that: creativity, like intelligence, exists to some degree in all people; creative behavior is learned and therefore can be taught; and children's creativity is built on the mental, aesthetic, and emotional patterns that have accumulated.[4]

When art for young children is viewed as a means of self-expression and also as a mode of communication with others, it becomes a perfect corollary to literature. Through many happy experiences with artistic, well-written children's books, young children grow to feel that beauty and color are important to their lives and that books are ever-present sources of information, inspiration, and aesthetic satisfaction.

Creative art-literature experiences occur in the classroom when boys and girls are moved by a good story well told or read, when art materials are made available, and when time and space are allowed for experimentation with the materials. On the other hand, true creativity is seldom expressed when each story is followed by the "en masse" assignment, "Use crayons to make a nice picture of your favorite part."

---

3. William H. Burton and Helen Hefferman, *The Step Beyond: Creativity* (Washington, D.C.: National Education Association, 1964), p. 1.

4. John A. R. Wilson and Mildred C. Robeck, "Creativity in the Very Young," *Teaching for Creative Endeavor,* ed. William B. Michael (Bloomington: Indiana University Press, 1968), pp. 55–56.

Most teachers of young children would agree that two keys to a successful art program for preschool and primary children are self-selection of art activities and freedom of expression. However, with increasing facility and maturity in the use of art materials, children can profit from planned art activities initiated and supervised by the teacher. Freedom of choice and expression need not be thwarted. Books make a natural springboard for such planned activities.

On the following pages are presented some art activities that have proven successful and appropriate for young children. Suggestions are also made for books that are well suited to introduce, accompany, or culminate the various art projects described. It cannot be overemphasized that many children will not be ready for a structured art activity. Those children should be encouraged to pursue individual interests until they choose to take part in the more directed art activities.

Mural Making

Murals, or wall paintings, go back to the time when prehistoric humans scratched pictures in outline on the rock walls of their caves. Drawings offer evidence that people have always been moved to creative endeavor by strong artistic impulses, and that group effort was and is a pleasant way to work. Mural making remains one of the most rewarding group activities for children of all ages.

The most popular medium for mural making in the elementary classroom is tempera paint applied with large soft brushes. Ordinarily, a long strip of white wrapping paper or shelf paper is spread on the floor of the classroom or hall and small groups of children gather around it to paint. Later the mural is attached to the wall for display.

The children will be much more pleased with the finished mural if they have planned sufficiently in advance and have an idea of what the overall composition will be like. If films, slides, or prints are available, they will enjoy seeing some of the great murals that they have been used to adorn buildings in various parts of the world. It should be emphasized before the children begin painting that shapes and forms on a mural must be large, bold, and with a minimum of small detail.

Opportunities for using literature in mural composition are almost limitless if children are encouraged to interpret favorite stories and poems in their own ways. Books that help to create strong mental images of the beauty in nature are excellent raw material for group paintings of the mural type. Such books might include: *A Tree Is Nice, The Little Island, The Little House, The Happy Owls, Time of Wonder, The Big Snow,* and *Switch on the Night.*

Frieze Construction

A frieze is a long, narrow, horizontal band or border used for decorative purposes. In Greek architecture, the frieze was richly carved with hundreds of figures of people, plants, and animals. This band of low-relief architectural sculpture was usually located at the top of the outer wall of ancient temples.

In today's classroom, the frieze consists of a long, narrow band of paper on which numerous objects and figures made by children have been pasted. Frieze making is unsurpassed as a group activity for young children. It provides practice in sketching, painting, cutting, and pasting. Above all, the children are given the satisfaction of creating something of beauty. When all the children have made original contributions to the frieze, it is always lovely to look at.

Any good tale of the accumulative type in which animals, objects, or events increase one after the other up to the climax offers an excellent entrée to the planning of a frieze. Children can then be given the privilege of making as many additions to the border as time and inclination will allow. Some books that have been used by teachers to initiate a frieze project are: *Millions of Cats, Caps for Sale, Mr. Popper's Penguins, A Sky Full of Dragons, The 500 Hats of Bartholomew Cubbins,* and *Alligators All Around.*

Collage

"Collage" comes from the French word "coller," which means to glue or paste something in place. Thus, a collage is made by pasting different textures and shapes of material to a flat surface such as paper, wood, or cardboard to form an interesting and pleasing arrangement.

Collage materials may include fabrics and papers of varying textures and colors, soft wire, ribbon, buttons, yarn, seeds, macaroni, small toys and boxes, excelsior, toothpicks, straws, cotton, wood shavings, and countless other materials that are interesting in pattern, texture, color, or shape (fig. 6.1).

Materials for collage should be collected over time by the teacher and students until an ample supply is available. The materials may then be sorted and filed in shoe boxes with the ends labeled as to contents. For children who cannot yet read, small scraps of the material, instead of labels, may be glued on the boxes to identify the contents.

The collage technique is especially good for those children who think that art must always be realistic representation. Collage lends itself to abstract and semiabstract design. Storybook characters and scenes make

Figure 6.1. Captain Cook, from
Mr. Popper's Penguins by Richard
and Florence Atwater, keeps cool in a
snowstorm of packing foam, an
excellent example of using found
materials for art projects.

fine subjects for collage projects. Such work should flow naturally from
the child's imagination and interests without undue influence from book
illustrations or teacher suggestions.

Fanciful animal stories in which the animal characters act like people,
and often like small children, afford popular subject matter for collage
construction. Such books might include: *Rabbit Hill, The Story of Ferdinand, Charlotte's Web, The Story of Babar, The Story of Ping, Make
Way for Ducklings, Angus and the Ducks,* and *Theodore Turtle.*

Mosaic

It has been said that Mesopotamian builders as early as the third mil-
lennium B.C. used small stones to cover the surface of their wood for
color and protection. Mosaic is used in exactly the same way today, to
cover a surface with small pieces of material in order to form an entirely
new covering that is more attractive and durable than the original.

Each small piece of material used in a mosaic is called a "tessera,"
which is Latin for square piece; the plural is "tesserae." Tesserae may be
composed of cut paper, cardboard, egg shells, pebbles, tile, seeds, lin-
oleum, or bits of wood. The design for the mosaic is drawn on heavy
cardboard or thin wood and each tessera is glued to the surface one at a
time until all the areas have been filled in.

Mosaics are fun to do and are easy enough for young children. The
finished product almost always turns out to be a handsome work of art
whether made by an individual or by a group of children.

Students enjoy selecting a favorite book character to be captured in mosaic form. Using a crayon or felt point pen, the children sketch the shape of a storybook character in bold outline directly on the surface to be covered. The shape is filled in with glued tesserae and the background is added last. The finished mosaic is then ready to be trimmed and matted for display.

Books that have strong central characters that can be easily depicted by children and therefore are suitable for mosaic include: *The Tale of Peter Rabbit, The Gingerbread Boy, Petunia, Veronica, Swimmy,* and *Johnny Crow's Garden.*

Montage

"Montage" comes from the French word "monter," which means "to mount." A montage is a composite picture of several pictures or photographs that create a new photographic image.

In the elementary classroom, a student creates a montage by cutting pictures from magazines and pasting them together (mounting them) on a surface with edges slightly overlapping, to illustrate an association of ideas. For example, if the student wished to illustrate the concept "red," he or she might use an advertisement of a bottle of catsup, a red car, a red dress, a glass of tomato juice, or any other picture that is basically red. The pictures then are pasted together to create a totally new image that says "red" with much greater impact than any single picture could convey.

The montage technique is not only enjoyable as an art process but also has the advantage of giving young children needed practice in eye-hand-mind coordination as they select, classify, cut, arrange, and paste. The finished montage will be meaningful to all who view it if it is labeled appropriately with the idea or feeling it is intended to convey.

Some books that have been used successfully to inspire the montage process are: *Hailstones and Halibut Bones* (montage of colors), *The Little Auto* (montage of cars), *Mr. Rabbit and the Lovely Present* (montage of fruit), *Peter's Chair* (montage of furniture), *A Baby Sister for Frances* (montage of babies), and *Daddies, What They Do All Day* (montage of men at work).

Easel Painting

Probably the single most significant art activity for young children is painting with tempera paint at an art easel. Every day, throughout the entire school day, the easel should stand ready and waiting for children to use when they feel the urge to create a picture with paint.

An ample supply of newsprint paper, cut to fit the size of the easel, should be made available. A large twelve-inch brush is needed for each color of tempera paint being used so that colors may stay bright and clear. The paint must be thick enough so that the brush can carry a full load of paint. A man's discarded shirt makes a fine artist's smock, and a low line with clothespins is a necessity for drying the large paintings.

Many times children will wish simply to experiment with bold splashes of color, but just as often they will want to paint a specific picture. Again, literature can provide the needed input for something to talk about, write about, and paint.

Folk literature of all types is an excellent catalyst for creative activity. Elements of folktales, myths, legends, and fables consistently appear in the spontaneous writing and painting of children. Adults who work with children should share their knowledge of folk literature with the children, and every experience with literature of this type needs to be accompanied by opportunities for the children to give personal expression to the story. Easel painting is always a ready outlet for such expression.

The following books are examples of the abundant wealth of riches available in the area of folk literature: *The Three Billy Goats Gruff, Cinderella, The Legend of the Willow Plate, Aesop's Fables,* and *A Book of Myths.*

Papier-Mâché Over an Inflated Balloon

An inflated balloon of either the round or oblong shape provides an excellent form or framework for paper sculpture, and it is easy enough for young children to execute. This type of sculpture may be used effectively to create prototypes of animal characters from favorite books and stories.

Newspaper or paper toweling strips are dipped into a bowl of wallpaper paste that has been thinned to the consistency of cream, and then are applied directly to the inflated balloon. The process should be repeated until the balloon is completely covered with four or five layers of the paper strips. If the strips run in different directions, the finished shape will be more durable.

Allow papier-mâché to dry thoroughly and paint it the desired color with tempera paint. Features may be added by using yarn, buttons, felt pieces, and other materials glued in place. Legs for animal figures may be made by forming cones from half-circles of construction paper (see fig. 6.2).

Figure 6.2.   This clown piñata was made by using papier-mâché over an inflated balloon according to step-by-step directions in the book *Piñatas* by Virginia Brock.

Familiar characters from literature that are quite suitable for papier-mâché sculpture are Charlotte and Wilbur, Curious George, Babar, Ferdinand, Peter Rabbit, Angus, and Frederick.

Shadowboxes

A popular art-literature activity with children is the old-fashioned shadowbox technique used to depict scenes from stories, poems, plays, and songs.

Background for the scene is made by lining a shoebox with colored construction paper. Younger children may find it simpler to paint the inside of the box. The easiest method of making mountains, trees, shrubs, houses, and barns for the foreground is to cut them from colored construction paper and stiffen each piece with cardboard so that it will stand alone when its base is glued to the bottom of the shadowbox.

Small animal and human figures can be fashioned of pipe cleaners, clothes pins, clay, or play dough and added last to the shadowbox as finishing touches.

Shadowboxes are more easily identifiable and thus more enjoyable to children if they are properly labeled before being placed on display.

Some examples of well-known scenes to consider for shadowboxes are:

Laura's Christmas in *The Little House in the Big Woods*
"Dividing Night" from *Rabbit Hill*
Mrs. Mallard teaching her ducklings to swim (*Make Way for Ducklings*)
The caterpillar emerging as a butterfly (*The Very Hungry Caterpillar*)
Mr. and Mrs. Bird safely at home (*The Best Nest*)

Painting with Yarn and String

By gluing yarn or heavy string to pieces of fabric or colored paper, textured paintings can be made by children as a creative response to literature. Such paintings are very beautiful when completed and look remarkably like stitchery.

The basic outline of a book character is first lightly drawn with chalk on burlap, felt, or colored paper (white paper may be used if yarn is of a dark color). Using white liquid glue in a plastic squeeze bottle, a thin stream of glue is dribbled along the chalk line. A length of yarn or string is then carefully placed on the wet glue and allowed to dry.

Background features may be added to the yarn paintings with crayons, colored chalk, or construction paper.

Characters that can be drawn with simple basic shapes and few details are the best subjects for yarn paintings, such as the characters from *Swimmy, Crictor, Georgie,* and *Frederick* (fig. 6.3).

Figure 6.3.   A third-grader's yarn painting makes effective use of shape, color, and texture. It was inspired by Leo Leonni's *Swimmy.*

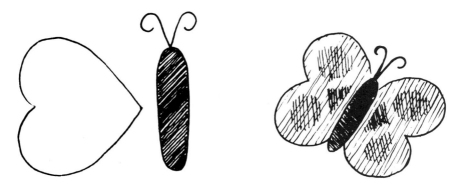

Figure 6.4.   Large heart shapes make attractive butterflies as a follow-up to the reading of *The Very Hungry Caterpillar* by Eric Carle.

Butterfly Mobiles

Read aloud *The Very Hungry Caterpillar* by Eric Carle and show children the illustrations. Discuss the metamorphosis from caterpillar to butterfly. Take advantage of student interest to initiate an art project in which they make butterfly mobiles to hang from the ceiling in the classroom.

Each child should cut two large hearts from thin white poster board. (Since the two hearts will form the butterfly's wings, they should be identical in shape and size.) The two hearts are glued together at the points. A cigar shape may then be glued on between the hearts to form a body for the butterfly. Pipe cleaner antennae may be taped to the body to finish the butterfly shape (see fig. 6.4).

The butterflies are now ready to be painted on both sides with tempera paint according to each child's own creative imagination. Attach strings to the butterflies and hang them from the ceiling for all to enjoy. Reread *The Very Hungry Caterpillar* (figs. 6.5, 6.6, 6.7).

Scrimshaw

Scrimshaw is the ancient art of crafting objects from the teeth and jaw bones of the sperm whale. It was mainly the handiwork of whaling sailors who, in the nineteenth century, collected whale blubber to make lamp oil. The men liked to while away the long idle hours on the ship by making scrimshaw buttons, letter openers, shoehorns, jewelry, and countless other decorative and useful objects. The name scrimshaw actually means "to avoid work." It comes from the British word "scrimshank," which means "to fool around."

Figures 6.5., 6.6., 6.7. Children using tempera paint and brushes paint large cutout butterflies to be hung as mobiles in a local shopping mall. (Courtesy Lamar University.)

Figure 6.8.   Scrimshaw may be carved from plastic as a project to accompany the reading of *Seabird* by Holling C. Holling.

In his book, *Seabird,* Holling C. Holling gives an accurate and dramatic account of scrimshaw as he describes the adventures of an ivory gull carved by a young crew member on an old-time whaling vessel. It is an outstanding book for reading aloud and may well be considered the young child's version of *Moby Dick.*

Today the whale is considered an endangered species and people are strongly discouraged from buying any whale scrimshaw work; however, it is interesting to view in museums. Quite satisfactory scrimshaw can be carved on plastic, using the following directions:

Provide students with smooth flat pieces of white plastic cut from dishwashing detergent bottles or bleach bottles. Have them draw a pencil design of their own choosing on the plastic. Show them how to carve the design by following the pencil lines with the point of a common 16-penny nail. To darken the etched lines, children should rub over them with a black crayon and polish off the excess with a paper towel (fig. 6.8). Small cardboard racks can be made to display the finished pieces of scrimshaw.

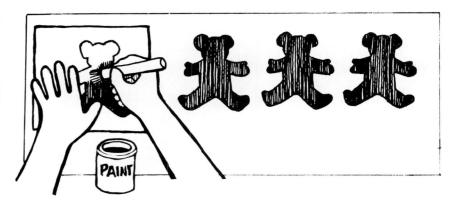

Figure 6.9.   Once children have mastered the art of cutting stencils, they use them for many purposes. Note: Avoid the use of commercial stencils; allow children to create their own.

Stenciling

A stencil is a piece of thin cardboard with a cutout shape in the center. When the piece is laid on a surface and color is applied through the opening, a desired figure is produced. The pattern or design created by such a procedure is also called a stencil (fig. 6.9).

It is possible for a stenciling project to be used with young children if it is simplified and adapted for them. It has the potential to be both creative and cognitive. Once mastered, stenciling becomes an effective technique for illustrating child-made books and other writing.

Show children how to draw a pencil outline of an animal (or other shape) on a tablet back. With scissors cut a slash from the edge of the cardboard into the line drawing so that scissors may be inserted. Once the shape is cut out, the slash may be taped back together (see fig. 6.10). The stencil is ready for use. Each design is original and the children have followed detailed directions to solve a problem.

Place the completed stencil on white paper and use crayons to color from the center of the opening. Colored chalk may also be used. It may be rubbed gently with a tissue for an interesting blurred, textured picture (see fig. 6.11).

Show children how to place the opening of the stencil slightly over the first design and continue the coloring. This creates an overlapping effect and gives the illusion of many animals or shapes.

 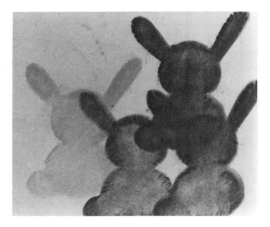

Figure 6.10.   Even the stencil itself is attractive and is often displayed alongside the stencil designs.

Figure 6.11.   Overlapping figures by placement of the stencil can create interesting effects when colored chalk is used.

Art for All Always

Some of the most beautiful books being published for today's young readers are books about art and artists—books that describe paintings, sculpture, crafts, manuscripts, machines, and other treasures found in museums throughout the world. Information in such books is presented in a clear, down-to-earth manner intended to teach children how to visit a museum and how to observe and understand the similarities, as well as the differences, in the way artists paint and sculpt.

A collection of art books in the kindergarten and primary classroom encourage children to look beyond the pages, beyond the reproductions and replicas, to a time when they will have the privilege of viewing the originals close up. In other words, such books help to develop a lifelong interest in art.

Art books can be obtained at local museums and loan libraries, school and public libraries, and the school's art department. It is not necessary for young students to be able to read every word in an art book to appreciate the great beauty to be found in it. The teacher's interest and enthusiasm are essential, however. Make the books available, discuss them, and replace and refurbish the display occasionally. Sit back and watch the beauty of the books weave its magic spell. (An annotated list of art books is given at the end of the chapter.)

Studying the Art in Children's Books

Many great artists have found in children's books a fertile field for their talents. They know children to be severe critics with a sure eye for banality, but also very receptive, appreciative, and completely honest in their appraisal. An audience of such perception is bound to stimulate an illustrator to his or her best effort. Such excellence has given today's children an unparalleled selection of artistic, well-written books from which to choose.

Not only are the best books entertaining and beautiful to look at, but they also offer an endless array of art media and processes for the child's consideration. The home or classroom that owns even a modest collection of fine picture books has a veritable art gallery at its disposal.

Unfortunately, with increased facility in printing and in art reproduction techniques, an outpouring of valueless books for children have been marketed. Every day it becomes more imperative that teachers, parents, and children find ways to ferret out the treasurers that do exist in literature. With fewer quiet hours available for reading, and with funds for books at a premium, it seems a tragedy to waste either on books that have no lasting value.

Probably the best way to gain skill in recognizing quality in children's books is to make a thorough study of some of the finest that have been published and use those as a measuring stick to judge others. The Caldecott Award books are examples of excellence.

The Caldecott Award

The American Library Association established a special award in 1937 to pay tribute to the artists who spend their time creating outstanding illustrations for children's books. The award was named for Randolph Caldecott, a nineteenth-century illustrator of children's literature. It is said that his illustrations designate him as the first artist to illustrate poems and stories from a child's point of view.

When the sculptor René Paul Chambellan (famous for his sculpture in Rockefeller Center) was commissioned to design the Caldecott Medal, he turned to Caldecott's own work for inspiration. Chambellan at once decided that he could not improve on the English artist's work and thus chose two of Caldecott's own drawings to be reproduced on the medal. One side depicts "John Gilpin's Ride" and the other illustrates a line from an ancient nursery rhyme, "four and twenty blackbirds baked in a pie." (See fig. 6.12.)

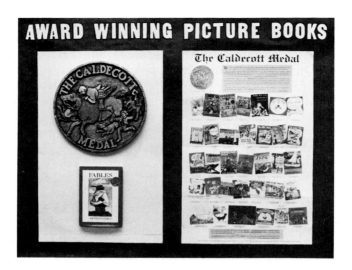

Figure 6.12.   A cardboard replica of the medal, a
Caldecott poster, and the jacket from a recent winner are
combined to create a beautiful, instructional literature
bulletin board. (Courtesy of Barbara Ellis.)

One of the requirements for winning the Caldecott Award is that an
artist be either a citizen or a resident of the United States. Daniel Melcher
is the donor of the medal, which was originally conceived and donated
by his father, Frederic Melcher. The award is administered and presented
by the Association for Library Service to Children, a division of the American Library Association. A replica of the bronze medal is attached to the
jacket of winning books for easy identification in bookstores and libraries. A complete list of the Caldecott Medal books, and their illustrators and publishers, is given in Appendix A.

The first Caldecott Award was presented to Dorothy P. Lathrop in 1938
for her distinguished black and white picture book *Animals of the Bible.*
Since that time the medal has been awarded annually. One illustrator has
won the award three times and five others have won it twice.

Marcia Brown was awarded the Caldecott Medal for *Cinderella*
(1955), *Once a Mouse* (1962), and *Shadow* (1983). Robert McCloskey
won the medal for *Make Way for Ducklings* in 1942 and for *Time of
Wonder* in 1958. Barbara Cooney won the medal for *Chanticleer and
the Fox* in 1959 and for *Ox-Cart Man* in 1980. Nonny Hogrogian was
awarded the medal for *Always Room for One More* (1966) and *One Fine
Day* (1972). The husband and wife illustrating team of Leo and Diane
Dillon made history by winning the medal two years in a row. They were

presented the award in 1976 for *Why Mosquitoes Buzz in People's Ears* and again in 1977 for *Ashanti to Zulu: African Traditions.* The most recent artist to win two Caldecott Awards was Chris Van Allsburg. His *Jumanji* won in 1982 and *The Polar Express* in 1986.

There are also books published each year with outstanding illustrations that do not win the Caldecott Award. The selection committee has chosen to name as "Honor Books" other fine picture books that have been contenders or runners-up for the medal. It is a splendid prize for an artist to have a book chosen as an Honor Book. Most schools and libraries collect the Caldecott Honor Books as well as the Caldecott Award books. And, fortunately, most of them are still in print.

Young children are curious about the Caldecott Award and often request information about the author and illustrator of winning books. They seem to find fascination in a book that has won an important award for its artwork. Additionally, an unusual feature of the Caldecott Award books is their appeal to all ages. Such attraction makes them excellent material for cross-age grouping. Older children read them aloud to younger children and, in the process, polish and refine their own reading skills.

Most of the Caldecott books remain popular with children, perhaps because they have been presented in a variety of ways by adults who like them. Children have always been drawn to great books when parents have read them aloud at home, when teachers have presented them in class for reading and discussion, and when librarians have found interesting ways to display them.

Significant adults in a child's life are responsible for providing him or her with a rich program of art and literature. Incidental exposure to a few moth-eaten library books will never meet the aesthetic needs of a child.

CHILDREN'S BOOKS FOR ART ACTIVITIES

Aesop's Fables, illustrated by Alice and Martin Provensen. New York: The Golden Press, 1967.

> Forty of the favorite tales of wise and foolish animals selected and adapted by a famous storyteller, Louis Untermeyer. The illustrations are humorous and clever, a perfect complement to the familiar old stories.

Alligators All Around, written and illustrated by Maurice Sendak. New York: Harper & Row, Publishers, 1962.

> A delightful nonsense alphabet book about alligators. A tiny book just right for small hands. Part of the Nutshell Library by Maurice Sendak.

Angus and the Ducks, written and illustrated by Marjorie Flack.
Garden City, N.Y.: Doubleday & Co., Inc., 1930.

> Angus, a curious little Scotty dog, goes to investigate the quacking sound.
> The quacking turns to hissing and Angus quickly loses his curiosity—for three
> minutes at least.

Art for Children: Pablo Picasso, by Ernest Raboff. New York: Harper
& Row, Publishers, 1982.

> The popular *Art for Children* series is now available in paperback editions
> and practical enough for everyday use in the elementary classroom. Each
> book contains a brief biographical sketch and an easy-to-read interpretation
> of the artist's paintings. Each title is filled with full-color reproductions of
> the artist's work along with many smaller sketches. The books are designed
> specifically to inspire in children a better understanding of the world of great
> art. The series presents the works and lives of sixteen of the world's most
> recognized artists: Renoir, Da Vinci, Rembrandt, Picasso, Van Gogh, Mi-
> chelangelo, Raphael, Chagall, Gauguin, Klee, Rousseau, Velasquez, Matisse,
> Remington, Dürer, and Toulouse-Lautrec.

A Baby Sister for Frances written by Russell Hoban; illustrated by
Lillian Hoban. New York: Harper & Row, Publishers, 1964.

> Watching her parents care for the new baby in the family, Frances feels alone
> and neglected until she finally decides to set things right by running away.
> Her parents understand her feelings and quickly take steps to make amends.

The Big Snow, written and illustrated by Berta and Elmer Hader. New
York: The Macmillan Co., 1948.

> A realistic story of how various animals prepare themselves for winter, and
> of a kindly couple who puts out food for them when the big snow arrives.
> A good book to help make children sensitive to needs of wild animals.

A Book of Myths, illustrated by Helen Sewell. New York: The
Macmillan Co., 1942.

> This is a selection of the most popular myths from Bulfinch's "Age of the
> Fable." It is a fine resource for storytelling in the middle grades. The line
> drawings are reminiscent of early Greek Art.

Caps for Sale, written and illustrated by Esphyr Slobodkina. New York:
William R. Scott, Inc., 1947.

> A cap peddler who carries all his wares on his head is surprised to find they
> have been whisked away by a band of mischievous monkeys. How he finally
> persuades them to give back the caps is delightful fun for young children.

Charlotte's Web, written by E. B. White; illustrated by Garth Williams.
New York: Harper & Row, Publishers, 1952.

> *Charlotte's Web* is a universally loved book of the modern talking beast tale
> variety. It is excellent for reading aloud, as a continued story, to eight-year-
> olds. Most children will then read the book for themselves—often more than
> once.

The Comical Celtic Cat, written and illustrated by Norah Golden.
Mountrath, Portlaoise, Ireland: The Dolmen Press, 1984.

> A comical Celtic cat lives in Kells with a young monk named Matthew who is busy painting a book, not just any book, but the Book of Kells. The artist enlists his cat to pose for the capital letter C, "scratching your back or biting your foot, the most comical capital in the book." Batik illustrations show the illumination of letters.

Crictor, by Tomi Ungerer. New York: Harper & Row, Publishers, 1968.

> As a birthday gift, Madame Louise Bodot receives a boa constrictor from her son who is studying reptiles in Africa. Crictor makes a good pet and rescues his mistress from a burglar. Some letters of the alphabet and the numerals through eight are reviewed as Crictor coils his body into various shapes for the amusement of his friends.

Da Vinci, written and illustrated by Mike Venezia. Chicago: Children's Press, 1989.

> This publication proves that an art book can be easy to read with large print and easy vocabulary, while at the same time be authentic and beautiful to see. Stories behind "The Last Supper," "The Mona Lisa," "The Virgin of the Rocks" and other of Leonardo's paintings make for fascinating reading. A list of museums where the originals are housed is given at the end of the book. A 32-page paperback.

Early Humans, written by Nick Merriman and photographed by Dave King. New York: Alfred A. Knopf, 1989.

> Ancient people and their ways of life are presented in this book by means of museum photographs with descriptive captions. An effective source to use in preparing children for a museum visit. Other titles in the series are: *Arms & Armor; Bird; Butterfly & Moth; Mammal; Music; Pond & River; Rocks & Minerals; Shell; Skeleton; Sports;* and *Tree.*

Faces, written by Giles Waterfield. New York: Atheneum, 1982.

> Artists believe that a face reveals more about its owner than any other part of the body. Artists from all cultures have concentrated on the face in sculpture, painting, drawing, and mask-making. This book presents a collection of faces from many periods and countries. The portraits range from realistic likenesses of great portraitists to the stylized masks of primitive cultures. The author recommends books for further reading and urges students to visit museums to look at portraits close up. Other books in the "Looking at Art" series are *People at Home* and *People at Work.*

Feelings, written and illustrated by Aliki. New York: Greenwillow Books, 1984.

> An array of faces show moods and emotions such as sorrow, fear, sadness, surprise, joy, anger, and many others. Excellent for discussion as children strive to verbalize their own feelings. Also serves as a point of departure for art activities as feelings are expressed in still another way.

The 500 Hats of Bartholomew Cubbins, written and illustrated by Dr. Seuss (Theodor Geisel). New York: The Vanguard Press, 1938.

> The king orders Bartholomew to remove his plumed hat out of respect to His Majesty, and Bartholomew is quite willing to do so, but every time he removes it, another appears in its place. Each new hat is more elaborate than the one before, and the last is the most wonderful hat of all.

Frederick, written and illustrated by Leo Lionni. New York: Pantheon Books, Inc., 1967.

> While the other field mice are working to store up nuts and grain for the long hard winter, Frederick is storing up words and colors to warm them during the cold days ahead. He is such a good storyteller they are able to see the colors "as clearly as if they had them painted in their minds."

A Greek Potter, written and illustrated by Giovanni Caselli. New York: Peter Bedrick Books, 1986.

> This book describes a potter at work during the time of the Olympics, a festival to Athena, and construction of the temples. It also shows the daily life of the potter's family. Other titles in the "Everyday Life" series are: *The Egyptian Craftsman, A Medieval Monk,* and *A Viking Settler.*

Hailstones and Halibut Bones, written by Mary O'Neill; illustrated by Leonard Weisgard. Garden City, N.Y.: Doubleday & Co., 1961.

> Twelve poems by Mary O'Neill are used to describe the colors of the spectrum. By using familiar objects and images, she shows that each color has its own story to tell. The artwork forms a perfect relationship with the poetry as each color is presented in picture form.

Inspirations: Stories About Women Artists, written by Leslie Sills and illustrated with photographs of museum paintings. Niles, Ill.: Albert Whitman & Company, 1989.

> Four artists are features in this book: Georgia O'Keeffe, Frida Kahlo, Alice Neel, and Faith Ringgold. Each chapter includes photographs of the artist, a biographical sketch, and color photographs of each artist's major works. Paintings are discussed in detail. The basic feature of each discussion is the source of inspiration that motivated the artist. Too difficult for the youngest readers, but an excellent source for teachers. It provides a gallery of paintings for young children to contemplate even if they are unable to read the text.

Johnny Crow's Garden, written and illustrated by Leslie Brooke. New York: Frederick Warne and Co., 1965.

> Johnny Crow stands out among the wise and foolish animals in the garden as having a unique personality. The book has been very popular with young children since the first edition was issued in 1903.

Journey Through History: The Greek and Roman Eras, written by Gloria and Oriol Verges; illustrated by Carme Peris. New York: Barron's, 1988.

> *The Greek and Roman Eras* is one of a series of six books written in an easy-to-understand style that introduces young readers to a study of history. Each

book focuses on people—their work, economics, government, art, games, and home life. Each book contains a glossary of terms and concepts. Titles in the series include: *Prehistory to Egypt; The Greek and Roman Eras; The Middle Ages; The Renaissance; Modern Times;* and *The Contemporary Age.*

Just Imagine: Ideas in Painting, written by Robert Cumming; illustrated with photographs of museum paintings. New York: Charles Scribner's Sons, 1982.

> The author believes that any person who is to enjoy art to its fullest should be able to "get into a painting and see what it is really about." He believes that the viewer must be prepared to use imagination to become involved with the painting. His tries to show museum goers how to look at paintings in a fresh, new way.

The Legend of the Willow Plate, written by Alvin Tresselt and Nancy Cleaver; illustrated by Joseph Low. New York: Parents' Magazine Press, 1968.

> Practically everyone has seen the blue willow design on dinnerware, but not all people know the ancient Chinese legend that it portrays. This book offers a sensitive, poetic retelling of the old story.

Let's Go to the Art Museum, written and illustrated by Virginia K. Levy. New York: Harry N. Abrams, Inc., 1988.

> A museum workbook that covers materials, media, and processes that are basic in the production of various art forms. Art terminology is carefully defined and a vocabulary list is given at the end of the book. The author's aims are to help children appreciate the art in museums and also to lead them to create some art of their own.

The Little Auto, written and illustrated by Lois Lenski. New York: Henry Z. Walck, Inc., 1940.

> Mr. Small drives the little auto exactly like a young child would like to do, with all the familiar gestures and movements. A simple story without plot, but one young children request again and again. Other books in the series are *The Little Train, The Little Airplane,* and *The Little Fire Engine.*

The Little House, written and illustrated by Virginia Lee Burton. Boston: Houghton Mifflin Co., 1942.

> A little country house is engulfed as the city gradually builds around it. The story shows some of the undesirable aspects of technological and industrial progress. Includes a lovely description of the four seasons as observed by the little house.

The Magic Fan, written and illustrated by Keith Baker. San Diego, Calif: Harcourt Brace Jovanovich Publishers, 1989.

> When Yoshi tires of building the common, everyday things such as wagons, fences, houses, stairs, tables, and walls, a magic fan unfolds to teach him how to build a boat to catch the moon, a kite to look over the world, and a bridge to arch like a rainbow. Once his aesthetic impulses have been satisfied, Yoshi returns to building the mundane items needed by his neighbors. Beautifully illustrated with unique fan-shaped folding pages.

Make Way for Ducklings, written and illustrated by Robert McCloskey. New York: The Viking Press, 1941.

> After Mr. and Mrs. Mallard have hatched out a fine family of eight ducklings, they must teach the little ones to swim, dive, walk in a line, to come when called, and to keep a safe distance from things with wheels.

A Medieval Feast, written and illustrated by Aliki Brandenberg. New York: Thomas Y. Crowell, 1983.

> A detailed description of the preparation and celebration of a medieval feast at an English manor house readied for a visit from the king and queen. Aliki's illustrations were inspired by the work of medieval artists and craftsmen whose illuminations, tapestries, and other works of art are preserved in museums. An authentic rendition that teaches customs, costumes, and art of the medieval period in history.

Meet Edgar Degas, written by Anne Newlands; illustrated with photographs of museum paintings. New York: J. B. Lippincott, 1988.

> The famous French artist walks us through museums of the world to examine some twenty of his own paintings. Based on the diaries kept by Degas, the author has written commentary on Degas' philosophy of life and art as though he is speaking to us from the nineteenth century. Brought back to life are the dancers, jockeys, ironers, café singers, and musicians who lived in Paris a century ago.

Meet Matisse, written by Nelly Munthe; illustrated by Rory Kee and Tom Simpson. Boston: Little, Brown and Company, 1983.

> When Matisse was an old man, ill and confined to bed and wheelchair, he created his greatest works. At that time he traded pen and paintbrush for a pair of scissors and began making the colorful cutouts that were to become his trademark. Inspired by a split philodendron growing in his studio, Matisse used the scissors to carve leaf shapes out of colored paper as a form of sculpture. Students are given step-by-step directions for creating cutouts in the Matisse manner.

Mufaro's Beautiful Daughters, written and illustrated by John Steptoe. New York: Lothrop, Lee & Shepard Books, 1987.

> This story is an African folktale collected from people living near the Zimbabwe ruins. Details in the illustrations are based on the architecture of the ruins and on the flora and fauna of the Zimbabwe region. *Mufaro's Beautiful Daughters* won a Caldecott Honor Book Award for John Steptoe. A fine book for reading aloud to young children and brief enough to be completed in one sitting. Allow children time to savor the beautiful paintings.

Peter Rabbit's Colors, with new reproductions from original illustrations by Beatrix Potter. New York: Frederick Warne & Co., 1989.

> Characters from the Beatrix Potter stories present colored objects from Peter Rabbit's blue jacket to Jemima Puddle-Duck's pink shawl as a way of teaching colors to very young children. A review at the end of the book asks, "Can

you remember the colors?'' It presents all the objects (without labels) on a double page. Children are given an opportunity to name not only the colors but the objects themselves.

The Polar Express, written and illustrated by Chris Van Allsburg. Boston: Houghton Mifflin Company, 1985.

> Dreamlike and mysterious pastel paintings in full color illustrate this appealing story of Christmas magic. An otherworldly train carries a young boy to the North Pole on Christmas Eve to receive a special gift from Santa Claus. Winner of the Caldecott Medal.

Mr. Popper's Penguins, written by Richard and Florence Atwater; illustrated by Robert Lawson. Boston: Little, Brown & Co., 1938.

> When he is not working at his job of house painting, Mr. Popper reads books on polar exploration. His life is changed completely when Admiral Drake sends him a penguin from the Antarctic, which he names Captain Cook. An aquarium sends Mr. Popper a mate for Captain Cook, and soon there are ten more penguins in the house!

Potato Printing, written and illustrated by Helen R. Haddad. New York: Thomas Y. Crowell, 1981.

> One of the best examples of a ''how to'' book. Gives a detailed description of ways to use an ordinary potato to print pictures, designs, and messages on paper or fabric. An easy-to-read text and graphic step-by-step illustrations make it a fine selection for the classroom collection. Each project contains a handy ''You will need'' list.

The Pottery Place, written and illustrated by Gail Gibbons. New York: Harcourt Brace Jovanovich, Publishers, 1987.

> This picture book describes the history, economics, and process of pottery making by following a truckload of pottery from artist to gift shop. The reader is taken inside the potter's studio to see the tools and skills needed in traditional pottery making. Directions are given for making a pinch pot, a coil pot, and a slab pot. Excellent for reading aloud as part of any clay modeling project.

Rabbit Hill, written and illustrated by Robert Lawson. New York: The Viking Press, 1944.

> A modern talking beast tale that is extremely popular with children in the middle grades. It teaches a reverence for all of nature's small creatures, from rabbits to field mice.

A Sky Full of Dragons, written by Mildred Whatley Wright; illustrated by Carroll Dolezal. Austin, Tex.: Steck-Vaughn Co., 1969.

> The story of how a Chinese boy named Lee Chow and his grandfather use rice paper and paint to make a sky full of dragon kites for Lee Chow's friends. What Lee Chow is given in return is something he wants more than anything. Beautifully illustrated.

The Story About Ping, written by Marjorie Flack; illustrated by Kurt Wiese. New York: The Viking Press, 1933.

> The adventures of a small duck who lives with his brothers, sisters, cousins, aunts, and uncles on a Chinese junk in the Yangtze River. Authentic Chinese legendry and background.

The Story of Babar, written and illustrated by Laurent de Brunhoff. New York: Random House, 1937.

> Translated from French for American children, Babar's adventures have been popular here for many years. Babar is an elephant who dresses in a business suit and acts very much like a man. This is the first of a dozen books about Babar and his friends.

Swimmy, written, and illustrated by Leo Leonni. New York: Pantheon Books, Inc., 1963.

> Swimmy, a frightened and lonely little black fish, explores the depths of the ocean to find a family he can adopt. When he finds a family of fish with whom he can swim, he uses his intelligence and creativity to teach his new brothers and sisters a way to protect themselves from larger fish. Lovely illustrations by a famous artist.

Switch on the Night, written by Ray Bradbury; illustrated by Madeleine Gekiere. New York: Pantheon Books, Inc., 1955.

> The story of a little boy who does not like the night. He is lonely and unhappy while the other children run and play in the dark. Finally, a little girl teaches him how to switch on the night with a light switch. He finds that in switching on the night he can switch on crickets, frogs, stars, and a great white moon.

The Tale of Peter Rabbit, written and illustrated by Beatrix Potter. New York: Frederick Warne & Co., Inc., 1901.

> One of the most perfect stories for early childhood. Young children see themselves in Peter as he disobeys, finds himself in serious trouble, repents, is punished, and is finally accepted and forgiven.

The Three Billy Goats Gruff, illustrated by Marcia Brown. New York: Harcourt Brace Jovanovich, Inc., 1957.

> One of the finest versions available of a folktale that has been a favorite of children for generations. Illustrated by one of the most versatile of all artists for children.

Time of Wonder, written and illustrated by Robert McCloskey. New York: The Viking Press, 1957.

> This beautiful book of watercolor paintings tells the story of life on a Maine island before and after a hurricane. Children go about exploring the seashore and the forests beyond, just as children have always done. An excellent account is given of the way parents protect children during a crisis.

A Tree Is Nice, written by Janice May Udry; illustrated by Marc Simont. New York: Harper & Row, Publishers, 1956.

> The text and pictures are combined to show every child who reads or looks at the book the joys and delights a nice tree has to offer. The book not only

gives childlike directions for planting a tree but also describes the pride that comes in watching it thrive and grow.

Veronica, written and illustrated by Roger Duvoisin. New York: Alfred A. Knopf, Inc., 1961.

> A hippopotamus named Veronica wants to become famous and conspicuous. She becomes very conspicuous by leaving the herd and walking boldly down the main street of a pink and white city. Trouble brews as Veronica becomes *too* conspicuous.

Visiting the Art Museum, written and illustrated by Laurene Krasny Brown and Marc Brown. New York: E. P. Dutton, 1986.

> One family's visit to an art museum introduces young children to fine art in a lighthearted and inviting way. It includes comments made by parents and children on the paintings and sculpture no matter how irreverent those comments might be. The book is illustrated with full-color reproductions of art from all over the world. Contains fourteen practical tips for enjoying an art museum.

The Warrior and the Wise Man, written and illustrated by David Wisniewski. New York: Lathrop, Leo & Shephard Books, 1989.

> When the author wished to dramatize the contrast between two approaches to solving a problem (blind force and reasoned action), he set his story in Japan. He has one twin brother represent the warrior class and the other represent the wise men. They are given the task of preserving the five universal natural elements: earth, water, fire, wind, and cloud.
>
> Cut-paper silhouettes layered one against the other are used to depict the natural beauty of the story. This is a fine book for group discussion and for introducing the technique of cut-paper collage.

• BIBLIOGRAPHY

Aller, Doris, and Diane Aller. *Mosaics.* Menlo Park, Calif.: Lane Book Co., 1959.

Brock, Virginia. *Piñatas.* New York: Abingdon Press, 1966.

Burton, William H., and Helen Heffernan. *The Step Beyond: Creativity.* Washington, D.C.: National Education Association, 1964.

Carlson, Ruth Kearney. *Literature for Children: Enrichment Ideas.* Dubuque, Iowa: Wm. C. Brown Co., Publishers, 1970.

Eisner, Elliot W., and David W. Ecker. *Readings in Art Education.* Waltham, Mass.: Blaisdell Publishing Co., 1966.

Gaitskell, Charles D., and Al Hurwitz. *Children and Their Art.* New York: Harcourt Brace Jovanovich Inc., 1970.

Gowan, John Curtis, George D. Demos, and E. Paul Torrence. *Creativity: Its Educational Implications.* New York: John Wiley & Sons, Inc., 1967.

Herberholz, Barbara. *Early Childhood Art.* Dubuque, Iowa: Wm. C. Brown and Company, 1974.

Larrick, Nancy. *A Teacher's Guide to Children's Books.* Columbus, Ohio: Charles E. Merrill, Books, Inc., 1963.

Linderman, Earl W., and Donald W. Herberholz. *Developing Artistic and Perceptual Awareness.* 3rd ed. Dubuque, Iowa: Wm. C. Brown and Company, 1974.

Lord, Lois. *Collage and Construction.* New York: Scholastic Book Services, 1958.

Lowenfeld, Viktor, and W. Lambert Brittain. *Creative and Mental Growth.* 4th ed. New York: The Macmillan Co., 1964.

Smith, Irene. *A History of the Newbery and Caldecott Medals.* New York: The Viking Press, 1957.

Wankelman, Willard F., Philip Wigg, and Marietta Wigg. *A Handbook of Arts and Crafts.* Dubuque, Iowa: Wm. C. Brown and Company, 1968.

Wilson, John A. R., and Mildred C. Robeck. "Creativity in the Very Young." In *Teaching for Creative Endeavor,* edited by William B. Michael. Bloomington: Indiana University Press, 1968.

Woolman, Bertha, and Patricia Litsey. *The Cladecott Award: The Winners and Honor Books.* Minneapolis: T. S. Denison and Company, Inc., 1988.

7

"Better Homes and Kindergartens Cookbook":

Books That Lead to Cooking Activities

Of all the learning experiences a teacher might plan for young children, none is more versatile than preparing food in the classroom. Children are fascinated by cooking and eating, and yet, it has been found that they know very little about the origin, preservation, and preparation of the food they eat every day. The fact that children do have strong feelings about food and actually understand so little about it makes cooking a very important area for teaching.

A reliable way to make each cooking experience a cohesive learning unit with interrelated steps is to have it spring naturally from an excellent piece of children's literature. Since authors are aware of children's interest in food, many good books have been written in which food and the acquiring of food is the main theme. As a matter of fact, storytellers were creating and telling tales about food long before such stories were recorded in print. The old folktales abound with the problems of earning bread and imaginary tables laden with rich and exotic foods. Such stories are extremely popular with modern children.

Reading aloud and discussing a good book in which food is an important element is usually all the motivation necessary to begin planning a cooking activity with young children. Cooking makes the book memorable, and in turn, the story serves to make cooking in the classroom even more important.

Some children can hardly wait to sample the finished product while others are satisfied with the cooking activity itself. (Courtesy of Anahuac Independent School District, Anahuac, Texas.)

If the cooking activities are appropriate to the developmental level of children and if they are introduced at an opportune time, all areas of the curriculum are enriched and enhanced in the process. Children acquire skills in language arts as they become involved with the exciting vocabulary of food. They learn sequential order in a natural way as they follow a recipe on the tape recorder or on a recipe chart made of rebus drawings.

Social studies concepts are gained as the children plan, organize, and cooperate to carry out the cooking tasks. They learn to set a table, to take part in appropriate conversation at the table, and to assume responsibility for cleaning up. They begin to understand that mealtime is a great socializing practice and is much more in our lives than the fulfillment of creature comfort.

Cooking experiences are rich in science and mathematics learnings. The children count, measure, estimate, add, subtract, multiply, divide, and learn about fractions. They observe and discuss the chemical reactions as ingredients are mixed together. They watch the changes in form that foods take when heated and cooled. They are able to examine gelatin as a powder, as a liquid, and as a solid. Voila! Chemistry in the kindergarten!

Food preparation is an excellent vehicle for teaching health and safety. Teaching nutrition to young children has always been difficult, and changing undesirable attitudes about food is an important objective in kindergarten cooking. Some children are poorly nourished simply because they refuse to try new foods, and variety in their diet is totally lacking. However, we know that they usually do eat, and with relish, what they have prepared—even vegetables!

All the necessary safety precautions should be emphasized when preparing food. Children can be taught to clean up spills promptly, to handle utensils correctly, and to follow safety rules to the letter. They can learn proper respect for any food or utensil that is hot. Cooking should always be carefully supervised by the teacher. In addition, an aide, a student teacher, or other interested adults may be asked to help supervise the cooking activities. The table range or hot plate should be placed at the child's eye level. Such precautions pay dividends in accident prevention, and subsequent learnings may carry over into life outside the classroom.

Learning theory tells us that young children prefer interesting work over entertainment or other activities. Cooking is interesting work. Some teachers have always believed that children and cooking go together. Others feel that children and cooking and literature go together—a recipe for fun and learning.

Hints to the Teacher

All cooking activities must be closely supervised and most teachers will want another adult present to help work with groups and with individual children. The helper might be a student teacher, an aide, an interested parent, or a cook from the school cafeteria. The teacher should review the procedures in advance so that the helper will be able to offer the right assistance and will not take over tasks that children should do for themselves.

Since so few classrooms are equipped with cook stoves, it is usually necessary to improvise. A table range, an electric fry pan, or a hot plate will usually suffice. Such small appliances offer an added advantage of being at the child's eye level. Other alternatives include the stove in the school cafeteria or the oven of a cooperative parent who lives near the school.

It is best to begin with simple cooking activities in which good results will be more or less guaranteed. The children are then ready to proceed to more complex recipes and to more detailed units of work.

It is a good idea to try each recipe before presenting it to the children. At such time the teacher might work out a sequence of steps for

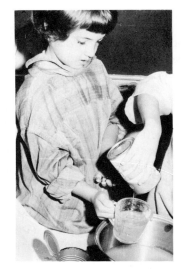

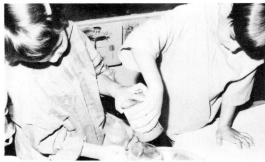

Cooperation in the cooking task brings social satisfaction. Two youngsters measure the broth, which shows graphic proof that there are two cups in each can. Another student shares the clean-up tasks. (Courtesy of Lamar University.)

each group of students and write them in a plan book for ready reference. A check-off list of needed materials and ingredients is always helpful.

Adults should recognize that the importance of cooking in the classroom lies in the doing and not necessarily in the finished product. In most cases, the cooking will provide a small snack for the children, and not a full meal.

If expense is a problem, the food prepared in the classroom may be used as part of the midmorning snack and paid for out of the funds provided. Many schools will allow teachers to requisition foods that are used as instructional material. Some foods, such as vegetables for soup, may be brought by children from home.

The Poppy Seed Cakes

The Poppy Seed Cakes is a nonsensical book made up of a series of stories built around the misadventures of a small boy named Andrewshek. It is easy for young children to identify with Andrewshek as he finds himself involved in one mishap after another. Each time he repents and promises to do better but finds it utterly impossible to stay out of mischief. These warm and human stories are excellent for reading aloud and perfect for storytelling. Auntie Katushka's good poppy seed cakes are referred to throughout the book and one story actually lists the ingredients:

> One lovely Saturday morning Andrewshek's Auntie Katushka took some butter and some sugar and some flour and some milk and seven eggs and she rolled out some nice little cakes. Then she sprinkled each cake with some of the poppy seeds which she had brought from the old country.[1]

Recipe for Poppy Seed Cakes

1 cup butter or margarine	2 cups flour
½ cup sugar	poppy seeds

Blend butter, sugar, and flour with fingers. Roll into small balls the size of a walnut. (Let each child work on a small piece of waxed paper sprinkled with flour.) Flatten each ball slightly with a floured spoon. Sprinkle cakes with poppy seeds. Bake in a slow oven, about 300°, until lightly brown around the edges. Cool and serve with a beverage at snacktime.

Related Activities

Language Arts

Tell or read aloud a story from *The Poppy Seed Cakes* each day until the series is completed.

Lead a discussion about Andrewshek's experiences and about his relationship with the kindly Auntie Katushka.

Make paper models of the butter, sugar, flour, milk, eggs, and poppy seeds for children to arrange on the felt board in sequential order as they appear in Auntie Katushka's recipe. Compare Auntie Katushka's recipe with the simpler one.

---

1. Margery Clark, *The Poppy Seed Cakes* (Garden City, N.Y.: Doubleday & Co., Inc., 1924).

Social Science

Study the illustrations by Maud and Miska Petersham and discuss the clothing worn by Andrewshek, Auntie Katushka, and Erminka.

Talk about the wondrous and rhythmic names of the characters. How are they different from names we hear every day?

Discuss ways in which children everywhere are alike.

Plan a tea party like Auntie Katushka's and serve the freshly baked poppy seed cakes.

Science and Mathematics

Measure ingredients. Study the markings on the measuring cups.

Count the cookies together and decide how to divide them evenly among the class.

Study the thermostat on the oven and set it at 300°.

Let children estimate the number of minutes it will take to brown the cakes. Watch the clock and count the minutes it actually takes to bake them.

Health and Safety

Emphasize the importance of cleanliness in handling food.

Supervise thorough washing of hands with soap before dough is kneaded.

Elect committees of children to wash the mixing bowl, measuring cup, and cookie sheets.

Art

Study the decorative designs that ornament the pages of *The Poppy Seed Cakes*.

Show children how to make similar designs. Have them repeat a simple flower drawing on a sheet of art paper that has been folded four times. When the paper is unfolded, there will be sixteen squares in which to repeat the chosen pattern. Display the designs as a border around the bulletin board.

Prepare a frieze showing the ducks that spoiled Erminka's red boots. Let each child draw, color, and cut out several ducks to paste on a large blue "pond" that the teacher has previously mounted on the bulletin board.

Blueberries for Sal

Little Sal and her mother go up one side of Blueberry Hill to pick blueberries for the winter while Little Bear and his mother come up the other side of Blueberry Hill to eat blueberries for the winter. Somehow

Little Sal gets lost and follows Little Bear's mother; at the same time Little Bear gets lost and follows Little Sal's mother. The two mothers are properly astonished when they discover the mistake. Little Sal and Little Bear take the mix-up in stride and all ends well.[2]

The exact parallelism in the story and also in the illustration makes an excellent book for reading and discussion in kindergarten. Robert McCloskey uses a beautiful blue ink, the color of blueberries, for the very realistic illustrations.

Recipe for Blueberry Cupcakes

1 package frozen blueberries
1 package blueberry muffin mix

Mix cupcakes according to directions on the blueberry muffin package. Pour batter into foil disposable muffin cups. Fill each only one-half full. Bake cupcakes in the classroom by using an electric fry pan. Place muffin cups on a wire rack in the fry pan and cover the pan while baking.

Thaw frozen blueberries while cupcakes are baking. While the muffins are still warm, spoon some of the blueberries on each one for a delicious and colorful topping. Serve with milk at snacktime.

Related Activities

Language Arts

Read *Blueberries for Sal* to the class and give the children an opportunity to study and discuss the illustrations.

Encourage the children to retell the story. Keep it moving by asking, "What happened next? And then what happened?"

By using the "fruits" page in a picture dictionary, compare blueberries with other berries.

Make a chart of berries by cutting pictures from old seed catalogues and from labels on cans of berries.

Make a list of new words used in the blueberry unit and review them with the children.

Social Science

Locate Maine on a large map of the United States. Discuss the fact that Robert McCloskey lived there and that blueberries grew near his home.

---

2. Robert McCloskey, *Blueberries for Sal* (New York: The Viking Press, 1948).

Collect travel folders and pictures of Maine.

Discuss the protective love that mothers feel for their young.

Read aloud *One Morning in Maine.*[3] Compare it with *Blueberries for Sal.*

Science and Mathematics

Compare the way in which Sal and her mother stored berries for the winter with the way Little Bear and his mother stored berries for the winter. Develop the concept of animal hibernation.

Study the end pages of the book *Blueberries for Sal,* which show Sal and her mother canning blueberries in glass jars. Bring a glass jar used for canning to show the children. If possible, show a lid with a red rubber sealing ring like the one pictured.

If several sealing rings are available, let the children count them the way Sal is doing in the picture.

Compare freezing with canning as a way of preserving the blueberries.

Health and Safety

Use the electric fry pan or portable oven as an exhibit in a discussion of safety precautions to be observed while using electrical appliances.

Involve the sense of sight, smell, and taste in sampling the blueberries. Develop a willingness to try new foods.

Art

Using crayons, decorate plain white paper napkins with a blueberry motif. With white paper towels, make matching place mats. Use the napkins and mats at snacktime.

Chicken Soup with Rice

Chicken Soup with Rice, by Maurice Sendak, is composed of hilarious nonsense rhymes promoting chicken soup with rice every month of the year. At the end of the twelfth month, the story is summarized with the following rhyme:

> I told you once
> I told you twice
> All seasons of the year
> are nice
> for eating chicken soup
> with rice![4]

---

3. Robert McCloskey, *One Morning in Maine* (New York: The Viking Press, 1952).

4. Maurice Sendak, *Chicken Soup with Rice* (New York: Harper & Row, Publishers, 1962). Available in paperback from Scholastic Book Services, New York.

In addition to the paperback edition, the book is also available in miniature form as part of the *Nutshell Library* by Maurice Sendak. Each one of the books in this set is 2½ inches by 3¾ inches, just the right size for small hands. The four books are housed in a decorative slip case.

Recipe for Chicken Soup with Rice

8 cups seasoned chicken broth
1 cup chopped celery
½ cup rice

Heat the broth in a boiler. Add chopped celery and cook until tender. Add rice and cook until it is fluffy and tender. Cool and serve in paper cups with packaged toast or crackers.

Related Activities

Language Arts

Read *Chicken Soup with Rice* aloud several times until children are able to join in on the refrain.

Discuss events associated with each month of the year and show how the rhymes and illustrations depict each month.

Compare illustrations in the paperback edition with the *Nutshell Library* version of *Chicken Soup with Rice*.

Social Science

Study the *Chicken Soup with Rice* calendar and repeat the names of the months in sequence.[5]

Talk about the meaning of "soup" and discuss soups that are popular in different parts of the country.

Science and Mathematics

Measure water in measuring cup.

Study the meaning of one-half cup.

Have children count out the needed number of paper cups.

Help children count out two crackers per person.

Examine grains of rice before and after heating. Show how they expand and soften when cooked.

---

5. The *Chicken Soup with Rice* calendar is available from Scholastic Book Services, New York.

Art

Let children look through old magazines for pictures of soups. They should be able to find cans, bowls, and cups of soup. Have them cut out the pictures and paste them on a large chart labeled "SOUP."

Health and Safety

Discuss the danger of boiling liquids. Show how the handle of a boiler should be turned toward the wall.

Wash hands before eating.

Emphasize the nutritional value of wholesome soup.

Bread and Jam for Frances

Frances is a young and very childlike badger who is unwilling to try any new food and insists on bread and jam three times a day. Her parents find a way to cure her of asking for bread and jam by serving her nothing else for a period of time. The Hobans have illustrated the book with soft charcoal drawings that give Frances and her family a delightful furry texture.

As Frances waits for the school bus, she sings:

> Jam on biscuits, jam on toast,
> Jam is the thing that I like most.
> Jam is sticky, jam is sweet,
> Jam is tasty, jam's a treat—
> Raspberry, strawberry, gooseberry,
> I'm very FOND . . . OF . . . JAM![6]

Recipe for Blackberry Jam

1 cup canned blackberries, drained
¾ cup sugar
1 tablespoon Sure-Jell

Mix Sure-Jell with berries in sauce pan. Bring mixture to boil, stirring occasionally. Add sugar and boil one minute, stirring constantly. Cool and serve on slices of bread cut in half.

---

6. Russell and Lillian Hoban, *Bread and Jam for Frances* (New York: Harper & Row, Publishers, 1964). Available in paperback from Scholastic Book Services, New York.

Related Activities

Language Arts

Read aloud the book *Bread and Jam for Frances*. Discuss the story. Why did Frances finally cry when given her favorite food, bread and jam?

Look at pictures of strawberries, gooseberries, blueberries, blackberries, and other berries. Discuss the differences in appearance.

Outline plans for making jam.

Write the recipe on a large chart. Read it to the children. Let them observe writing of the chart. Show them how to follow a recipe in sequential order.

Social Science

Read aloud the other "Frances" books to show wholesome family relationships.

Explain how blackberries are a native American fruit but were considered only a weed by early settlers.

Science and Mathematics

Show shape of bread before cutting it in half (square).

Examine shape of bread after cutting at an angle (triangle).

Show other examples of "one-half."

Measure ingredients in calibrated containers. Show markings.

Health and Safety

In discussing *Bread and Jam for Frances,* ask children to explain why parents want them to eat many kinds of food.

Talk about the taste of blackberry jam and show how the sampling of a new food can be an exciting adventure.

Emphasize the importance of washing hands before eating finger foods.

Outline safety precautions to be observed when heating liquids.

Art

Using colored chalk, allow children to make large pieces of fruit on the want-ad sections of newspapers. Have children cut out the fruits and paste them (slightly overlapping the pieces) on a large chart to make a colorful collage. Label the chart, "Fruits We Like."

Old Black Witch

Nicky and his mother purchase a neglected, broken-down house with plans for turning it into a cozy tearoom. They are surprised to find it inhabited by a cranky old witch who has no intention of vacating the premises. In the long run, she turns out to be a good cook and whips up batches of delicious blueberry pancakes for the tearoom guests. Nevertheless, even a helpful witch must make some concessions to her own meanness, and she does so by demanding "days off to be nasty."[7]

Recipe for Bewitching Blueberry Pancakes

1¼ cups flour	1 egg
2½ teaspoons baking powder	¾ cup milk
3 tablespoons granulated sugar	3 tablespoons melted fat or oil
¾ teaspoon salt	½ cup washed blueberries

As you stir in the blueberries (this is the magic part) say three times:

Gobble dee gook
With a wooden spoon,
The laugh of a toad
At the height of the moon!

Pour on a hot griddle and watch.[8]

Related Activities

Language Arts

Write creative stories about witches and other Halloween symbols and transfer them to shape books—booklets cut into the shape of a witch's hat, a jack-o-lantern, a ghost, and so on.

Make a vocabulary chart of interesting words used in *Old Black Witch:*

tearoom	scorched
rafters	crooked
beams	rude
cauldron	quaint
brew	greedy

Prepare a rebus chart of the recipe for Bewitching Blueberry Pancakes.

---

7. Wende and Harry Devlin, *Old Black Witch* (New York: Parents' Magazine Press, 1963).

8. Reprinted by permission of Four Winds Press, A division of Scholastic Inc. from *Old Black Witch* by Wende and Harry Devlin. Copyright © 1963 by Wende and Harry Devlin.

Social Science

Study the origin of Halloween and the meaning of its various symbols.

Science

Discuss the unscientific basis of witchcraft.

Art

Draw and color the Halloween symbols on stiff paper. Cut and hang them as mobiles.

Using tempera paint on black paper, make a colorful Halloween mural.

Make autumn leaf witches. Glue a large tree leaf onto colored construction paper. Add witch hat and broom cut from black paper. (Leaf forms witch's cloak.) (See fig. 7.1.)

Make collages by using precut black witch's hat glued on paper as a visual starter. Felt pens, yarn, and fabric scraps are then used to complete the pictures. (See figs. 7.2 and 7.3.)

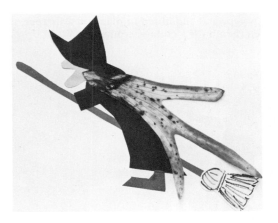

Figure 7.1. An autumn leaf of interesting shape and color provided the "visual starter" for this flying witch.

Figures 7.2. and 7.3.   These two witches were created from visual starters. A large black hat was precut and glued in place on art paper; using fabric and paper, the children then built a collage around it.

Figure 7.4.   A circle of black paper cut in half and shaped into a cone forms the base for this free-standing version of "Old Black Witch."

Beginning with a half-circle of black construction paper, form a cone shape. Add witch hat and features to free-standing cone (fig. 7.4).

Cranberry Thanksgiving

Maggie and her grandmother prepare for Thanksgiving and Maggie looks forward to her grandmother's good cranberry bread, which she makes from a very old and secret recipe. Grandmother has been offered a good sum of money for her famous recipe but refuses to sell, thinking it will be something wonderful to leave to Maggie.

Two unusual guests arrive for Thanksgiving dinner, and a crisis builds as the secret recipe turns up missing.

Cranberry Thanksgiving is an adventure story with just enough intrigue and mystery to suit children, but it also reflects deep friendship and forgiveness of one's enemies, very appropriate themes for a Thanksgiving story.[9]

Recipe for Grandmother's Famous Cranberry Bread

2 cups sifted all-purpose flour
1 cup sugar
1½ teaspoons baking powder
1 teaspoon salt
½ teaspoon baking soda
¼ cup butter or margarine
1 egg, beaten
1 teaspoon grated orange peel
¾ cup orange juice
1½ cups light raisins
1½ cups fresh or frozen cranberries, chopped

Sift flour, sugar, baking powder, salt, and baking soda into a large bowl. Cut in butter until mixture is crumbly. Add egg, orange peel, and orange juice all at once; stir just until mixture is evenly moist. Fold in raisins and cranberries.

Spoon into greased 9 × 5 × 3-inch loaf pan. Bake at 350 degrees for 1 hour and 10 minutes, or until a toothpick inserted in center comes out clean. Remove from pan; cool on wire rack. If you choose, you may substitute cranberries for the raisins to have an all cranberry bread.[10]

---

9. Wende and Harry Devlin, *Cranberry Thanksgiving* (New York: Parents' Magazine Press, 1971).

10. Reprinted by permission of Four Winds Press, a division of Scholastic Inc. from *Cranberry Thanksgiving* by Wende and Harry Devlin. Copyright © 1971 by Wende and Harry Devlin. Originally published by Parents' Magazine Press.

Related Activities

Language Arts

Study the end pages in which portraits of the four characters appear in old-fashioned oval frames. Look at the same portraits at the end of the book and review the names and personalities of the characters.

Discuss what Mr. Whiskers meant when he said, "Don't trust a man because he smells of lavender and has a gold cane."

Social Science

Locate New England on the map.

Study the illustrations and discuss the traditional New England Thanksgiving as it is shown in the pictures.

Discuss the idea of a "secret recipe" to be handed down from one generation to another.

Compare the appearance of Mr. Horace who smells of lavender with Mr. Whiskers who smells of clams and seaweed.

Science

Using the encyclopedia, read about a "cranberry bog" and how cranberries are grown and harvested.

Art

With crayons and manila paper, make an all-over pattern of cranberries similar to the small design on the book cover. Use the artwork as place mats when the cranberry bread is served.

Study the silhouettes of the story characters sitting before a roaring fire. Cut similar silhouettes from black paper and mount the shapes on an orange background.

The Thanksgiving Story

The Thanksgiving Story, by Alice Dalgliesh, is a fictional account of the first Thanksgiving, beginning with the voyage of the Mayflower and ending with the first feast between the Pilgrims and the Indians.[11] Since the story is developed around the experiences of one family, it appeals to young children and brings the story closer to the present time.

The illustrations are colorful and authentic, a perfect complement to the traditional story. They include a cross-section diagram of the Mayflower.

---

11. Alice Dalgliesh, *The Thanksgiving Story* (New York: Charles Scribner's Sons, 1954).

Making a crumb crust involves all the senses. (Courtesy of Port Arthur Independent School District, Port Arthur, Texas.)

This is a very good book to read aloud as a continued story, and it is also excellent for storytelling. The illustration of the Thanksgiving feast can be a springboard for many creative activities in the classroom, including the cooking of traditional foods.

Recipe for Individual Pumpkin Pies

The following ingredients will be needed for each child:
2 graham crackers
1 teaspoon sugar
1 tablespoon melted butter
1 small plastic bag
1 foil muffin cup

Let each child crush his two crackers in a small plastic bag. Add the sugar and melted butter and mix thoroughly. Have children press the crumb mixture into the muffin cup. The crust is then ready for filling.

The following recipe for filling should be prepared at home by the teacher and chilled overnight:

Pumpkin Mallow Pie Filling

2 cups pumpkin	1 tsp. cinnamon
2 pkgs. marshmallows	1 tsp. (scant) salt
2 cartons "Cool Whip"	

Cook mixture of pumpkin, marshmallows, and spices over low heat until marshmallows melt. Cool. Chill two cartons of "Cool Whip" and beat until fluffy. Fold in pumpkin mixture. Take the filling to the classroom and allow each child to spoon some of the mixture into his or her pie shell. The pies may be topped with whipped cream or trimmed with chocolate chips. Cut recipe in half for a small class. Serve with milk at snacktime.

Related Activities

Language Arts

Read aloud or tell *The Thanksgiving Story* and give children an opportunity to talk about their own understandings of the Thanksgiving holiday.

Prepare an exhibit of books and pictures about Thanksgiving. Encourage browsing.

Make a vocabulary chart of Thanksgiving words. Illustrate each one with a rebus drawing.

Compare a real pumpkin with a picture of a pumpkin and with the printed word "pumpkin."

Social Science

Plan and teach a simplified unit of the Thanksgiving holiday. Emphasize the meaning of the holiday.

Use a globe to trace the voyage of the Mayflower and a map to locate Plymouth.

In a dramatic play, act out *The Thanksgiving Story*.

Science and Mathematics

Measure ingredients for the pie crusts. Count out the graham crackers needed. Involve all the senses in making pie crusts.

Using the diagram in *The Thanksgiving Story*, study the parts of a ship.

Health and Safety

Discuss all the foods that were said to have been served at the first Thanksgiving dinner.

Art

Arrange a Thanksgiving centerpiece for the classroom.

Create a Thanksgiving collage by pasting pictures of foods cut from magazines on a large chart in the shape of a harvest table.

The Duchess Bakes a Cake

The Duchess Bakes a Cake is a book to be read aloud to children for pure fun. An impish duchess bakes a cake so light and fluffy that it lifts her up into the clouds. Gunhilde, the youngest of her thirteen daughters, suggests that they all begin eating the "light luscious delectable cake" to get her mother down. "How lovely!" the Duchess says. "Come let us sup. I'll start eating down; you start eating up."[12]

Flat posterlike folk art in brilliant colors is used to illustrate the hilarious story.

Recipe for One-Two-Three-Four Cake

1 cup shortening	3 cups sifted flour
2 cups sugar	3 teaspoons baking powder
¼ teaspoon salt	1 cup milk
4 eggs, separated	1 teaspoon vanilla

Preheat oven to 375° F. Use two 9-inch round cake pans. Baking time is 35 to 40 minutes.

Cream shortening, sugar, and salt together until light and fluffy. Add beaten egg yolks and blend until smooth. Sift flour and baking powder together three times and add to first mixture with milk and vanilla. Fold in the stiffly beaten egg whites. Pour into greased and floured cake pans. Bake. Remove from pans immediately after baking. Cool on wire racks. At snacktime, serve the cake while still warm with cups of cold milk.

---

12. Virginia Kahl, *The Duchess Bakes a Cake* (New York: Charles Scribner's Sons, 1953).

Related Activities

Language Arts

Reread *The Duchess Bakes a Cake* during the waiting period while the cake bakes.

If the oven in the school lunchroom is used for baking, compose a thank-you note to the manager. The teacher can serve as recorder for the children's language.

Promote conversation at snacktime.

Social Science

Help children learn to take turns.

Teach cooperation and organization needed to carry out the complex task of baking a cake.

Practice setting the table.

Science and Mathematics

Add baking powder to water and observe chemical reaction.

Help children to hypothesize about what will happen to the batter as it bakes.

Measure the depth of the batter before baking. Record. Measure thickness of cake after baking. Compare the two figures.

Set oven timer. Synchronize with clock. Set alarm to go off when the cake is done.

Show the children how to test for doneness.

Health and Safety

Teach safety precautions regarding hot stove and hot pans. Demonstrate the use of insulated mittens. Caution: An adult should put the cake in the oven and also remove it.

Art

Make place mats by trimming edges of paper towels with a crayon border. Slices of cake may be served directly on mats.

The Gingerbread Man

The rhythm of the language in this old folktale has fascinated young children for ages. The gingerbread man repeats the same impertinent reply to all who try to stop him:

Kindergarten girls make gingerbread men by rolling the dough into small balls. (Courtesy of Brad Hogue.)

> Run, run
> As fast as you can.
> You can't catch me.
> I'm the gingerbread man.[13]

Each time he gains another pursuer, the gingerbread man adds one more line to his song until he is finally outwitted by the fox, and both the song and the gingerbread man come to an end. True to the folktale style, the story ends abruptly and is tied up neatly with a flourish: "And that was the end of the gingerbread man!"

Recipe for Gingerbread Men

4 cups sifted flour	½ cup shortening
1 tablespoon cinnamon	½ cup firmly packed brown sugar
1 teaspoon salt	1 egg
1 teaspoon baking powder	1 cup molasses
1 teaspoon ginger	

---

13. Ed Arno, *The Gingerbread Man* (New York: Scholastic Book Services, 1967).

Sift first five ingredients together and set aside. Cream shortening. Gradually add brown sugar, creaming until fluffy after each addition. Continue creaming while adding egg. Blend in molasses. Stir in dry ingredients. Chill dough overnight in the refrigerator.

Pinch off a ball of dough for each child who is working at the table. Let the children roll or pat dough to ¼-inch thick on a lightly floured surface. (If they have a tendency to roll too much flour into the dough, powdered sugar may be substituted for flour.) Cut dough with gingerbread man cookie cutter or cut around cardboard pattern of a gingerbread man. A very good plan for making a more creative gingerbread man is to form a ball for the head, one for the body, and four smaller ones for the arms and legs. Flatten and mash them together slightly so the pieces will adhere. No two gingerbread men will be alike, and that is part of the fun. Using a large spatula, transfer each cookie to a large cookie sheet that has been lightly greased. Each child's cookie may be marked with a small piece of foil on which his or her name has been printed with a magic marker.

Bake at 350° for 10 to 15 minutes. Cool and serve with milk during snacktime.

Related Activities

Language Arts

Discuss the new words learned, such as knead, dough, ginger, spatula, cinnamon, and so on.

Make a bulletin board of the recipe. Read and interpret it to the children. Emphasize the importance of sequential order.

Dramatize the story while cookies are baking to help occupy the waiting time.

Social Studies

Work together as a team, share utensils, and take turns. Have students assume responsibility for cleanup. Relate cooperative team efforts to other activities.

Distribute duplicated copies of the recipe.

Science and Mathematics

Help children to measure the ingredients. Study the meaning of "one-half cup."

Set timer for fifteen minutes. Watch clock hands to see if timer and clock coincide.

For most children, cooking in the kindergarten will be their first opportunity to become actively involved in the preparation of the food they eat. (Courtesy of Anahuac Independent School District, Anahuac, Texas.)

Show one-to-one correspondence by serving each child his or her own cookie.

Involve the senses of sight, touch, smell, and taste in preparation and discussion.

Art and Music

Provide clay or play dough for children to re-create the cooking experience.

Cut gingerbread men from brown paper. Mount on colored construction paper. Use as cover for gingerbread recipe to take home.

Play the record, *The Gingerbread Man.*

Health and Safety

Stress the importance of cleanliness in cooking and eating.

Emphasize the need for cleaning up spills.

Talk about the new taste of ginger and show children that sampling a new flavor can be an exciting adventure.

Journey Cake, Ho!

Journey Cake, Ho![14] is an old mountain folktale about a boy who chases a journey cake that jumped from the oven and ran away. He finally retrieves the cake and also the farm animals that follow the cake. This is

---

14. Ruth Sawyer, *Journey Cake, Ho!* (New York: The Viking Press, 1953).

a "cumulative" tale based upon repetition and accumulation. Robert McCloskey's humorous illustrations in browns and blues are a perfect backdrop for the lively story.

Since *Journey Cake, Ho!* is a variant of *The Pancake* and *The Gingerbread Man,* the three stories lend themselves to comparison of the content and language.

Journey cake is sometimes known as Johnnycake. Johnnycake was a type of corn bread widely made as this country's frontier was settled. The pioneer food was also sometimes called journey cake, as it could be made with water and taken on long journeys without fear of spoiling. The story is also told that at one time the Indians made such a bread, called Shawnee cake.

Recipe for Journey Cake

1 cup sweet milk
1 cup buttermilk
1 teaspoon salt
1 tablespoon shortening
cornmeal
melted butter

Mix the first five ingredients together, using enough cornmeal to make the batter of a consistency suitable to be rolled into a sheet ½-inch thick. Spread the batter on a buttered cookie sheet. Bake in a moderate oven (350°).

As soon as the journey cake begins to brown, baste it with melted butter. Repeat the basting several times until the cake is brown and crispy. Serve while still warm.

Related Activities

Language Arts

Study and compare the three terms Johnnycake, journey cake, and Shawnee cake.

Read *Journey Cake, Ho!* to the children and give them an opportunity to study the illustrations.

Have children discuss the likenesses and differences in the three folktales, *Journey Cake, Ho!, The Pancake,* and *The Gingerbread Man.*

Social Science

Tell the story of Indian corn and how it was ground into meal.

Make a study of different kinds of bread and the people who make them.

Science and Mathematics

Make a chart of the recipe and allow children to use a measuring cup and measuring spoons for the ingredients.

Examine the texture of dry cornmeal and compare it with the texture of cornmeal after it has been mixed with the liquids.

Make journey cake with water instead of milk, store for a few days, and then check to see if it is edible. Discuss findings of the experiment.

Bring in some ears of corn for children to examine.

Health and Safety

Discuss the need for refrigeration of many foods. Why would pioneer families need a bread like journey cake?

Locate bread on a chart of the four basic food groups. Discuss the nutritional value of bread.

Have a tasting party and sample many kinds of bread.

Art

Help children make mosaics of dry grains of corn glued on cardboard. These will be more effective if many shapes and colors of grains are used, such as popcorn, yellow corn, Indian corn, and so on.

Stone Soup

Stone Soup is an old folktale in which three hungry French soldiers trick an entire village into providing them with vegetables for their "stone soup."[15]

The gay red and black illustrations are filled with people, animals, and much activity. They serve to give children a glimpse of French village life, and they are organized in such a way that it becomes easy for young children to retell the story.

---

15. Marcia Brown, *Stone Soup* (New York: Charles Scribner's Sons, 1947).

Recipe for Stone Soup

3 qts. water	4 small onions, chopped
1 lb. ground meat	¼ head cabbage
4 carrots, peeled and sliced	1 can tomatoes, chopped
4 potatoes, peeled and diced	salt
4 stalks celery, chopped	

Simmer ground meat in water 30 minutes (a smooth river-washed agate stone may be added to the water just for fun). Add vegetables and simmer until done. Make a small ceremony of removing the stone. Salt to taste before serving. "Hot" paper cups may be used for serving. When salted crackers are served with the soup, it might replace the morning snack.

Related Activities

Language Arts

Read aloud *Stone Soup* and lead a discussion on the meaning of the stone in the soup. Encourage children to explore the battle of wits between the soldiers and the peasants.

Compare the plot, theme, characters, and illustrations in *Stone Soup* with those in *Nail Soup* by Harve Zemach.[16]

Make a vocabulary chart of all the vegetables that children can name. Beside each word, place a rebus drawing to illustrate it.

Arrange pictures of fruits and vegetables into categories on a large chart to give children practice in distinguishing between the two.

Make an arrangement of wax or plastic models of vegetables.

Have children put together jigsaw puzzles of vegetables.

Social Studies

Explain the meaning of the term "folktale."

Discuss the houses, clothing, and cobblestone streets pictured in the illustrations.

Allow children to express their opinions about what magic the stone brought to the soup.

Make a study of vegetables from the garden to the dining table. Consider all the people who work to make vegetables available to the consumer.

Provide an opportunity in the playhouse center for boys and girls to re-create the story of *Stone Soup*.

---

16. Harve Zemach, *Nail Soup* (Chicago: Follett Publishing Co., 1964).

Science and Mathematics

Help children to discover that vegetables have different sizes, colors, shapes, textures, smells, and flavors.

Have children count out salted crackers to go with the soup.

Health and Safety

Categorize foods into the four basic food groups needed for good nutrition. Show that vegetables, in some form, should be eaten every day.

Art

Use air-hardening clay to model different vegetables. When dry, paint each the appropriate color with tempera paint.

Nail Soup

Nail Soup is a Swedish folktale about a tramp who asks a rather selfish old woman for food. He is told that there is not a bite in the house. The tramp declares he will make soup for both of them. He puts water in a pot and drops in a nail. When he needs meat, potatoes, and other vegetables to make it a "feast fit for the king and queen," the old woman happens to "remember" where she has hidden these ingredients.

When the delicious soup is eaten and the tramp starts to leave, the woman tells him, "And thank you for teaching me how to make soup with a nail, because now that I know how, I shall always live in comfort."

"That's all right," said the tramp. "It's easy if you remember to add something good to it."[17]

School-made soup helps to dispel the idea that all soup comes in cans. (Courtesy of Beaumont Independent School District, Beaumont, Texas.)

---

17. Ibid.

Recipe for Nail Soup

3 qts. water	4 stalks celery, chopped
1 lb. ground meat	4 small onions, chopped
4 carrots, peeled and sliced	¼ head cabbage
4 potatoes, peeled and diced	1 can tomatoes, chopped

Simmer ground meat in water 30 minutes (a large aluminum common 16-penny nail may be added to the water just for fun). Add vegetables and simmer until done. Make a small ceremony of removing the nail. Salt to taste. "Hot" paper cups may be used for serving. The soup, accompanied by crackers, might replace the morning snack.

Related Activities

Language Arts

Read *Nail Soup* to the children at story time. Lead a discussion of the trickery involved. Help children to see that the tramp was able to make the old woman a little less selfish.

Allow children to express their ideas about the value of the nail in the soup.

Discuss the humor in the title *Nail Soup.*

Social Science

Study the illustrations and discuss the clothing worn by the characters.

Talk about what the old woman meant when she said, "Such people don't grow on trees."

Science and Mathematics

Estimate the time it will take to bring the water to a boil. Time the water by a clock in the classroom.

Test the water with a food thermometer when the water is cold and then after it begins to boil. Show children the difference in the two readings.

Health and Safety

Teach safety precautions to be observed in using a knife and vegetable parer. A plastic knife with serrated edge is a safe tool for children to use.

Emphasize the necessity of washing raw vegetables before eating them.

Art

Make a large collage of vegetable pictures cut from magazines and seed catalogues.

The Carrot Seed

In the face of discouragement from his parents and from his big brother, a small boy plants a carrot seed. "It won't come up. It won't come up," they tell him; but every day he sprinkles the ground with water and, sure enough, it *does* come up.[18]

This is an excellent book to use with young children because it shows them as they are—incurable optimists.

Recipe for Buttered Carrots

Wash eight to ten carrots and remove outer surface with a vegetable parer. Place carrots on chopping board and slice (teacher activity). Run two inches of water into saucepan. Add one teaspoon salt. Place pan over high heat and bring to boil. Add carrot slices. Cover with lid and lower heat. Cook fifteen minutes or until tender. Pierce with fork to test tenderness. Drain. Empty carrots into bowl. Dot with plenty of butter and salt to taste. Serve while still warm.

Related Activities

Language Arts

Read *The Carrot Seed* to the children. Give them a chance to express their ideas about the story.

Take apart a paperback edition of the book. Let children put the pages in sequential order on the chalk ledge. Help them retell the story.

Move from concrete to abstract by showing a real carrot, a model of a carrot, a picture of a carrot, and finally the word "carrot."

Social Science

If possible, make a field trip to the grocery store to buy the carrots. Talk to the grocer and ask him or her to leave on the tops. Look at other vegetables in the store. Find out how many of them the children recognize by name.

Encourage children to express their feelings about the little boy as he waits and waits for the seed to come up. Also let them describe their feelings about the ending of the story when he hauls his carrot home in a wheelbarrow!

Listen to the record of *The Carrot Seed.*

---

18. Ruth Krauss, *The Carrot Seed* (New York: Harper & Row, Publishers, 1966). Available in paperback from Scholastic Book Services, New York.

Science and Mathematics

Make a collection of seeds, from the smallest, such as carrot seeds, to the largest, such as coconuts. Display them in graduated order from smallest to largest.

Make a collection of seed catalogues.

Plant the top of the carrots, cut side down, in a dish of water.

Study the vegetable page in picture dictionaries.

Classify pictures of vegetables that grow below the ground, and vegetables that grow above the ground.

Discuss the eating of roots, stems, and leaves of various vegetables.

Health and Safety

Review safety precautions to observe when cooking is in progress.

Locate carrots on a chart of the four basic food groups.

Make an effort to improve children's attitudes about eating vegetables.

Art

Make pictures of carrots.

Dip twelve-inch pieces of yarn in liquid starch and help each child to arrange a piece into the shape of a carrot on a piece of cardboard. When thoroughly dry, let them paint the carrot bright orange with a green top. These can be mounted on a bulletin board labeled, "We Like Carrots."

The Egg Tree

Easter traditions in a Pennsylvania Dutch family are the theme of this book. It is an entertaining story of cooking, decorating, hiding, hunting, and eating Easter eggs. Directions are given for making the lovely Easter egg tree.

The Egg Tree is a story of adventure, fun, and excitement, but it is also a book of art. The pages are decorated with authentic Pennsylvania Dutch designs created by the author. Even the prereading child can enjoy an aesthetic experience just by turning through the pages. Katherine Milhous won the Caldecott Award for *The Egg Tree* in 1951.[19]

Recipe for Easter Eggs

Gently place one dozen clean white eggs into a large saucepan. Add cold water until it is one-half inch above top of eggs. Cover with lid. Heat slowly to boiling. Turn heat very low and cook twenty minutes. Place pan in sink and run cool water over eggs until they are cool enough to handle. Eggs are now ready for dyeing or painting.

---

19. Katherine Milhous, *The Egg Tree* (New York: Charles Scribner's Sons, 1950).

Related Activities

Language Arts

Study the book *The Egg Tree* and prepare the story for telling. It may be necessary to abbreviate it somewhat for young children.

Provide children time and opportunity to study the illustrations.

Make plans to create an egg tree for the classroom. Prepare invitations to be sent to parents and friends. The teacher might duplicate the notes and then let children decorate them with Easter designs.

Social Science

Discuss the Pennsylvania Dutch folk art as it appears on the borders of the pages in *The Egg Tree*.

Invite friends in to see the egg tree as did the Pennsylvania Dutch.

Science and Mathematics

Break a raw egg into a dish and encourage children to examine it. Break one of the cooked eggs and examine it. Discuss what happened in the cooking process.

Count the eggs and study the concept of "a dozen." Count the spaces in an empty egg carton.

Count out six eggs and study the concept of "one-half dozen." Cover one-half the spaces in an egg carton and count the remaining spaces.

Health and Safety

Discuss the need for refrigerating eggs.

Review safety precautions to be observed while eggs are cooking on the hot plate in the classroom.

Illustrate the fact that eggs are included in the four basic food groups.

Art

Practice making Pennsylvania Dutch designs by using those in *The Egg Tree* as a guide. Mount on the bulletin board.

Use wax crayons to make designs on the cooked eggs before dipping them in vegetable dye or before painting them with watercolors. The wax will resist the dye, and the designs will show through. The children can make polka dots, stripes, and zigzag designs.

Make an egg tree by letting children cut and color paper eggs to hang on a branch that has been wedged into a flower pot. Have children bring Easter toys from home to place under the tree, just as the children did in *The Egg Tree*.

Rain Makes Applesauce

This picture book was named a runner-up for the coveted Caldecott Award in 1965. The lovely, ethereal illustrations are a perfect complement to a book of nonsense with its silly talk for young listeners. The language patterns are delightful and children love to repeat the refrain, "O, you're just talking silly talk." They recognize the nonsense as very similar to the silly talk they like to make up and say to each other.

The nonsense in *Rain Makes Applesauce* is balanced with the necessary realism to make it palatable to children. Hidden in the lower right-hand corner of each nonsense drawing is a small segment of the true story of applesauce. The sequence begins with the planting of an apple tree and ends with the making and eating of applesauce. An excellent book for reading aloud and for rereading many times.[20]

Recipe for Applesauce

6 sour apples
⅔ cup white granulated sugar
1 cup water

Wash apples and cut them into quarters. Use a cutting board and show children how to cut away from themselves. Since cutting must be closely supervised, allow only a few children to work at one time. Carefully remove cores. Put apples and sugar in saucepan. Add 1 cup water. Cover with lid and cook slowly 30 minutes or until tender. Stir occasionally. Cool. Press through a colander. A few drops of red coloring may be added to make a rosy red applesauce. Serve on graham crackers at snacktime. Note: It is not necessary to peel the apples.

Related Activities

Language Arts

Compare pictures of apples, wax and plastic models, and real apples (include some yellow ones). Make a list of all the adjectives children use in describing the pictures, the models, and the real apples. Read all the words on the list back to the children.

Write the word "apple" on chart paper and have children cut apples from seed catalogues to paste on the chart.

---

20. Julian Scheer, *Rain Makes Applesauce* (New York: Holiday House, 1964).

Social Science

Take a field trip to a grocery store to survey the various apple products available. Buy a few to bring back to the room for sampling.

Science and Mathematics

Discuss and illustrate the meaning of "quarter."

Measure ⅔ cup of sugar in measuring cup.

Measure one cup water in measuring cup.

Have children count the apples.

Using apples of different sizes, show "greater than," "smaller than," and so on.

Sample apple juice and apple butter. Discuss the difference in consistency.

Art

Make a large tree for the bulletin board and allow children to cut paper apples to hang on it.

White Snow Bright Snow

This is a beautifully illustrated and poetic story of a big snow, written by Alvin Tresselt. From the falling of the first lacy flakes to the point where everything is buried under the white drifts, people go about their appointed tasks. Adults are busy making preparations for being shut in, but the children build a snowman.

Spring finally arrives and brings an end to the big snow: fence posts lose their dunce caps, the snowman's arms drop off, and running water gurgles in gutters and rain pipes.

The brilliant colors of the houses against the white snow and blue sky helped to win the Caldecott Award for Roger Duvoisin, the illustrator.[21]

Recipe for a Snowman Cake

1 box white cake mix
Seven-minute frosting mix
1 can shredded coconut

assorted gumdrops
candy cane

Mix white cake according to directions on the box and bake in two 8-inch round pans. Cool. Arrange the cakes together on a tray. One cake forms the head of the snowman and the other the body.

21. Alvin Tresselt, *White Snow Bright Snow* (New York: Lothrop, Lee & Shephard Co., Inc., 1947).

Decorating with chocolate chips, gumdrops, or raisins is a way of expressing individuality. (Courtesy of Anahuac Independent School District, Anahuac, Texas.)

Frost the cakes with frosting mix (or seven-minute frosting) and sprinkle generously with coconut. Make buttons, eyes, nose, and mouth from gumdrops. Cut the snowman a top hat from black paper and fasten on with toothpicks. Add a big candy cane for trim.

Related Activities

Language Arts

Read *White Snow Bright Snow* to the children. Lead a discussion centered around the building of a snowman.

Read *The Snowy Day* by Ezra Keats[22] and *Frosty the Snowman,* retold by Annie North Bedford.[23] Compare the snowmen in these two books with the one in *White Snow Bright Snow.*

Play the record of *Frosty the Snowman* and help the children to learn the words of the song.

Social Science

Show pictures of a mail carrier, a police officer, a farmer, and a parent. Talk about their work. What kinds of jobs would they do to prepare for a storm?

22. Ezra Jack Keats, *The Snowy Day* (New York: Viking, 1962).
23. Annie North Bedford, *Frosty the Snowman* (New York: Golden Press, 1950).

On a large wall map of the United States, point out the areas where snowfall is the heaviest. Locate the warmer zones where snow is seldom seen. Help children to find their own state on the map and talk about the average amount of snowfall in that particular part of the country.

Compile a scrapbook of snow scenes from newspapers, magazines, travel folders, and postcards.

Make booklets about the snowman cake (including the recipe) for children to take home. Let each child draw and color a picture of the snowman cake as a cover for his or her booklet.

Invite another kindergarten or first grade class in to share the snowman cake. If cut in small squares, it will serve thirty-five to forty children.

If the school cafeteria oven is used for baking the cake, write a thank-you note to the manager. The teacher can serve as recorder for the children's sentences.

Science and Mathematics

Count the strokes used in mixing the cake batter.

Show children the baking temperature printed on the cake mix box. Write the numeral on the chalkboard. Show them how an adult would set the oven thermostat accordingly.

The teacher or a lunchroom cook can show the children how to test for doneness.

Health and Safety

Emphasize the danger of working near a hot oven. Let children examine the asbestos-lined mittens used for removing hot pots from the ovens. Allow children to watch removal of hot cakes from the oven.

Art

Paint a mural of *White Snow Bright Snow.* Spread a strip of black tar paper from the lumber yard on the floor. With white chalk, draw a base line the full length of the tar paper about six inches from the bottom. Mix tempera paint in one-pound coffee cans to the consistency of thick cream.

Using large soft brushes, let each child paint a house on the base line. Emphasize the fact that everything on a mural should be *large.*

When the houses are completely dry, the children can pile "snow" on the roofs by using thick white tempera paint. White dots of paint may be sprinkled over the entire mural to simulate snowflakes.

The brilliantly colored houses and white snow will stand out against the black background and children can experience the satisfaction of working together to create a beautiful snow scene.

Five O'Clock Charlie

With the publication of *Five O'Clock Charlie* in 1962, young children were at last able to enjoy one of Marguerite Henry's wonderful horse stories. It serves as an excellent introduction to her other books that are so widely read by students in the middle and upper grades.

Charlie is a lovable old horse who is retired by his master. He finds a way to make a useful, interesting life for himself by ringing the bell at the Boar's Head Inn every day precisely at five o'clock to notify the countryside that Bertie's good apple tarts are hot out of the oven. Of course, he is rewarded for his effort with the "biggest, brownest, juiciest tart of all."[24]

Recipe for Easy Apple Tarts

2 cans crescent dinner rolls
1 can apple pie filling

Make each rectangle of dough slightly larger and thinner by rolling it gently with a floured rolling pin. Cut five circles from each piece with a 2½" cookie cutter or drinking glass. Place one tablespoon of pie filling on 20 circles. Top with remaining circles and seal edges together with the tines of a fork. Place on ungreased baking sheets and pierce each tart with a fork. Bake 15 to 20 minutes at 375° in preheated oven. Cool and serve with milk.

These small round tarts baked golden brown look very much like those Bertie served each day to Five O'Clock Charlie. Wesley Dennis features them several times in his illustrations.

Related Activities _____

Language Arts

Read aloud the book *Five O'Clock Charlie*. Discuss the story. What kind of a horse was Charlie? What is a "work" horse? Why was Charlie retired by Mister Spinks? How does a horse of twenty-eight years compare with a person of that age? What is meant by the term, "put out to pasture"? Why did retirement make Charlie unhappy? How could Charlie know when to ring the bell? What is an inn? What was the most popular food served at the Boar's Head Inn? Why?

---

24. Marguerite Henry, *Five O'Clock Charlie* (Chicago: Rand McNally & Company, 1962).

Prepare a vocabulary chart of descriptive words used by Marguerite Henry in reference to Charlie—frisky, bored, useless, forlorn, free, stately, bold, good-for-nothing, happy.

Social Science

Study the illustrations for a realistic look at the English countryside.
Locate England on a map or globe.
Compare Charlie's retirement with that of elderly people in our society.
Discuss the emotions of loneliness and boredom.

Science and Mathematics

Discuss Charlie's rheumatism as a characteristic of the aging process. At age twenty-eight, why was it so remarkable that Charlie could still roll over, "not just half way, but a complete once over"!

Point out the three geometric shapes to be seen in the crescent dinner roll dough, two triangles placed together to form a rectangle, and a rectangle cut into circles.

Art

Study the illustrations of Wesley Dennis in *Five O'Clock Charlie* and in Marguerite Henry's other books.

Make a collection of horse pictures, prints, and posters for the bulletin board.

Mr. Rabbit and the Lovely Present

Mr. Rabbit helps the little girl to decide on a gift for her mother's birthday. A basket of fruit is the perfect solution. It is a gift that any child can appreciate and any mother would be happy to receive. In the trial and error process, many less suitable gifts are considered and abandoned, a behavior common to all who face the problem of selecting just the right gift for an important person. The ensuing dialogue is childlike, humorous, and extremely sensible.

Mr. Rabbit and the Lovely Present might be called a book of color. Charlotte Zolotow vividly describes the three primary colors (and one secondary), and Maurice Sendak has illustrated the book in the soft blue-green colors of springtime. As with all beautiful books, this one wears very, very well.[25]

---

25. Charlotte Zolotow, *Mr. Rabbit and the Lovely Present* (New York: Harper & Row Publishers, 1962).

Recipe for Fruit Salad

2 delicious apples	2 bunches of grapes
2 fresh Bartlett pears	1 carton "Cool-Whip"
2 ripe bananas	

Wash apples and pears. Cut them into bite-sized pieces in a large mixing bowl. Slice bananas into fruit mixture. Add grapes that have been washed and stemmed. Toss fruit lightly. Spoon into 20 to 24 small paper cups and top each one with one tablespoon whipped topping. According to the age of the children, the salad may be eaten with either a fork or a spoon.

Note: There is no need to peel the apples and pears for this recipe. The peels are both nutritious and colorful. If there is to be a delay in serving the cut fruit, sprinkle it with lemon juice to avoid discoloration.

Related Activities

Language Arts

At story time, read *Mr. Rabbit and the Lovely Present* to children two or three days in succession. Lead a discussion of the story, its characters, and illustrations.

Prepare a display of books illustrated by Maurice Sendak.

As a vocabulary experience, ask children to compare a piece of artificial fruit with a real one. Make two lists of adjectives.

Make primary color charts with pictures cut from magazines—a good committee project.

Create sock puppets to represent Mr. Rabbit and the little girl. The dialogue in the story is very easy for young children to paraphrase and provides excellent material for an informal puppet show.

Develop a language chart of the fruit salad recipe and illustrate it with rebus pictures for easier reading.

Social Science

Discuss the ancient tradition of birthday celebrations and the custom of gift giving. An excellent resource book to use for this project is *Birthdays* from the Garrard Holiday Series.[26]

---

26. Lillie Patterson, *Birthdays* (Champaign, Ill.: Garrard Publishing Company, 1969).

Science and Mathematics

Allow children to explore the different sizes, colors, shapes, textures, and smells of the fruit to be used in the salad.

As one-to-one correspondence, count out a paper cup and a fork (or spoon) for each child in the class.

Show the larger fractional parts of each piece of fruit before cutting it into smaller pieces.

Health and Safety

Emphasize the importance of fruit in the diet as part of the basic four food groups.

Art

Using colored chalk on newspaper, children can make large pieces of fruit for a bulletin board display. The teacher should prepare a large paper basket to be fastened on the board before pieces of fruit are tacked in place. For vocabulary, reading, and spelling purposes, each piece of fruit made by the children may be appropriately labeled with a black felt point pen.

The Funny Little Woman

The funny little woman from Old Japan likes to do two things. She likes to laugh and she likes to make good dumplings out of rice. One day, one of her plump dumplings rolls away, and the funny little woman follows it all the way to the land of the wicked "oni." There, the oni teaches her how to use a magic paddle to stir up a pot full of rice from only one grain.

How the funny little woman escapes from the wicked oni and claims the magic paddle for herself makes a humorous story of high adventure. *The Funny Little Woman* is a Caldecott Award winner.[27]

Recipe for Rice Dumplings

Sift together 1 cup flour, ½ teaspoon salt, and 1½ teaspoons baking powder; add ½ cup milk, 1 cup cooked rice, and 2 tablespoons melted fat or salad oil to make soft dough.

Empty one large can beef stew into pan; bring to a boil; drop dumplings from spoon onto stew. Cover tightly and steam without lifting cover 12 to 15 minutes. Makes 8 to 10 small servings.

---

27. Arlene Mosel, *The Funny Little Woman* (New York: E. P. Dutton and Company, Inc., 1972).

Related Activities

Language Arts

Read aloud *The Funny Little Woman*. Discuss the characteristics of a folktale.

Make plans to cook rice dumplings. Prepare a recipe chart for children to follow.

Read related books such as *Crow Boy* and *Umbrella* by Taro Yashima. Read some Japanese haiku poems and help children create some of their own.

Social Science

Locate Japan's islands on the map.

Make a collection of travel folders featuring Japan. Include the picture of Mount Fuji with cherry blossoms in the foreground.

Prepare an exhibit of Japanese realia such as a kimono, chopsticks, lacquered bowls, tea cups, dolls, fans, and so on.

Science and Mathematics

Make a study of how rice is grown.

Plant some rice seeds.

Examine some examples of Japanese rice paper.

Study fractions listed in the recipe for rice dumplings.

Measure ingredients.

Art

Using a beginner's guide to origami, help children to try their hand at this ancient art of paper folding.

With soft brush and thin black tempera paint, paint some characters from the Japanese language, following those in *Umbrella* as a guide.

Study Blair Lent's paintings in *The Funny Little Woman,* and discuss why they might have been chosen for the Caldecott Award.

Examine some Japanese watercolor paintings done on rice paper and on closely woven silk.

Strega Nona

Strega Nona is a variation on a popular folktale told in many countries. Big Anthony, the hired hand, thinks he has learned the secret of Strega Nona's magic pasta pot, but finds that he has omitted one important ingredient. Authentic illustrations offer a realistic view of the costumes and customs of Italian village life.[28]

---

28. Tomie dePaola, *Strega Nona* (Englewood Cliffs, N. J.: Prentice-Hall, Inc., 1975).

Recipe for Spaghetti

To three quarts boiling water, add 2 teaspoons salt. Dip long strands of spaghetti, a handful at a time, into the briskly boiling water. (Note: This must be done by an adult.) As it softens, curl it around in the pan until the whole length is under the water. Use one box of spaghetti. Cook at a fast boil until tender. Drain. Serve warm and sprinkle with grated Parmesan cheese.

The children will enjoy trying to eat spaghetti Italian style. Hold the fork in the right hand, spoon in left; spear spaghetti on fork. Hold end of fork against spoon, and turn until strands are wound into a ball on the end of the fork.

Related Activities

Language Arts

Read aloud the book *Strega Nona*. Compare this folktale with "Boil, Little Pot, Boil" and "Why the Sea Is Salt."

Prepare a chart of Italian words and phrases to give children some exposure to the appearance and sound of another language. Some commonly used words and phrases of greeting are:

Buon giorno (Bwon joŕ-noh) Good morning.
Addio (Ad-deé-joh) Good-bye.
Come sta? (Kó-meh-stah) How are you?
Scusi (Skoó zee) Pardon me.
Per favore (Per fah-voh-reh) Please.
Prego (Preh-goh) You're welcome.
Arrivederci (Ahr-ree-veh-deŕ-chee) I'll be seeing you.

Social Science

Locate Italy on the map or globe. Talk about its unusual bootlike shape, with Sicily being the football just off the toe of the boot.

Discuss the meaning of Strega Nona's expression, "Let the punishment fit the crime."

Study the end pages of the book for a realistic picture of Italian architecture with its red-tiled roofs and graceful arches.

Science and Mathematics

Look at several types of pasta and discuss the various shapes.

Discuss folk medicine as practiced by Strega Nona with her "potions and cures."

Art

Cut white paper pigeons similar to those shown on the end pages. Fasten them together as mobiles to hang in the classroom.

Paint stylized plants and animals like those featured in the illustrations.

Hollow, dry noodles of various shapes may be strung together to form decorative necklaces and bracelets. The noodles may be strung on either string or pipe cleaners, and some of the pieces may be colored with a felt marker to provide color and interest.

Using Rebus Charts with Cooking Experiences

A *rebus* is a representation of a word or phrase with a picture or symbol. Rebuses used with young children consist of small realistic pictures used in place of key words (or along with them) to suggest what the words are and what they mean.

Many children's magazines, papers, and game books employ rebus pictures to make the material more colorful and appealing, and easier to read and understand. Classroom teachers use them for exactly the same reasons.

To teach literal comprehension, the ability to read and follow directions, recipe charts may be illustrated with labels, drawings, or cutout pictures. Even a child at the prereading level can follow a well-made chart to carry out a task precisely or to make something correctly according to instructions.

After the cooking experience is over, the rebus recipe chart may be left in place a few days to allow children opportunity to reread it. The chart then makes excellent material to reproduce and send home for parent and child to read together as a graphic record of the experience with cooking and literature. Figure 7.5 offers several examples of rebus charts.

The "Little House" Books and Frontier Foods

The leading characters in Laura Ingalls Wilder's Little House books are well known to children whether or not they have ever opened one of the books. "Little House on the Prairie" had the distinction of being one of the longest running and most popular shows on television.

Long-time lovers of the Little House books were dismayed at the prospect of having them rewritten for television, and many watched the pilot program with some trepidation. But most of the same people have

Rice Dumplings and Stew

1 large can beef stew

Sift together flour, salt, baking powder, milk, rice, and oil to make a soft dough.

Empty can of stew into pan; bring to a boil; drop dumplings from spoon onto stew. Cover tightly and steam without lifting cover for 12 to 15 minutes. (8 to 10 small servings).

Journey Cake

corn meal

Mix together. Use enough corn meal to make batter thick enough to roll into 1/2 inch thick sheet. Spread batter on buttered cookie sheet. Bake at 350°.

When cake browns, baste with melted butter. Bake again until brown and crispy.

Fruit Salad

2 🍎 s   2 bunches 🍇

2 🍐 s

2 🍌 s   2 cartons whipped topping

Wash apples and pears. Cut into bite-sized pieces in mixing bowl. Slice bananas into bowl. Add washed and stemmed grapes. Toss. Spoon into paper cups and top each with whipped topping.

Vegetable Soup

3 quarts water
1 lb. ground 🥩
4 🥕 s sliced
4 🥔 s diced
4 🌽 s chopped
1/4 🥬 chopped
4 small 🧅 s chopped
1 can 🍅 chopped
🧂 to taste

Simmer 30 minutes.

Figure 7.5. Rebus charts may enhance the cooking experience for children.

Applesauce

6 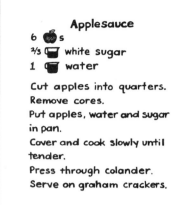s
²/₃ 🥤 white sugar
1 🥤 water

Cut apples into quarters.
Remove cores.
Put apples, water and sugar
in pan.
Cover and cook slowly until
tender.
Press through colander.
Serve on graham crackers.

Chicken Soup with Rice

8 cups
chicken broth

½ cup rice

⅓ cup celery

Buttered Carrots

10 🥕s
1 🥤 water
1 🥄 🧂
🧈

Wash and pare carrots.
Let your teacher slice them.
Put water and salt into saucepan and bring to a boil. Add
sliced carrots. Cover with lid
and lower heat. Cook 15 minutes
or until tender. Drain. Put in
bowl and dot with butter.
Salt to taste. Serve warm.

Gingerbread Men

4 🥤s sifted 📦   1 🥄 ginger
1 🥄 cinnamon   1 🥄 salt
1 🥄 baking powder

½ 🥤 shortening   1 ◯
½ 🥤 brown sugar
     (packed)   1 🥤 molasses

Sift first 5 ingredients together.
Set aside. Cream shortening.
Continue creaming while slowly adding sugar, egg and molasses.
Add dry ingredients. Chill.
Pinch off ball of dough. Pat to
¼ inch thick on lightly floured
surface. Cut cookie shape. Cook on
lightly greased cookie sheet at 350°
for 10-15 minutes.

Figure 7.5.   cont.

since acknowledged that the series caused more children and adults to know and appreciate the books than the author could ever have imagined in her lifetime.

It is only natural that people living in a highly technological and mechanized society would be drawn toward a quieter and simpler time—to a time when a family could pack up and move when things got too crowded. Legend has it that at one time in Wisconsin the forest was so dense that a squirrel could hop from limb to limb for a thousand miles without ever touching the ground. It was in those woods that Laura's Pa made a clearing to build the little house for his family. Laura was later to describe her childhood impression of the big woods:

> So far as the little girl could see, there was only the one little house where she lived with her Father and Mother, her sister Mary and baby sister Carrie. A wagon track ran before the house, turning and twisting out of sight in the woods where the wild animals lived, but the little girl did not know where it went, nor what might be at the end of it.[29]

Without a doubt, the major reason why both the books and the television show hold so much appeal for people of all ages is that Laura Ingalls Wilder was a remarkably gifted writer who had the ability to transport her readers to her own time and place. The television shows, even though many of the episodes were radical departures from the original story, remained surprisingly faithful in showing her philosophy: . . ."the real things haven't changed. It is still best to be honest and truthful; to make the most of what we have; to be happy with simple pleasures; and to be cheerful and have courage where things go wrong."[30]

Whatever its shortcomings, the television version of "Little House on the Prairie" deserves to be cited as an excellent example of the medium's capacity for enhancing and extending children's experiences with literature.

Many primary teachers introduce their students to the Little House books by reading aloud *Little House in the Big Woods* or *Little House on the Prairie,* both suitable for younger children. Either book is enough to capture the interest needed to complete the series of nine, which can then be read independently as children mature in reading over a period of years.

---

29. Laura Ingalls Wilder, *Little House in the Big Woods.* New York: Harper & Row, Publishers, Inc., 1932, p. 2.

30. Excerpted from a letter Laura Ingalls Wilder wrote to some of her young readers. Courtesy Harper & Row, Publishers, Inc.

Figure 7.6.   This is the house in Mansfield, Missouri that Laura and Almanzo Wilder built more than ninety years ago. It is now open to the public, and the Laura Ingalls Wilder Museum is adjacent to the house.

A fascinating part of each book, for readers of all ages, is the frontier food so graphically described in both the text and illustrations. Over one-hundred recipes from Laura's pioneer childhood have been compiled into a handsome book entitled *The Little House Cookbook,* by Barbara M. Walker, published by Harper & Row. It is an important resource to accompany the Little House series and should be included in both the school library and the classroom collection.

A cooking activity based on the Little House books is a very natural followup to the reading and gives children insight into the social pleasures of preparing and eating a meal in a pioneer setting. See figures 7.6, 7.7, and 7.8.

Figure 7.7. Order blanks are available from the Rocky Ridge Farm in Mansfield, Missouri, for ordering Laura Ingalls Wilder books, artifacts, and recipes.

Figure 7.8. Authentic recipes of dishes described by Laura Ingalls Wilder in the "Little House" books are included in this volume. It is illustrated with Garth William's drawings from the books.

CHILDREN'S COOKBOOKS

Come and Get It: A Natural Foods Cookbook for Children, written by Kathleen M. Baxter; illustrated by Mimi Orlando. Ann Arbor, Mich.: Children First Press, 1989.

> A spiral-bound cookbook written in calligraphy and illustrated with line drawings. The cookbook opens with a preface to "Big People" introducing them to a practical plan for teaching cooking and nutrition to their children. Recipes explain how to grow alfalfa sprouts, how to make sun tea, trail mix, thumb pies, and other fascinating dishes. The book contains one-hundred-fifty recipes for children of all ages to prepare and to share with friends and family.

Cooking in the Classroom, written by Janet Bruno and Peggy Dakan. Belmont, Calif.: Fearon Pitman Publishers, Inc., 1974.

> The authors of this small cookbook believe that a love for cooking starts early for both boys and girls when they are allowed to work in the kitchen. And being teachers, they tested their recipes in the classroom, teaching chemistry, mathematics, reading, and spelling in the process. Each recipe is printed in a language experience chart format and is accompanied by a comic cartoon illustration.

Cool Cooking for Kids, written by Pat McClenahan and Ida Jaqua. Belmont, Calif.: Fearon Pitman Publishers, Inc., 1976.

> This cookbook is designed for teaching cooking and nutrition to preschoolers. It contains lesson plans and enrichment activities along with the recipes to aid teachers and parents in working with children two to eight years of age. One of the most helpful chapters for parents is called "Real Cool Cooking: Recipes That Don't Use Heat." Preschool teachers will enjoy the wealth of ideas for bulletin boards, charts, posters, puppets, and other materials for teaching nutrition.

My Cooking Spoon, written by Joanne Barkan; illustrated by Jody Wheeler. New York: Warner Books, Inc., 1989.

> A cardboard toy-book that describes familiar kitchen tools for children ages 2 and up. A metal pin holds the spoon-shaped pages together, similar to the way measuring spoons are fastened together, allowing them to be opened in a fan shape. Each page (front and back) features a different type of spoon and explains its uses. Other books in the "My First Kitchen Gadget Books" are: *My Cooking Pot; My Frying Pan; My Rolling Pin; My Measuring Cup;* and *My Spatula.*

Peter Rabbit's Cookery Book, compiled by Anne Emerson and illustrated by Beatrix Potter. New York: Viking Penguin, Inc., 1987.

> All twenty-one recipes were suggested by food mentioned in Beatrix Potter's Peter Rabbit stories. Each recipe has been developed simply and in step-by-step order for young cooks. An excellent discussion of safety procedures in the kitchen is given at the beginning of the book. Beatrix Potter's illustrations are as appealing as ever.

The Popcorn Book, written and illustrated by Tomie dePaola. New York: Holiday House, 1978.

> One twin cooks the popcorn while the other reads about it. By the time the popcorn book is finished, the kernels are ready to eat. Popcorn stories and legends are included, along with recipes and storage tips.

• BIBLIOGRAPHY

Cox, Carole. *Teaching Language Arts.* Needham Heights, Mass.: Allyn and Bacon, Inc., 1988.

Donoghue, Mildred. *The Child and the English Language Arts.* Dubuque, Iowa: Wm. C. Brown Publishers, 1990.

Ellis, Arthur, Timothy Standal, John Pennau, and Mary Kay Rummel. *Elementary Language Arts Instruction.* Englewood Cliffs, N. J., 1989.

Huck, Charlotte, Susan Helper, and Janet Hickman. *Children's Literature in the Elementary School.* 4th edition. New York: Holt, Rinehart and Winston, 1987.

Mangiere, John, Nancy K. Staley, and James A. Wilhide. *Teaching Language Arts: Classroom Applications.* New York: McGraw-Hill Book Co., 1984.

Norton, Donna. *The Effective Teaching of Language Arts.* 3d edition. Columbus, Ohio: Merrill Publishing Co., 1989.

Phelan, Patricia. *Talking to Learn.* Urbana, Ill.: National Council of Teachers of English, 1989.

Stewig, John Warren. *Children and Literature.* 2d edition. Boston: Houghton Mifflin Company, 1988.

Sutherland, Zena, and May Hill Arbuthnot. *Children and Books.* 7th edition. Glenview, Ill.: Scott, Foresman & Company, 1986.

8

"A Circle of Celebrations":

Books to Enrich the Holidays

The major holidays of the school year have always provided curriculum content at the preschool, kindergarten, and primary levels. Children as well as parents and teachers are drawn to them as naturally as they are to other kinds of folklore and legend. There is probably no better way to develop a certain "world mindedness" in young children than to have them study the celebrations and festivals of people everywhere, because a culture's values are mirrored in its festivals.

This chapter presents nine major American holidays that occur during the school year: New Year's Day, Valentine's Day, St. Patrick's Day, Easter, Cinco de Mayo, Halloween, Thanksgiving, Christmas, and Hanukkah. Each holiday is discussed briefly, its symbols are listed and explained, and suggestions are given for classroom activities. An annotated list of holiday books is given at the end of the chapter along with a bibliography of references for the teacher.

New Year's Day

New Year's Day is a holiday that has been celebrated all over the world for thousands of years. It seems that nearly everyone celebrates New Year's Day, the year's birthday, but not all in the same way. It all depends on how time is measured. Some people celebrate the harvest, some the shortest day of the year or the longest, still others the beginning of the spring season.

In America, time is measured by the sun. It takes 365¼ days for the earth to go around the sun. That gives our year 365 days. Every four years (Leap Year) an extra day is added to take care of the quarter days.

Figure 8.1.   The Roman god Janus ruled over gates and doors. He had two faces to see people either entering or leaving the gates. Caesar named the first month for him thinking he could look back at the old year and ahead to the New Year.

The Romans named January for Janus, their two-faced god who was the keeper of doors and gates. He could look both ways to see who was coming and going through the gates. The Romans thought he would also be able to look back at the old year and ahead to the new one (fig. 8.1). They named January 1 as New Year's Day about two thousand years ago.

No matter how New Year's day is celebrated, all consider it a new beginning.

New Year's Day Customs and Symbols

New Year's Resolutions. Since the new year provides a fresh, clean start, most people decide to improve themselves—to make the new year better than the old. In Madagascar and Burma, people pour cold water over their heads to symbolize a fresh, clean start. It is said the Babylonians made resolutions some five thousand years ago.

Father Time.   Kronos was the Greek god of Time. An old man with a long white beard, he is dressed in flowing robes and always carries a scythe for reaping the years. The image is also used to designate the old year just past.

New Year Baby.   The baby is the most popular of all symbols to signify a new year. He wears only a diaper and a top hat. In cartoons, he usually carries a badge or streamer with the new year's number printed on it. The New Year Baby comes from the Greek god Dionysus, who was born new again at the beginning of every year.

Firecrackers, Horns, and Whistles.   Based on an ancient belief that the old year will not leave of its own accord, it must be driven out with loud noises so that the new one can enter. Some people still open their doors at midnight to let the old year out and the new one in.

Bells.   Used to "ring out the old, ring in the new."

Open House.   Dutch settlers brought the tradition to this country. They invited friends in on New Year's Eve for food and drink. The favorite drink was wassail. They lifted their wassail glasses in a ceremonial toast to good friends.

Midnight Watch.   Many people celebrate New Year's Eve in church services. When midnight arrives they welcome the New Year with hymns and prayers.

Suggested Activities

- Make a study of New Year's Day customs around the world. An excellent resource book is *New Year's Day* by Lynn Groh.

- Make New Year's Day greeting cards that feature Father Time and Baby New Year. Mail them to parents and friends.

- Prepare a New Year timeline on which students can designate their own birthdays and other significant events.

- Arrange a collection of books that feature the months of the year. *Chicken Soup With Rice* by Maurice Sendak, *The Golden Circle* and *A Book of Months* by Hal Borland, and *A Time to Keep* by Tasha Tudor are examples.

- Make a study of our calendar and its origins. Use the topic as a springboard to a unit on Greek and Roman mythology as they relate to the calendar.

- Acquire enough free new calendars to give each student a personal one to keep. Teach them to read it properly and to mark important events.

- Make New Year's resolutions for improving life in the classroom. Record them on an experience chart.

- Let upper primary children write their personal resolutions in illustrated booklets to be taken home and posted for future reference.

Valentine's Day

The giving of Valentine messages goes back to the time of the Roman Empire. St. Valentine was imprisoned because he refused to honor the Roman gods. It is said that he had been very kind to children and they in turn brought messages of love and friendship to him in prison.

Figure 8.2. A heart shape is the most common romantic symbol and has been since antiquity. The fanciest valentines often contain hearts on top of hearts, surrounded by still more hearts.

For his defiance, St. Valentine was beheaded on February 14. When he was buried, the story goes, a pink almond tree near his grave burst into bloom as a symbol of lasting love.

Valentines became romantic love messages in thirteenth-century England. It is mainly the United States and Great Britain that keep the Valentine's Day celebration alive. In both countries, people of all ages enjoy Valentine parties and the exchange of valentine messages.

Valentine Customs and Symbols

Heart. The heart shape is the most common of all romantic symbols. It represents love and affection wherever it is seen. Candy, cookies, and even cakes are made in heart shapes for valentine parties (fig. 8.2).

Fan. A fan on a valentine means "Open up your heart to me."

Ribbon. A ribbon on a valentine means "You are all tied up." "You are mine."

Lace. In Latin, "lace" and "net" are the same, hence a lace ruffle on a valentine means "You have caught my heart in a net."

Rice. Symbolic of a wedding, rice is used to decorate some valentines.

Ring. A ring also represents a wedding or an engagement.

Coin. A coin on a valentine means that you will marry someone wealthy.

Red Mitten. A humorous symbol that teases. It says "I do *not* like you."

Flowers, Birds, Butterflies, Lambs.   All signs of spring, which represent new life and romance.

Angels and Children.   An angel or child on a valentine are symbols believed to bless a happy marriage.

Harps and Lyres.   Any musical instrument shown on a valentine is used to suggest romantic music.

Cupid.   One of the most famous valentine symbols is Cupid with his bow and arrow. He goes back to Roman times. Here is a story the Romans told about him: Cupid was the son of a beautiful goddess Venus; wherever Venus went, Cupid went too. He was a joyful little god and he liked to see people happy. He went around shooting gold-tipped arrows into the hearts of humans to make them fall in love.

Suggested Activities

- Prepare address books for students and a classroom mailbox for posting handmade valentines.
- Teach students how to cut heart shapes from folded paper (practice on newspaper for economy's sake). *Appolonia's Valentine* by Katherine Milhous is an excellent reference for making valentines.
- Use white paper napkins folded several times for cut-paper doilies. Use them for mounting the heart shapes.
- Collect valentines that show the different symbols. Paste them in a valentine scrapbook.
- Arrange a collection of valentine books for the classroom library center.
- Tell the myth of Cupid and Psyche as a feltboard story.

St. Patrick's Day

In Ireland, St. Patrick's Day (March 17) is a holy day. The churches are filled to overflowing and a chorus of voices can be heard singing "Hail Glorious St. Patrick." A parade usually follows the service, often forming at the doors of the church, and celebrants march through the heart of the city.

Later in the day children are told the legends of St. Patrick. One of their favorite stories tells how snakes were banished from the Emerald Isle. It seems that after St. Peter had banished all the snakes except one, he enticed that one into a box with an offer of wine. Chiding the saint

Figure 8.3.   The shamrock is a three-leaved plant used as a floral emblem by the people of Ireland. It is closely associated with the belief that the Irish are people of good fortune, and that the shamrock brings "the luck of the Irish."

for his lack of fair play, the snake begged to be released. "I promise to let you out on the morrow," said St. Patrick as he threw the box into the lake. Ever since, it is said that children often hear the voice of the snake rising from some mountain lake "Is this day the morrow . . . is this day the morrow?"

Irish Americans traditionally celebrate St. Patrick's Day with parades in cities all over the United States. They usually sport bright green jackets and top hats with shamrocks pinned on them (fig. 8.3). Some family groups choose to march together carrying a banner with the name of their clan. Many other ethnic groups join their Irish neighbors in a remarkable show of friendship.

St. Patrick's Day Customs and Symbols

The Irish Flag.   The Irish flag is composed of three vertical stripes of equal width. The colors are green (displayed next to the staff), white, and orange. Green stands for Catholics (old Ireland), orange stands for Protestants (new Ireland), and white for the peace and brotherhood between them.

The Claddagh.   The "claddagh" (cladder) design is a very old Irish symbol consisting of two hands holding a heart topped by a crown. The beautifully simple design holds a great deal of meaning for all who understand it. The hands represent friendship; the crown, loyalty; and the heart, love. At one time the claddagh was worn by both men and women on their wedding bands, but because of its history and unique design the claddagh symbol is now being used internationally as a token of great love and friendship. The design may be seen on bangles, bracelets, pins, necklaces, watches, and rings.

The Harp.   In early times the harp was referred to as a *cruit,* which may have been a lyre instead of a harp. According to legend, an early Irish king took the harp of the Psalmist David as his badge. It is still used as an official symbol on coins, the presidental flag, and on state seals and government documents.

The Book of Kells.   The Book of Kells, one of Ireland's most important treasures, resides in the Library of Trinity College, Dublin, and is considered one of the greatest illuminated manuscripts ever produced. It was written in the Monastery of Kells in the early ninth century and contains the four Gospels of the New Testament, written in Latin. Various letters of the alphabet in the *Book of Kells* are illuminated with brilliant colors, elaborate flourishes, and miniature designs. When only a few people knew how to write, it was considered important to make the writing as decorative as possible.

Suggested Activities

- Make replicas of the Irish flag by cutting rectangles of equal size from green, white, and orange construction paper. Paste the edges together in proper sequence (fig. 8.4).

- Display a large map of Ireland and point out its unusual shape. The outline of the map looks very much like a prehistoric bird with its beak above Dublin, eye at Belfast, and topknot feathers at Donegal. Its swept-back wings are at Westport and Galway and the forked tail is represented by the Dingle and Bantry Peninsulas. Once children have visualized the exotic parrot-like bird, they remember the distinctive shape of Ireland similar to the way they associate Italy with the shape of a boot (fig. 8.5).

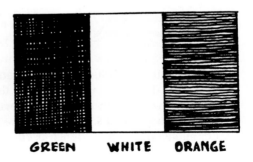

GREEN   WHITE   ORANGE

Figure 8.4.   The Irish flag is composed of three vertical stripes of equal width. The colors are green (next to the staff), which stands for Catholics (Old Ireland), orange which stands for Protestants (New Ireland), and white for the peace between them.

Figure 8.5.   Children are intrigued by maps of all kinds when they are presented in relevant and interesting ways.

Figure 8.6.   Children enjoy the idea of illuminating letters and find it a natural thing to do at a time when they are learning about the alphabet.

- Provide examples of illuminated letters for children to study. Show them how to make large letters for illumination. Encourage them to decorate several letters, including their own initials. Finished illuminations may be pasted on cardboard to make attractive bookmarks (fig. 8.6).

Figure 8.7.   A shamrock, or three-leaved clover, is made from hearts cut from colored paper.

Figure 8.8.   The Claddagh is a very old Irish symbol that has become an international symbol of friendship. The hands represent brotherhood, the crown loyalty, and the heart love.

- Make over-sized shamrocks from green construction paper by cutting three hearts and gluing the points together and adding a stem. Mount shamrocks on the bulletin board (fig. 8.7).

- Assist children in creating claddagh designs as an art project for St. Patrick's Day. Ask them to trace around both their left and right hands and to cut out the handprints. Next, they should cut a large heart from colored paper and mount it on a white background. Have them paste a handprint on either side of the heart. Last, make a crown for the top of the heart. Provide opportunity for children to retell the story of the claddagh design (figs. 8.8, 8.9, 8.10).

Figure 8.9.   Claddagh designs made by kindergarten children were sent home to parents along with a story of the design's meaning. (Courtesy Lindsey Hudson, age 5, Helena Park Elementary School, Nederland, Texas.)

Figure 8.10.   Two tempera-painted handprints add the finishing touch to a claddagh design. (Courtesy Helena Park Elementary School, Nederland, Texas.)

Easter

The greatest festival of the Christian church commemorates the Resurrection of Christ. It is not always celebrated on the same date, however. The church Council of Nicaea in A.D. 325 decided that Easter should be celebrated on the first Sunday after the first full moon on or after the vernal equinox on March 21; Easter can come as early as March 22 or as late as April 25.

The Easter services are the most elaborate of the church year. The message "The Lord is risen" is expressed in ceremonies, prayer, and music. Besides the services in churches, sunrise services are held outdoors in many places. Some, such as those at Pike's Peak in Colorado and in the Grand Canyon of Arizona, have won national fame because of the beauty of their surroundings.

Fact and mythology combine to make Easter a day of glad tidings. Ancient Egyptians, Persians, Phoenicians, and Hindus believed the world began as an enormous egg. Hindu myth holds that the "world egg" broke in two, half turning to gold—the sky—and half to silver—the earth. Mountains, rivers, and oceans were formed from layers under the shell. The sun was "hatched" from this egg. Thus, each dawn became a new life, a new beginning.

Samoan Islanders believed their god Tangaloa-Langi was hatched from an egg and that broken bits of shell became the islands of the Pacific Ocean. Gifts of eggs were exchanged by ancient Greeks and Chinese during spring festivals in celebration of new life around them.

Today, many Chinese parents, on the birth of a child, send eggs dyed red to relatives and friends, announcing the event. Thus, the egg remains a symbol of new life and is a favored decoration on Easter greeting cards (fig. 8.11).

Our name Easter comes from "Eostre," an ancient Anglo-Saxon goddess, originally of the dawn. In pagan times an annual spring festival was held in her honor.

Figure 8.11.   The Easter egg is a highly favored decoration. Gifts of eggs were exchanged by ancient people during the rites of spring. It remains a symbol of new life.

Easter Customs and Symbols

The White Easter Lily.   The symbol of the Resurrection, the white Easter lily is the special Easter flower and is one of the oldest known flowers. The early Madonna lily was cultivated at least three thousand years ago in parts of the Old World. It can be seen in ancient Cretan wall paintings. The flowers of today's hybrid Easter lilies are pure white, with large funnel-shaped blooms and a strong, sweet aroma.

Colored Eggs, Rabbits, and Chicks.   From pagan antiquity, they represent new life. The Easter rabbit comes from pre-Christian fertility rites where it was recognized for its ability to reproduce, becoming the symbol of new life each spring.

Easter Monday Egg Rolling on the Lawn of the White House.   This is a European custom said to have been introduced in Washington by Dolly Madison.

Easter Parade.   Traditionally, new clothing was worn to the special Easter services in the churches. Now promoted mainly by the fashion industry.

The Egg Tree.   A Pennsylvania Dutch custom of trimming a tree with decorated egg shells. Easter toys and cakes were placed underneath. Neighbors were invited in to see the egg tree. *The Egg Tree* by Katherine Milhous won the Caldecott Award in 1951 for the beautiful Pennsylvania Dutch designs painted on Easter eggs. It contains directions for making an egg tree.

Easter Fires Pageant.   The custom of lighting Easter fires on the hilltops of central Texas was brought to this country by German immigrants. Legend holds that when the immigrant families were under siege by the Comanches in 1847, the hills were lit at night with Indian signal fires. As Easter approached, the mothers of Fredericksburg made up a story to explain the fires to their frightened children. The fires, they told the children, were lit by the Easter rabbit and his helpers, who were boiling and dyeing Easter eggs in giant cauldrons of boiling water. Today the legend is still told, and each Easter Eve the hills are set ablaze.

Fabergé Eggs.   Peter Carl Fabergé was a goldsmith who created priceless ornaments for the imperial family of Russia four centuries ago. His Easter eggs have always been the most popular items in the extravagant collection of trifles now housed in museums around the world. The eggs were highly ornamental, lavishly trimmed with gold, silver, and jewels. However, the most intriguing part of each egg was the surprise mechanical contraption concealed inside. For example, when a secret button was pressed on one of the eggs, leaves unfolded and a tiny bird rose and sang for the owner. It became a great challenge for Fabergé and his workers to create designs for the eggs that would continue to surprise and delight the royal family.

Although the gaudy extravagance represented by the Imperial Eggs does not appeal to us today, the eggs are a part of history and afford fine examples of the art of the goldsmith.

Suggested Activities

- Construct an egg tree. Fill a coffee can with wet plaster and, when partially hard, insert a sturdy branch. Hang blown eggs or paper eggs on the tree.

- Design Easter hats by using paper plates for the brims and paper cups for the crowns. Decorate them with paper flowers and Easter toys.

- Create an Easter basket by attaching a handle to a cut-down milk carton or oatmeal box. Cover it with pastel construction paper and decorate it with pictures of flowers, chicks, rabbits, and eggs.

- Make an Easter piñata by attaching papier-mâché strips to an inflated oval-shaped balloon. Cover it with ruffles made of pastel-colored tissue paper. A fine reference book for this project is *Piñatas* by Virginia Brock.

- Dye Easter eggs by one or more of the following methods:

  Draw a light-colored crayon design on an egg and dip the egg in dye.
  Put narrow masking tape around an egg and then dip it in dye to make a plaid egg.
  Drip melted wax on an egg and then dip it in dye. Add more wax and a second color of dye, and so on. This is the Russian "pysanky" technique of decorating eggs.
  Wrap an egg in a piece of cloth and tie both ends. Dip in dye and let it dry overnight while still in the cloth. Unwrap the egg for a tie-dyed effect.

- Make a collection of Easter books for a holiday library center in the classroom.

- Create books in the shape of an egg for the creative writing of Easter stories. (See chapter 5 for directions in making shape books.)

Figure 8.12.   Toys are always a part of the Easter tradition and toys made by children are usually their favorites.

- Arrange a bulletin board of Easter symbols with brief captions explaining the origin and meaning of each symbol.

- Construct a Rockin' Egg, using the following directions:

  Scraps of fabric, a little glue, and imagination can turn an ordinary plastic egg into a creative, one-of-a-kind Easter toy. Provide each student with a large plastic egg of the type that separates at the middle. Take the egg apart and fill one half with sand. Replace the other half and tape the egg together securely.

  Show students how to decorate the weighted egg to represent a person or an animal—the more humorous the better. The egg will stay in many different positions as it is rocked and rolled from side to side and end to end (fig. 8.12).

- Create Fabergé eggs in the classroom by using plastic eggs, scraps, and glue. Children may trim eggs with rick-rack, ribbon, scraps of paper or cloth, sequins, buttons, beads, and so on. A small Easter toy should be placed inside to provide the element of surprise. Cut a small ring of cardboard in which to stand the decorated egg.

Cinco de Mayo

Cinco de Mayo is the Mexican Independence Day. It literally means the "Fifth of May" and marks the anniversary of the 1862 Battle of Puebla, in which a Mexican army defeated the French forces of Napoleon III, winning freedom for Mexico. For Americans of Mexican ancestry, the holiday reminds them of their cultural heritage and provides a special

Figure 8.13.   Instructed to settle where they were to see a sign—an eagle sitting on a cactus and devouring a serpent—the ancient Aztecs saw such a sign and settled in Mexico. There they grew and prospered to become the dominant people.

opportunity to celebrate Hispanic customs. Cinco de Mayo is also celebrated by Hispanics from the other Central American countries as well as from South America and the Caribbean Islands.

The celebration of Cinco de Mayo in the classroom offers non-Hispanic children a chance to become better acquainted with Hispanic traditions and promotes respect for a culture other than one's own (fig. 8.13).

Cinco de Mayo Customs and Symbols

Flowers.   On Cinco de Mayo, flower fairs and festivals are held in all parts of Mexico. Both fresh and handmade paper flowers are used to decorate booths, floats, and costumes. Even pets and farm animals are adorned with flowers and ribbons.

Native Crafts.   Mexican artisans take pride in craftsmanship and their work is displayed as an important feature of the Cinco de Mayo celebration. Some of the crafts they produce are wrought silver, hand-hammered jewelry, carved wood, glassware and tile, hand-tooled leather, pottery, lacquered articles, hand-twisted palm baskets, and woven textiles.

Piñatas.   The piñata is a colorful decoration and a symbol of gaiety. Any party theme can be dramatized by its use and the Cinco de Mayo celebration is no exception. Piñatas are broken to spill their hidden treasures for family and friends and unbroken ones are sold as souvenirs to visitors. Directions for making papier-mâché piñatas are given in chapter 6.

Traditional Foods.   Typical Mexican food is rich and colorful. Many of the dishes are hot and spicy, derived from Indian, Spanish, and Moorish influences. The staple ingredient of all Mexican meals is the *tortilla,* a thin pancake made of coarse cornmeal, which is eaten plain or spread with various spicy toppings.

Suggested Activities

- Make Mexican paper flowers from colored tissue paper. The large flimsy flowers are easier for children to handle if they are glued to paper plates. Provide each child a cardboard pattern for the center and one petal of a flower. Ask them to cut a center and several petals from colored tissue paper. The center should be glued to the middle of the plate. Note: Use glue sparingly; a small dab will hold the tissue in place. Glue petals around the center, allowing each one to slightly overlap the next. Construction paper stems and leaves may be added last (fig. 8.14).
  These huge, colorful flowers are gorgeous when displayed together on a long frieze of white wrapping paper—a veritable flower garden. One is immediately reminded of the flower markets and bazaars of Mexico.

- Create clay beads and medallions in the Mexican style. Roll moist Mexican clay into small round balls. Push a toothpick through the ball while it is still soft. When the beads are dry and hard, paint each one with tempera paint. Once the beads are completely dry, use a blunt darning needle and heavy thread to string them as necklaces.

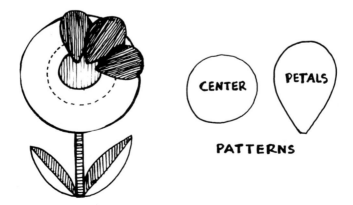

Figure 8.14.   Paper flowers can be made by even the youngest children as they celebrate the Mexican festival of Cinco de Mayo.

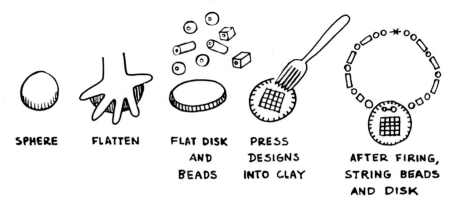

SPHERE   FLATTEN   FLAT DISK   PRESS
                     AND   DESIGNS
                     BEADS   INTO CLAY   AFTER FIRING,
                                              STRING BEADS
                                              AND DISK

Figure 8.15.   Beads and medallions made from air-hardening clay offer children a satisfying craft project.

To make a clay medallion, roll out a larger ball of Mexican clay and mash it flat to form a coin shape. Engrave a design on the disc with the tines of a fork. Push a toothpick through the disc for the string. Allow the medallion to dry thoroughly before stringing it with a length of yarn. The handmade medallion is complete and ready to be worn as a necklace (fig. 8.15).

- Cook tortillas in the classroom. Buy masa harina (corn flour) and mix it with enough water to hold it together. Form a ball the size of an egg. Press it into a flat pancake with a tortilla press or pat it flat with the hands. Cook in an electric skillet with enough cooking oil to brown the tortilla.

- Arrange a collection of books having a Mexican theme. Read aloud *Amigo* by Byrd Baylor Schweitzr and *Song of the Swallows* by Leo Politi.

- Prepare Mexican folktales for telling to children. A good source of tales is *Stories From Mexico* by Edward and Marguerite Dolch. It is an easy-to-read book with an emphasis on good storytelling and literary quality. The book is one in a series entitled "Folklore of the World."

- Tell the story of the "God's Eye" symbol and provide materials for students to try their hand at God's Eye weaving.
  Mexican Indians once held the belief that the God's Eye was a sacred decoration that brought good fortune, luck, health, and long life. God's Eye weaving is a simple form of weaving that can be mastered by children and accomplished quickly. The results are especially attractive when hung together as colorful mobiles.

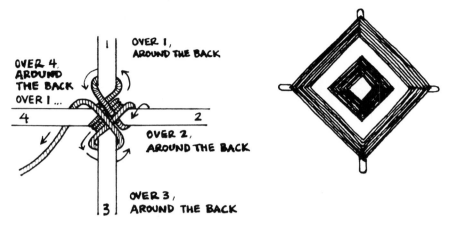

Figure 8.16.   Mexican Indians once held the belief that the God's Eye was a sacred decoration that brought good fortune and long life. It is a simple form of weaving easily mastered by children.

Make God's Eyes by gluing two crossed Popsicle sticks together. Tie a piece of variegated yarn around the crossed sticks at the center. Hold the frame in one hand and the yarn in the other. Weave the yarn over one leg of the frame then under, around, and over the same leg. Go to the next leg and repeat the procedure. Continue until the frame is filled (fig. 8.16).

Halloween

The Halloween celebration goes back in history to the ancient Celts. At the end of summer, they celebrated the end of the sunny weather and prepared for the season of cold and darkness. The Celts believed that winter was the season of death because the flowers and trees "died." The festival not only served as a time of thanksgiving for summer crops, but also to please the "Prince of Darkness."

In A.D. 835 the Roman Catholic Church made November 1 a church holiday to honor all saints—"All Saints' Day," "Hallowmas," or "All Hallows." The evening before (October 31) was called "All Hallow Even," and finally "Halloween." It was, and remains, a time of magic, superstition, and gathering of spirits.

Halloween Customs and Symbols

Black Cats.   Belief that on Halloween the dead could return in some other form. The wicked chose to return as black cats.

Costumes and Masks. Goes back to the time when the Celts wore masks and costumes to frighten away the evil spirits.

Ghosts. Early belief that the dead came back to their homes on October 31. They returned in the form of ghosts and played scary tricks on the living.

Lanterns. To keep away the ghosts, the living carried a light.

Skeletons. Ghosts leave their skeletons in the graveyard, and the bones dance a wild dance on Halloween.

Witches. Old and ugly females who were given magic powers by evil spirits. They traveled on brooms and brought bad luck to people. They kept company with bats and owls.

Warlock. The male counterpart of a witch.

Cauldron. A black pot that held the witches' magic brew. One of William Shakespeare's plays tells of three witches mixing a magic brew:

> Fillet of a fenny snake,
> In the cauldron boil and bake;
> Eye of newt, and toe of frog,
> Wool of bat, and tongue of dog,
> Adder's fork, and blind-worm's sting,
> Lizard's leg, and owlet's wing,
> For a charm of powerful trouble,
> Like a hell-broth boil and bubble.
> Double, double toil and trouble;
> Fire burn, and cauldron bubble.

Jack-O-Lantern. Lanterns to frighten away the evil spirits were carved from large turnips. Some people carved grinning faces on the turnip. Later pumpkins were used and they became known as "jack-o-lanterns" (fig. 8.17). The most famous "jack-o-lantern" story is the "Legend of Sleepy Hollow" by Washington Irving.

Figure 8.17. The Jack-O-Lantern symbol is based on a story from Ireland: Old Jack was so mean that when he died, the Devil threw him a turnip and a burning coal to make himself a lantern. Jack still carries his lantern and roams the world looking for a place to stay.

Trick-or-Treat.   In England, the poor went begging on Halloween. In return for food they promised to pray for the dead of the household. Housewives gave them coins, apples, and candy. They played mischievous pranks if the housewives failed to give them treats.

Orange and Black.   Representative of orange pumpkins and black cats and bats.

Wee Folk.   When the Celts became Christians they hated to give up their old ways. They had always believed in "Little People," and Halloween was their special time to appear. Some wee folk played mischief and others did good deeds.

Apples.   From "Apples of Pomona." Pomona was the goddess of fruits and gardens (Roman mythology). In addition to bobbing for apples, children like to play the following game: Peel an apple without breaking the paring, toss it over your left shoulder, and recite:

> With this peeling
> I hope to discover
> The first initial
> Of my true lover.

Suggested Activities

- Designate a permanent area in the classroom as a Halloween center. Stock it with Halloween games, puzzles, worksheets, stories, poems, and books.

- Make a midnight Halloween mural by painting ghosts, jack-o-lanterns, witches, and so on, on a large sheet of black craft paper. (See chapter 5 for directions on making a mural.)

- Make a series of booklets in the shape of a ghost for the writing of Halloween ghost stories.

- Cut black bats and cats from construction paper. Pin them around the bulletin board as a border.

- Prepare story boards by drawing and painting the Halloween symbols on pages of poster board. To the back of each story board, attach a copy of the legend behind the symbol.

- Follow the directions in chapter 7 to make several different kinds of witches.

- According to directions in *Old Black Witch* by Wende and Harry Devlin, make "bewitching blueberry pancakes." (See chapter 7 for additional information.)

- Prepare, "Queer Company" for storytelling on the felt board. (See chapter 2 for script and directions.)

Figure 8.18. Faces printed by kindergarten children reveal various moods and emotions. An effective activity to follow the reading of *Feelings,* written and illustrated by Aliki. (Courtesy Tia Webb, teacher.)

- Print dozens of circles on computer printout paper by using a grapefruit half dipped in a shallow pan of orange tempera paint. When circles have dried, use swabs dipped in black tempera paint to make eyes, nose and mouth for each jack-o-lantern face. Encourage children to show as many emotions as possible on the faces. Display the finished product as a frieze in the hallway or classroom (fig. 8.18).

Thanksgiving

Harvest festivals go back to ancient times when most countries of the world celebrated a bountiful harvest or gave thanks for a victorious battle. The Thanksgiving holiday, as we know it, was brought to this country by the Pilgrims. In the fall of 1621, they celebrated their first harvest with a bountiful feast and invited the Indians who lived nearby to share the turkey, deer, roast corn, Indian pudding, and fresh fruits.

The custom of Thanksgiving Day spread from Plymouth to other New England colonies. On November 26, 1789, President George Washington issued a general proclamation for a day of thanks. An official annual Thanksgiving Day holiday, the last Thursday of November, was set aside by Abraham Lincoln in 1863. In 1941 Congress ruled that the fourth Thursday of November would be observed as Thanksgiving Day and would be a legal holiday.

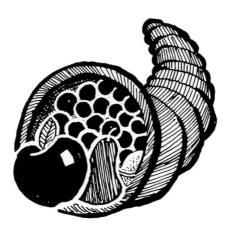

Figure 8.19. The cornucopia symbol is from Greek mythology. It is a horn containing food, drink, and treats in endless supply, said to have been a horn from the goat Amalthaea. It is popular at Thanksgiving time as a symbol of abundance.

Today Thanksgiving is a time of reunion between family and friends, of feasting and good cheer, of football and parades. It is also a day to give thanks.

Thanksgiving Customs and Symbols

Pilgrims. Thanksgiving was introduced to America by the Pilgrims, who celebrated a bountiful harvest and their new freedom by preparing a large feast.

Indians. Friendly Indians were invited to the first Thanksgiving feast. They stayed to take part in the games and parades that followed the meal.

Turkeys. Because it is believed that roast wild turkey was one of the main dishes served at the first Thanksgiving feast, it has become the most familiar and popular symbol of the holiday.

Cornucopia. The ancient Greeks believed in a magic horn that supplied an endless array of food and drink. Today the cornucopia, or horn of plenty, represents abundance (fig. 8.19).

Corn. Ears of corn and corn shocks are symbols of Thanksgiving to remind us that the Indians taught the Pilgrims how to raise corn successfully.

Football. It is customary to attend football games after the Thanksgiving meal or to watch the games on television. This tradition harks back to the first Thanksgiving when the Pilgrims and Indians played games and danced following the feast.

Suggested Activities _____

- Make a study of the ways in which the Thanksgiving festival is celebrated in different parts of the world. A good reference book that contains a chapter entitled "Customs Around the World" is *Thanksgiving* by Lee Wyndham.

- Prepare traditional Thanksgiving foods and act out the first Thanksgiving.

- Create an experience chart based on the cooking experience. Illustrate it with student artwork. (See chapter 5 for information on making language experience charts.)

- Cut a large harvest table from brown craft paper. Fasten it to the bulletin board and let children pile it high with traditional Thanksgiving food shapes that have been cut from construction paper.

- Cut a large circle of brown paper for a turkey body and a smaller one for the head. Attach them to a bulletin board and make the tail feathers from men's discarded neckties. This will result in a giant turkey to fill the bulletin board.

- Make leaf prints. Collect autumn leaves with interesting shapes. Place a leaf, vein side up, on a soft surface. Over the leaf place a sheet of thin white paper, hold it in place, and color over the leaf with the side of a crayon. Make all strokes go in the same direction. Cut along the leaf outline and mount it in a "Leaf Peeper's Scrapbook." Repeat the process with a different leaf and a different autumn-colored crayon. Older students may label each leaf by referring to a tree guidebook.

Christmas

Christmas is the most popular holiday in the Western world and certainly the favorite of children. Surprisingly, they know very little about the customs, traditions, and symbols of the holiday. Since the traditions originated in countries all over the world, and many are thousands of years old, they present a natural subject of study to foster cultural understanding and to enrich the holiday season for children.

Christmas Customs and Symbols

The Legend of the Poinsettia.   In Mexico it is the custom to bring gifts to the church on Christmas Eve to lay at the feet of the Christ Child. The story tells of a little boy who wanted to give a gift to the Child, but

Figure 8.20.   The evergreen tree is one of the most popular of all Christmas symbols. American Sunday schools began using decorated Christmas trees in the 1850s. When children saw them at church they wanted one at home.

he was poor and had no gift to give. "But I can at least pray," he thought. And so he knelt down outside the church window where he could hear the organ music and see people kneeling inside and sent up his prayer to the clear midnight skies. When he rose to his feet, in the spot where he had knelt was a beautiful red plant. He reverently picked the red flower and laid it at the feet of the Christ Child in the church. The Mexicans called the plant the "Flower of the Holy Night" ("Flor de la Noche Buena"). Years later, an American Ambassador to Mexico, Dr. Poinsett, brought the flower to the United States, where it was called the poinsettia.

The Christmas Tree.   The Christmas tree had its start somewhere in Germany, so the legend goes, and it may have been Martin Luther who brought the tradition about. It seems that Luther, walking alone in the late evening, was struck by the beauty of a tall fir thrust like a turret into the night. All around it were the blinking lights of the stars. He cut down a small tree for his house and decorated it with candles. As Christmas trees became a thriving tradition, other decorations were added: cookies, candy, fruit, tinsel, and today, twinkling electric lights and shiny balls (fig. 8.20).

In 1841 Prince Albert, Queen Victoria's husband, set up a Christmas tree in the Windsor Castle, and thus England became addicted to the practice. It was the homesick Hessian soldiers who, during the Revolutionary War, introduced the Christmas tree to this country.

Most Christmas trees are now grown on tree farms where they are planted as seedlings and left to grow for six to sixteen years. They are pruned, fertilized, and sprayed. When the trees are finally ready, they are sold by civic groups, garden shops, and grocery stores. The leading Christmas tree-growing states are Michigan, Wisconsin, Minnesota, and Washington.

Holly.   Many superstitions abound regarding this popular Christmas symbol. Ancients thought it sacred because it stayed green year round. They believed it would heal the sick, repel evil spirits, and protect homes. The Druids of ancient Britain decked their halls with boughs of holly to shelter sylvan spirits threatened by frost and winter winds. Early Christians believed that the crown of thorns was made of holly and that Christ's blood turned the berries red.

Mistletoe.   Kissing under the mistletoe is an ancient pagan custom that is derived from the marriage rite. The Druids in Gaul, Britain, and Ireland, before the time of Christ, considered the mistletoe sacred to love and marriage. Romans thought it a symbol of peace and hope. When enemies met under it, they laid aside their weapons, kissed each other, and made a truce until the next day. Mistletoe is the state flower of Oklahoma.

Christmas Greens.   Christmas greens have been used as symbols of the earth's fertility and eternal life since ancient pagan days. Teutonic peoples believed that certain greens could frighten away evil spirits. Red and green are color symbols of Christmas because of the red and green poinsettia, holly, and other evergreens with red berries.

Christmas Candles.   Candles and their light represent the "Light of the World." In ages past, torches, lamps, and fires were used to celebrate joyous occasions and festivals. Candles were notched and used to tell time. In medieval Europe a huge Christmas candle was burned to celebrate the festivities each night until Twelfth Night. It was considered bad luck if the candle burned out before the Twelfth Night.

The della Robbia Wreath.   Ceramic wreaths were used more than four hundred years ago in Italy as a border for a family's crest or coat of arms. This large, heavy ring was placed beside the front door as a sign or house marker, similar to the way numbers are used today.

A family of sixteenth-century artists named della Robbia began to decorate the wreaths with ceramic fruits and flowers in bright colors. The rings were so heavy they had to be set into the walls with concrete. Most of the existing wreaths are now preserved in museums throughout the world, but we have come to call any wreath decorated with fruits and flowers a "della Robbia" wreath.

Construct della Robbia wreaths for the bulletin board or for gifts to take home to parents. Cut fruits, flowers, and vegetables from seed catalogs and glue them around the border of a paper plate. Make a coat of arms for the center of the wreath by using symbols or initials. The della Robbia family often used religious themes in their wreaths (fig. 8.21) and your students may wish to use old Christmas cards for that purpose (fig. 8.22).

Figure 8.21.   An original ceramic wreath made by Luca della Robbia in the sixteenth century. (Courtesy of Houston Museum of Fine Arts.)

Figure 8.22.   A satisfactory replica of a della Robbia wreath can be made by pasting cutouts around the edge of a paper plate. A Christmas card angel is pasted inside the frame.

Christmas Stockings.   Stockings as containers for Christmas gifts are traced to an old story. Santa Claus dropped some old coins down a chimney one night. Instead of falling into the hearth, the money was dropped into a stocking that had been drying by the fireside. Since then, Santa is expected to fill all the stockings he finds by the fireplace on Christmas Eve. In Holland, wooden shoes are still placed by the fireplace on Christmas Eve in the belief that St. Nicholas will fill them with presents for good children and switches for naughty ones.

The Name "Christmas."   In medieval England it was called "Christes Masse," then "Christ's Mass," until it acquired its present spelling. In many European countries the day is still known as "Christ's Birthday" and is called "Noel" by the French, "Yulen Jul" by the Scandinavians, "Natale" by the Italians, and "Weihnacht" by the Germans.

Christmas Cards.   In the early 1800s, English schoolboys penned holiday letters to their parents as an exercise. In 1846 Sir Henry Copley, too busy to write his greeting, sent out the first printed cards.

Over four billion cards are exchanged in this country every year because of the mobility of the American people. Cards are a way to keep in touch with family and friends at Christmas time.

Christmas Carols.   In thirteenth-century Italy, the first Christmas carols were sung. They were later carried to Spain, France, and England by wandering musicians and sung between the acts of miracle plays. Inspired Britishers in turn composed "Hark, the Herald Angels Sing," "Joy to the World," and "God Rest Ye Merry Gentlemen." "Silent Night," was written in 1818 by Josef Mohr, a parish priest in Oberndorf near Salzburg, Austria, for his Christmas Eve services.

Christmas Foods.   The favorite Christmas foods in this country are turkey, dressing, and cranberry sauce, but other nations have different preferences as to Christmas meals. In Armenia, boiled spinach is eaten because it is believed that Mary did so the night before her Son was born. In Holland, small gifts are hidden in puddings and sausages. In Scandinavian nations, a large rice pudding containing a single almond is prepared in the belief that the person receiving the portion with the almond will be married before the following Christmas. In Poland, wafers are exchanged between friends instead of gifts, and hay is spread under the Christmas dinner tablecloth. In French Canada, the cat is always fed well at Christmas time because it is considered bad luck if there is a meow on Christmas Eve.

The Legend of the Animals at Christmas.   All nations honor those humble beasts who were close to Jesus at the time of His birth, sharing their stable with Him.

One of the best-loved legends tells us how the barnyard animals fell to their knees in adoration of the Christ Child just at midnight on Christmas Eve. Another legend has it that the animals were given the power of speech at midnight on Christmas Eve to announce the birth of Christ to the world.

In Spain, the cows are specially honored on Noche Buena because of the way the Little Jesus was kept warm by the cows breathing on him.

Lambs play a large part in the Nativity because of the shepherds who traveled so far to see the Baby Jesus. And when we place the little figures of donkeys and oxen, sheep and lambs, in our crèche, it keeps fresh in our hearts the part they played in the First Christmas.

In *Hamlet,* Shakespeare wrote about the cock crowing on Christmas Eve: "Some say that ever 'gainst that season comes wherein our Savior's birth is celebrated, this bird of dawning singeth all night long."

Christmas Bells.   Bells are symbolic of the joyous announcement of the birth of Christ. In medieval times on Christmas Eve, church bells tolled as they did for the dead. This was to warn the devil of the imminent birth of Jesus. At the stroke of midight, after ominous tolling, the bells rang joyously.

"I Heard the Bells on Christmas Day" was written by Henry Wadsworth Longfellow on Christmas Day in 1863 while the Civil War was still raging. "Peace on earth, good will to men" reflects the feelings of the author and his countrymen.

The Manger Scene (Crèche).   Manger scenes may have been used first by St. Francis of Assisi. More than seven hundred years ago, he had a farmer build a miniature manger at Christmas. St. Francis filled it with straw and added painted figures of the Baby, the Mother, the donkey, ox, the shepherds, and the three kings.

Santa Claus.   Santa Claus was brought to America by Dutch settlers. He was at that time pictured as a pale-faced bishop in ancient robes and called Saint Nicholas (Dutch children shortened "Nicholas" to "Claus," and the Spanish influence in the Netherlands changed "Saint" to "Santa"). St. Nicholas was known for his generosity in giving to the poor, especially to children.

In Clement Clark Moore's poem, "A Visit from St. Nicholas" or "Twas the Night Before Christmas," St. Nicholas evolved into a plump, jolly man with a nose like a cherry. He came wearing a red suit trimmed with white fur and riding in a sleigh drawn by eight reindeer.

Reindeer.   Reindeer, made popular by Clement Clark Moore's poem, now symbolize Christmas. More recently Rudolph the red-nosed reindeer has become a symbol. The poem about Rudolph was written by

Robert L. May for his daughter. Later the poem was set to music and is now enjoyed by children at each Christmas season. Rudolph, with his familiar nose that lights up, is frequently used in outdoor displays.

Suggested Activities _____

- Arrange a collection of Christmas books for the classroom library center.
- Prepare a file of Christmas poems for a "Poetry Aloud Allowed" center.
- Make booklets in the shape of a Christmas tree, stocking, candle, gift, and so on for creative writing. (See chapter 5 for directions on making shape books.)
- Design a collection of Christmas cards in class for students to send to parents and friends. Let them represent all the Christmas symbols.
- Arrange a bulletin board of the Christmas symbols. Write a brief caption under each one explaining its significance and origin.
- Prepare Christmas stories for puppetry and Readers Theatre presentations. (See chapter 3 for a discussion of puppetry and Readers Theatre.)
- Illustrate Christmas stories for feltboard presentations. (See chapter 2 for storytelling suggestions.)
- Prepare a wassail bowl for the class and sing traditional Christmas carols.

Hanukkah

Hanukkah, also known as the "Festival of Lights," is an eight-day holiday commemorating a victorious religious rebellion by Jews against the Greeks in 165 B.C. It also represents a great miracle that was said to have occurred when the triumphant Jews recaptured the Holy Temple in Jerusalem. Judah (the Macabee), leader of the Jews, found a small amount of oil to light the lamp that was to always burn in the temple. Even though there was only enough oil for one day, the lamp kept on burning for eight days. The Jewish people decided to celebrate each year the miracle of the oil that burned eight days.

Today when Jewish people celebrate Hanukkah, they do so by lighting the candles in a menorah, a candlestick that holds nine candles (fig. 8.23). On the first night of Hanukkah, the middle candle, called the "Shammash," is lit and used to light one of the other candles. Each night after

Figure 8.23.   The menorah is a candleholder that holds eight small candles for Hanukkah and one larger one (called a "shammash") to light the others.

that, another candle is lit until, on the last night, all nine candles are burning brightly. Wherever the Jewish people live throughout the world, Hanukkah is celebrated.

Hanukkah Customs and Symbols

Star of David.   The six-pointed star is formed by two equilateral triangles that have the same center and are placed in opposite directions. The star is the official emblem of Judaism and is the central feature of the flag of Israel.

The Dreidel.   The dreidel, a favorite toy of Jewish children, is a cube that spins. Directions for making dreidel tops and for playing the dreidel game are given in the activities section.

Latkes.   Potato pancakes, called "latkes," are a traditional dish served at Jewish holiday celebrations. The recipe for latkes is also given in the activities section.

Gelt.   Jewish boys and girls receive gifts of "gelt" or money during Hanukkah. It usually consists of chocolate candy coins covered with gold paper.

Suggested Activities

- "Spin the dreidel" (drad'l) is a holiday game played by Jewish children during the Hanukkah celebration. It is a game well suited to the classroom. Construction of the dreidel tops is a worthwhile crafts activity for children and the dreidel game teaches while it entertains.

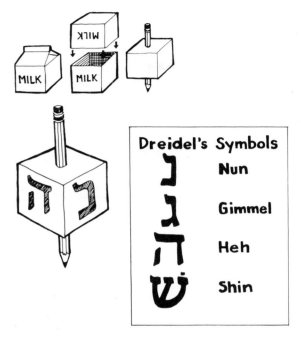

Figure 8.24.   Construction of dreidel tops and the playing of a dreidel game are effective activities for creating interest in the Hanukkah Celebration. (Drawing courtesy of Barbara Ellis.)

The dreidel is actually a cube that spins (fig. 8.24). The sides of the block contain four letters—*nun, gimmel, heh,* and *shin.* Each letter stands for the first letter in a four-word Hebrew message, "Nais gadol hayah sham," which means "A great miracle happened there."

Make the dreidel tops by inserting one small milk carton inside another to form a six-sided cube. Cover the block with white paper and glue it in place. Insert a sharpened pencil through the cube to form a spinner. Using a felt point pen, draw the Hebrew symbols on the four sides of the cube. The dreidel is complete.

To play the dreidel game, each player needs six markers. To begin, each player puts one marker in the center pile. The first

Figure 8.25.   Two papier-mâché egg cartons make a handy menorah. Twelve-inch candles fit snugly in spaces between the egg cups when the cartons are turned upside down.

player spins the dreidel. The letter that turns upward when the dreidel stops tells the player what to do as follows:

> *Nun,* nothing. The player passes.
> *Gimmel,* everything. Player takes all from center pile.
> *Heh,* half. Player takes half of center pile.
> *Shin,* put in. Player puts one marker into center pile.

The next player takes a turn in the same manner. If the center pile becomes empty, every player must add one marker from his or her pile. The game is over when one person holds all the markers; that player is declared the winner. Note: The dreidel game may be modified and simplified for very young children by using stick-on letters of the English alphabet on the dreidel. A child spins the top and then says a word beginning with the letter that turns upward.

- Create a menorah for the classroom by using two egg cartons turned upside down. Insert eight small candles and one large one between the egg cups. Using the large candle as a lighter, light one candle each day for eight days. Tell the story of the oil that burned for eight days (fig. 8.25).

- Make the Star of David design by gluing white drinking straws onto paper (fig. 8.26).

- Follow the recipe below to make latkes for children:

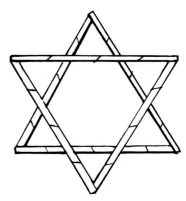

Figure 8.26.   The Star of David is the
official emblem of Judaism and is the
central feature of the flag of Israel.
Children find it an easy design to make
from six drinking straws.

Latkes

2 large potatoes, grated
1/4 c. flour
1 egg
1 tsp. salt

Drop the mixture by spoonfuls into a hot pan coated with vegetable
oil. Brown the pancakes on both sides. Serve with applesauce.

CHILDREN'S BOOKS FOR HOLIDAYS

NEW YEAR'S DAY

Chicken Soup with Rice, written and illustrated by Maurice Sendak.
New York: Scholastic Book Services, 1962.

> A book of months in poetry form. Excellent to use in January as an intro-
> duction to the months in a year. (See chapter 7 for teaching activities.)

The Chinese New Year, written and illustrated by Cheng Hou-Tien.
New York: Holt, Rinehart and Winston, 1976.

> The Chinese New Year holiday goes on for days as a celebration to winter's
> end and spring's beginning. This story of the celebration is illustrated with
> scissor cuts by the author. Excellent for reading aloud.

The Little House, written and illustrated by Virginia Lee Burton.
Boston: Houghton Mifflin Company, 1942.

> This story covers the four seasons in text and pictures and thus lends itself
> to a discussion of the New Year with its coming seasons. A Caldecott Award
> book.

New Year's Day, written by Lynn Brom and illustrated by Leonard
Shortall. Champaign, Ill.: Garrard Publishing Company, 1964.

New Year's parties have been celebrated for more than five thousand years,
and countries all over the world have influenced the traditional festivities.
Contains the story of the Roman calendar we now use in America.

New Year's Poems, selected by Myra Cohn Livingston and illustrated
by Margot Tomes. New York: Holiday House, 1987.

This is an excellent collection of old and new poems created to celebrate
the New Year. Poets include Alfred Lord Tennyson, David McCord, Myra Cohn
Livingston, and Jane Yolen. New Year's celebrations from various cultures
and various geographic areas are featured.

The Sick-in-Bed Birthday, by Linda Wagner Tyler; illustrated by Susan
Davis. New York: Viking Penguin, Inc., 1988.

Tucky Pig has spent hours preparing for his birthday party, but on the eventful
day he breaks out in chicken pox. He thinks it is the worst day of his life—
until the cards arrive from his classmates. An excellent selection to use in
the classroom as a source of inspiration for children who frequently create
get-well cards for a classmate who is ill.

A Time to Keep: The Tasha Tudor Book of Holidays, written and
illustrated by Tasha Tudor. New York: Rand McNally & Company,
1977.

One of the loveliest of all holiday books, with two full pages dedicated to
each month of the year. Excellent to read at the New Year as a preview of
good things to come.

VALENTINE'S DAY

Appolonia's Valentine, by Katherine Milhous. New York: Charles
Scribner's Sons, 1954.

Appolonia, a Pennsylvania Dutch girl, learns to paint beautiful, intricate valentines as tokens of her love and friendship. Features Jean-Jacques, her pen
pal from Brittany, and his cut-paper valentine. One of the illustrations shows
readers how to fold and cut valentines. By the author and illustrator of *The
Egg Tree.*

Arthur's Valentine, by Marc Brown. Boston: Atlantic Monthly Press,
1980.

Arthur finds a way to turn the tables on a secret admirer who sends him un-
signed romantic valentines. She asks for kisses; he gives her candy kisses.

The Valentine Bears, written by Eve Bunting; illustrated by Jan Brett.
New York: Houghton Mifflin Company, 1983.

Mr. and Mrs. Bear wake up from hibernation long enough to celebrate Valentine's Day with a box of chocolate-covered ants (her favorite) for Mrs.
Bear and two handmade valentines for Mr. Bear. They then go back to sleep
until spring. A fine selection to add to the "Valentine Books" collection in
the classroom and excellent for reading aloud at one sitting. Older primary
children probably will be able to read it for themselves.

Valentine Poems, selected by Myra Cohn Livingston and illustrated by Patience Brewster. New York: Holiday House, 1987.

> A collection of twenty poems celebrating Valentine's Day. Both contemporary and traditional poems are included. Other holiday anthologies by Myra Cohn Livingston are: *Thanksgiving Poems, Easter Poems, Christmas Poems, New Year's Poems,* and *Poems for Jewish Holidays.*

Valentine's Day, written by Elizabeth Guilfoile; illustrated by Gordon Laite. Champaign, Ill.: Garrard Publishing Company, 1965.

> This book tells the story of Saint Valentine, some of the legends that grew up around him, and how the date of his death became the official Valentine's Day we still celebrate.

St. Patrick's Day

Celebrations, written by Myra Cohn Livingston; illustrated by Leonard Everett Fisher. New York: Holiday House, 1985.

> A book of simple, appealing poems written to commemorate various special days throughout the year.

Clever Tom and the Leprechaun, retold and illustrated by Linda Shute. New York: Scholastic Inc., 1988.

> An old Irish folktale retold from "The Field of Boliaune" included by folklorist T. Croften Croker in *Legends and Traditions of the South of Ireland* (1825).
>
> Tom finds a tiny leprechaun in a field of boliauns (ragweed) and weaves an elaborate scheme to capture his gold. The manner in which the leprechaun is able to outwit Tom and save his fortune makes for a humorous story that has been handed down from one generation to another in Ireland. The book may be read aloud or used as background for storytelling.

St. Patrick's Day in the Morning, written by Eve Bunting; illustrated by Jan Brett. New York: Houghton Mifflin Company, 1980.

> Everyone thinks that Jamie is too young to walk the distance in the St. Patrick's Day parade, but what do they know? He gets up before the others are out of bed, tucks an Irish flag into his hat and hikes the route of the parade. He plants the flag at the end and hikes back. A true adventure story for young readers and listeners. Jan Brett's illustrations have captured the spirit of rural Ireland's rock-walled houses with slate roofs, cobblestone streets running through quiet villages, and stone fences separating one tiny green pasture from another.

Easter

Easter, written by Lillie Patterson; illustrated by Kelly Oechsli. Champaign, Ill.: Garrard Publishing Company, 1966.

> The story of the familiar Easter symbols—eggs, rabbits, flowers, and foods. Includes the history of the Easter celebration and describes customs in other countries.

The Easter Egg Artists, by Adrienne Adams. New York: Charles Scribner's Sons, 1976.

> Orson Abbott the rabbit decorates cars, bridges, houses, and airplanes to look like giant Easter eggs. An excellent book to share with young children as they begin decorating their own eggs.

The Egg Tree, written and illustrated by Katherine Milhous. New York: Charles Scribner's Sons, 1951.

> A decorative book of Pennsylvania Dutch art. It is also a story with a strong plot that appeals to young children as they plan their own Easter celebrations. (See chapter 7 for teaching activities.)

My First Easter Book, by Annetta E. Dellinger; illustrated by Linda Hohag. Chicago: Children's Press, 1985.

> A simply told, easy-to-read poetic story of Easter symbols and traditions—eggs, chicks, flowers, butterflies, and new clothes for the Easter Parade. Good to place in the holiday center for children to read and reread.

My Mother Sends Her Wisdom, written by Louise McClenathan; illustrated by Rosekrans Hoffman. New York: William Morrow and Company, 1979.

> In true folktale style, a clever peasant woman and her young daughter outwit a greedy moneylender. Detailed illustrations show rural life in a Russian setting. A good book to read aloud at Easter time because many pysanky eggs are shown.

Cinco de Mayo

I'm in Charge of Celebrations, by Byrd Baylor; illustrated by Peter Parnall. New York: Charles Scribner's Sons, 1986.

> A Southwest desert dweller finds enough events in the "sparse" environment to give herself one hundred and eight celebrations—besides the ones they close school for. She tells us, "I celebrate with horned toads and ravens and lizards and quail . . . And, Friend, it's not a bad party." Peter Parnall has captured the special spirit of the desert in his illustrations.

Piñatas and Paper Flowers: Holidays of the Americas in English and Spanish, by Alma Flor Ada; illustrated by Victoria de Larrea. Boston: Houghton Mifflin, 1983.

> A book written in both Spanish and English for use in classrooms on each side of the border. It describes the major holidays celebrated in North, South, and Central America. Two-color illustrations.

Tortillitas Para Mama and Other Nursery Rhymes, Spanish and English, written by Margot C. Griego; illustrated by Barbara Cooney. New York: Holt, Rinehart & Winston, Inc., 1981.

> A selection of rhymes from Latin America accompanied by illustrations reminiscent of Mexican murals. Text is written in both Spanish and English with suggestions for finger plays.

HALLOWEEN

A Ghost Named Fred, written by Nathaniel Benchley; illustrated by
Ben Shecter. New York: Harper & Row, Publishers, 1968.

> An easy-to-read ghost story that takes place in a friendly haunted house. The
> fun and humor make it only semiscary and just right for preschool and pri-
> mary children. An easy-to-read mystery story.

Ghost's Hour, Spook's Hour, written by Eve Bunting; illustrated by
Donald Carrick. New York: Houghton Mifflin Company, 1987.

> Midnight happens to be the hour that a dog and his young master are awak-
> ened by a scary thunderstorm. The house is dark and empty. Why won't the
> lights turn on? Where are Mom and Dad? All is resolved in a safe and satisfying
> manner. Mom explains, "Don't worry about being scared." "Everyone's
> scared sometimes."

Grinkles: A Keen Halloween Story, by Trish Collins. New York:
Franklin Watts, 1981.

> Ghost and witch team up to make a magic brew from grinkles (wrinkled
> grapes). Contains a recipe for oatmeal sprinkled with grinkles (some folks
> call them raisins). An easy-to-read book.

Halloween, written by Lillie Patterson; illustrated by Gil Miret.
Champaign, Ill.: Garrard Publishing Company, 1963.

> Included in this book are many stories and poems to enrich the Halloween
> holiday for children. Also a rich source of multicultural information for
> teachers.

Halloween Parade, written by Mary Lystad; illustrated by Cindy
Szekeres. New York: G. P. Putnam's Sons, 1973.

> A humorous, realistic story of a boy's dilemma about what costume to wear
> in the Halloween parade. The night before the parade, he finds the perfect
> answer.

Little Witch's Black Magic Cookbook, by Linda Glovach. Englewood
Cliffs, N.J.: Prentice-Hall, Inc., 1972.

> Little Witch likes to cook and here she offers children a special collection
> of easy-to-prepare recipes that call for a minimum of supervision from adults.

In the Witch's Kitchen, Poems for Halloween, compiled by John E.
Brewton, Lorraine A. Blackburn, and George M. Blackburn III and
illustrated by Harriet Barton. New York: Thomas Y. Crowell, 1980.

> An excellent collection of Halloween poems by some of the most out-
> standing of children's poets. Contains forty-six poems of fun and fright. Il-
> lustrated with humorous line drawings.

It's Halloween, written by Jack Prelutsky; illustrated by Marilyn
Hafner. New York: Greenwillow Books, 1977.

> Thirteen Halloween poems selected for beginning readers. Illustrated with
> colorful, detailed pictures to complement each poem.

*My Mama Says There Aren't Any Zombies, Ghost, Vampires,
Creatures, Demons, Monsters, Fiends, Goblins, or Things,* written by
Judith Viorst; illustrated by Kay Chorao. New York: Macmillan
Publishing Company, 1973.

> Can Nick trust his mother to be right about monsters and ghosts when she's
> obviously been mistaken about other things? Sometimes she makes him wear
> boots and it doesn't even rain. But then, on the other hand, his mother has
> been right about some things. A good book to read aloud at Halloween time.

Old Black Witch!, written by Wende and Harry Devlin; illustrated by
Harry Devlin. New York: Parents' Magazine Press, 1963.

> A popular story of fun and magic. The leading character is the most de-
> lightful witch to come along in many a day. (See chapter 7 for teaching ac-
> tivities.)

Scary, Scary Halloween, written by Eve Bunting; illustrated by Jan
Brett. New York: Houghton Mifflin Company, 1986.

> A rhyming story of Halloween trick-or-treaters in costume making the rounds
> in their neighborhood. A mother cat and her kittens, original "prowlers of
> the night," turn the tables on the children and reclaim the streets for them-
> selves. The book's illustrations show all the familiar symbols of Halloween
> and provide ideas for many kinds of classroom art projects.

The Teeny, Tiny Witches, written by Jan Wahl; illustrated by Margot
Tomes. New York: G. P. Putnam's Sons, 1979.

> There are all kinds of witches—cross witches and happy witches, but what
> kind of witch is Sam Witch? Where does he fit in? An easy-to-read book.

The Witch's Magic Cloth, written by Miyoko Matsutani, English
version by Alvin Tresselt; illustrated by Yasuo Segawa, New York:
Parents' Magazine Press, 1969.

> The author is a specialist in the field of Japanese folklore. Here he retells the
> ancient legend of Grandmother Asaka and the witch who gave her a bolt of
> golden cloth and a promise of eternal good health for the people of the vil-
> lage.

THANKSGIVING

Cranberry Thanksgiving, by Wende and Harry Devlin. New York:
Parents' Magazine Press, 1971.

> Thanksgiving is a time to forgive one's enemies—even the recipe robber
> who tried to steal Grandmother's "Famous Cranberry Bread" recipe (story
> includes the recipe). (See chapter 7 for teaching activities.)

The First Thanksgiving, written by Lena Barksdale; illustrated by Lois
Lenski. New York: Alfred A. Knopf, 1942.

> The story of a little Pilgrim girl named Hannah who was present at the first
> Thanksgiving feast. A handsome 58-page hardback book with colorful illus-
> trations of the Pilgrim and Indian families.

How Many Days to America?, written by Eve Bunting; illustrated by Beth Peck. New York: Houghton Mifflin, 1988.

> This is a moving story of modern day refugees coming to America from a Caribbean island. The hardships and fears they endure on the voyage are described by a young child traveling with her parents. They call their safe arrival, "coming to America" day, which also happens to be Thanksgiving Day.

Thanksgiving, written by Lee Wyndham; illustrated by Hazel Hoecker. Champaign, Ill.: Garrard Publishing Company, 1963.

> The author shows how harvest festivals go back to ancient times and how they are now celebrated throughout the world. The American Thanksgiving is a combination of a celebration for harvest and for freedom.

The Thanksgiving Story, written by Alice Dalgliesh; illustrated by Helen Sewell. New York: Charles Scribner's Sons, 1954.

> An excellent reference book on Thanksgiving for both students and teachers. Contains a detailed drawing of the Mayflower and a map of Cape Cod Bay. (See chapter 7 for teaching activities.)

Things to Make and Do for Thanksgiving, by Lorinda Bryan Cauley. New York: Franklin Watts, 1977.

> A collection of Thanksgiving games, puzzles, recipes, crafts, and stories. Large print and step-by-step directions make it well suited to the primary classroom.

CHRISTMAS

Baboushka and the Three Kings, written by Ruth Robbins; illustrated by Nicolas Sidjakov. Berkeley, Calif.: Parnassus Press, 1960.

> Adapted from an ancient Russian folktale, this book tells the story of Baboushka, who leaves gifts for Russian children as she journeys through the countryside seeking the Child.

The Boy Who Waited for Santa Claus, written and illustrated by Robert Quackenbush. New York: Franklin Watts, 1981.

> Dirk waits for Christmas and unenthusiastically celebrates all the other holidays along the way. A story that provides a basis for class discussion of Dirk's priorities.

The Black Snowman, written by Phil Mendez; illustrated by Carole Byard. New York: Scholastic Inc., 1989.

> A magical cloth called a "kente" brought its kindly magic to the Ashanti tribe in Africa many years ago. As the brightly colored cloth was handed down through the ages, it became tattered and torn but retained its magical power. An impoverished black family living in a modern city eventually becomes the beneficiary of the kinte's magic when it brings their sooty snowman to life, and an embittered young boy learns to appreciate the beauty of his black heritage. Full-page, richly textured illustrations form a perfect accompaniment to this story of warm family relationships. A fine selection to be read aloud as a continued story at the second and third grade levels.

Christmas Feasts and Festivals, written by Lillie Patterson; illustrated by Cliff Schule. Champaign, Ill.: Garrard Publishing Company, 1968.

> This book explores the history of Christmas celebrations and describes the customs and traditions of the holiday as it is celebrated in various parts of the world.

Christmas in America, written by Lillie Patterson; illustrated by Vincent Colabella. Champaign, Ill.: Garrard Publishing Company, 1969.

> The author explains how traditions, customs, legends, and symbols celebrated in this country have been borrowed from Europe and other parts of the world. Includes a subtle account of the way in which customs mix and change.

December Decorations, A Holiday-How-To Book, by Peggy Parish. New York: Macmillan Publishing Company, Inc., 1975.

> Simple step-by-step illustrations make this a good book to improve the literal reading comprehension of young readers. Also valuable as a resource and idea book for teachers.

The Joys of Christmas, written by Kathryn Jackson; illustrated by Jenny Williams. Racine, Wis.: Western Publishing Company, Inc., 1976.

> A picture book for primary children that describes Christmas customs, legends, festivals, pageants, traditional foods, and music from all parts of the world. An additional feature is the "Merry Christmas" greeting in some twenty different languages.

Make it Special, by Esther Hautzig; illustrated by Martha Weston. New York: Macmillan Publishing Company, 1986.

> Provides step-by-step directions for making cards, decorations, party favors, and small gifts for holidays, birthdays, and other special home and school celebrations. Easy-to-read text and informational drawings make it a valuable resource for primary and middle grade students.

Merry Christmas, Strega Nona, written and illustrated by Tomie dePaola. New York: Harcourt Brace Jovanovich, 1986.

> One of a series of books about a kindly, humorous witch and her bungling assistant, Big Anthony. Strega Nona refuses to use her witchcraft to fix the Christmas feast. Other books in the series are *Strega Nona* (Caldecott Honor Book), *Big Anthony and the Magic Ring,* and *Strega Nona's Magic Lesson.*

Mince Pie and Mistletoe, written by Phyllis McGinley; illustrated by Harold Berson. Philadelphia; J. B. Lippincott Company, 1961.

> In skillful verse form, Phyllis McGinley tells of contributions made to our Christmas celebration by the English, Spanish, Dutch, and French. Illustrated in soft tones of blue and reddish brown.

The Night Before Christmas, written by Clement C. Moore; illustrated by Arthur Rackham. Philadelphia: J. B. Lippincott Company, undated.

> A favorite narrative poem of children and adults. Made even more appealing by the flawless artistry of Arthur Rackham.

The Night Before Christmas, written by Clement Moore; illustrated by Tomie dePaola. New York: Holiday House, 1980.

>The most popular of all Christmas poems illustrated by one of the best-known artists for children. Captures the images of Santa Claus, his sleigh, and reindeer as they were depicted by Moore over a hundred years ago.

Tomie dePaola's Book of Christmas Carols, written and illustrated by Tomie dePaola. New York: G. P. Putnam's Sons, 1987.

>More than thirty favorite carols selected by the author. His paintings illuminate every carol and, for six of the carols, a foldout page opens up to reveal an illustration across three pages similar to an ancient triptych. Excellent for reading aloud at Christmastime to preschool and primary children and as part of the seasonal holiday book center in the classroom.

HANUKKAH

All About Jewish Holidays and Customs, written by Morris Epstein; illustrated by Arnold Lobel. Hoboken, N. J.: KTAV Publishing House, Inc., 1970.

>A complete reference book for the classroom or school library. Offers a history of all the major Jewish holidays and customs. The book opens with the following questions: "A holiday is on its way! Which will it be: a gay and fun-filled one like Purim or Hanukkah? A solemn and sobering one like Yom Kippur?" The readability level is too difficult for most beginning readers, but the book provides excellent background information for parents and teachers.

Holiday Tales of Sholom Aleichem, selected and translated by Aliza Shevrin and illustrated by Thomas di Grazia. New York: Macmillan Publishing Company, 1979.

>Sholom Aleichem was a humorist, satirist, and most beloved of Yiddish writers. Some of his stories formed the basis for "Fiddler on the Roof." The seven stories in this collection deal with Hanukkah, Passover, and other Jewish holidays. Excellent for storytelling and as a reference for teachers.

It Could Always Be Worse: A Yiddish Folk Tale, written and illustrated by Margot Zemach. New York: Farrar, Straus, 1977.

>A popular folktale about a poor man who thinks his household is entirely too crowded. He goes to the rabbi to ask for advice, but his life gets much worse. Margot Zemach's illustrations never fail to fascinate children. Named a Caldecott Honor Book and winner of the New York Times Best Illustrated Book.

Jewish Holidays, Facts, Activities, and Crafts, written and illustrated by Susan Gold Purdy. New York: J. B. Lippincott Company, 1969.

>This book describes and explains the history of sixteen major Jewish holidays from their ancient origins to their modern celebration. It also provides twenty-four craft ideas and activities related to the significance of each holiday. Diagrams and easy-to-follow directions make the projects especially suitable for busy classrooms.

Joseph Who Loved the Sabbath, written by Marilyn Hirsh; illustrated by Devis Grebu. New York: The Viking Press, Inc., 1986.

> The retelling of a traditional Jewish story about a poor man who brings the finest gifts he can acquire to celebrate the Sabbath. He lives to reap his own reward.

My First Hanukkah Book, written by Aileen Fisher; illustrated by Priscilla Kiedrowski. Chicago: Children's Press, 1985.

> A collection of poems relating to Hanukkah, in large print and easy-to-read vocabulary. The poems feature latke potato cakes, "Spin the Dreidel" game, the menorah, Star of David, and other symbols of Hanukkah. The origin of the Miracle of Lights is told from a child's point of view. Excellent for use at the kindergarten and primary levels and for reading aloud at home to preschoolers.

A Picture Book of Hanukkah, by David A. Adler; illustrated by Linda Heller. New York: Holiday House, 1982.

> Just what the title implies, a picture book for very young children that discusses (in brief text) how the celebration of Hanukkah came about, what it signifies, and the ways in which it is celebrated by today's children.

The Power of Light, by Isaac Bashevis Singer; illustrated by Irene Lieblich. New York: Farrar, Straus & Giroux, 1980.

> This Nobel Prize-winning author has written a series of eight tales—one for each night of Hanukkah. The stories contain familiar symbols and motifs of Hanukkah: the lamp, the dreidel, the pancakes, and the menorah. Each story shows events affecting the lives of Eastern European Jews and the manner in which they celebrate Hanukkah.

Stories from the Jewish World, written by Sybil Sheridan; illustrated by Robert Geary. Morristown, N. J.: Silver Burdett Press, 1987.

> A collection of stories that have been handed down by word of mouth from one generation to the next. One of the tales is the story of Hanukkah. It is written in a storytelling format but may be read by students at the upper primary level.

The Story of the Jews, written by Julia Neuberger; illustrated by Chris and Hilary Evans. New York: Cambridge University Press, 1986.

> A history of the Jewish people, their cultural and religious practices, holidays, and symbols. It features a section titled "The Jews of Today" and contains a helpful glossary of Jewish terms. Recommended as a reference book for teachers; a 32-page paperback.

There's No Such Thing as a Chanukah Bush, Sandy Goldstein, written by Susan Sussman; illustrated by Charles Robinson. Niles, Ill.: Albert Whitman & Co., 1983.

> A young Jewish girl is having guilt feelings about participating in her school's Christmas activities. Her wise grandfather helps her understand "the difference between celebrating something because *you* believe in it, and helping friends celebrate something because *they* believe in it."

A Torah Is Written, written by Paul Cowan; photography by Rachel Cowan. New York: The Jewish Publication Society, 1986.

> In each generation scribes have written by hand the words of the Torah, the scroll that contains the laws and history of the Jewish people. This book describes the training and the tools of the scribes and the process they use to transcribe the handwritten scrolls. Each step of the process is illustrated with a black and white photograph.

The Treasure, written and illustrated by Uri Shulevitz. New York: Farrar, Straus and Giroux, 1976.

> A man named Isaac wears out his shoes traveling over mountains and through forests seeking his treasure. At last, he gives up the search, returns home, and finds treasure under his own stove. In thanksgiving he builds a house of prayer, and on the wall he places an inscription: "Sometimes one must travel far to discover what is near." A Caldecott Honor Book.

BIBLIOGRAPHY

Alexander, Sue. *Small Plays for Special Days.* New York: The Seabury Press, 1977.

Barth, Edna. *A Christmas Feast.* New York: Houghton Mifflin, 1979.

———. *Lilies, Rabbits and Painted Eggs: The Story of Easter Symbols.* New York: The Seabury Press, 1970.

———. *Turkeys, Pilgrims and Indian Corn: The Story of the Thanksgiving Symbols.* New York: Clarion Books, 1975.

Borland, Hal. *The Golden Circle: A Book of Months.* New York: Thomas Y. Crowell, 1977.

Burnett, Bernice. *The First Book of Holidays.* New York: Franklin Watts, 1974.

Coffin, Tristram Potter. *The Book of Christmas Folklore.* New York: The Seabury Press, 1973.

———. *The Illustrated Book of Christmas Folklore.* New York: The Seabury Press, 1974.

Cutler, Katherine N., and Katie Cutler Bogle. *Crafts for Christmas.* New York: Lothrop, Lee and Shepard Company, 1974.

Dobler, Lavinia. *Customs and Holidays Around the World.* New York: Fleet Publishing Corporation, 1962.

Dostal, June. *Elementary Teacher's September-June Book of Classroom Activities: An Almanac for Every Day in the School Year.* West Nyack, New York: Parker Publishing Company, Inc., 1977.

Emmens, Carol A., ed., and Harry Maglione, associate ed. *An Audio-Visual Guide to American Holidays.* Metuchen, N.J.: The Scarecrow Press, 1978.

Foley, Daniel J. *Christmas the World Over.* Philadelphia: Chilton Books, 1963.

Frankson, Carl E., and Kenneth R. Benson. *Crafts Activities Featuring 65 Holiday Ideas.* West Nyack, N.Y.: Parker Publishing Company, Inc., 1970.

Gater, Joseph. *Holidays Around the World.* Boston: Little, Brown Company, 1953.

Hopkins, Lee Bennett, and Misha Arenstein. *Do You Know What Day Tomorrow Is? A Teacher's Almanac.* New York: Scholastic Inc., 1990.

Ickis, Marguerite. *The Book of Christmas.* New York: Dodd, Mead and Company, 1960.

Jones, Beverly, ed. *The Fall Book: Creative Learning By the Month.* Houston, Texas: Learning Innovations, 1979.

Krythe, Mamie R. *All About Christmas.* New York: Harper and Brothers, 1954.

Linton, Ralph and Adelin. *Halloween Through Twenty Centuries.* New York: Henry Schuman, 1950.

McSpadden, Walter J. *The Book of Holidays.* New York: Thomas Y. Crowell, 1958.

Metcalf, Edna. *The Trees of Christmas.* New York: Abingdon Press, 1969.

Muir, Frank. *Christmas Customs and Traditions.* New York: Taplinger Publishing Company, 1977.

Newmann, Dana. *The Teacher's Almanac: Practical Ideas for Every Day of the School Year.* West Nyack, N.Y.: The Center for Applied Research in Education, Inc., 1973.

Palmer, Peggy. *Classroom Craft Activities Featuring 50 Seasonal Ideas.* West Nyack, N.Y.: Parker Publishing Company, Inc., 1977.

Ray, John B. *Christmas Holidays Around the World.* New York: Comet Press Books, 1959.

Rice, Susan Tracy, compiler; Robert Haven, ed. *Our American Holidays: Easter.* New York: Dodd, Mead and Company, 1953.

Rinkoff, Barbara. *The Family Christmas Book.* Garden City, N.Y.: Doubleday and Company, Inc., 1969.

Rogers, Barbara Radcliffe. *The Forgotten Art of Creating an Old-Fashioned Family Christmas.* Dublin, N.H.: Yankee, Inc., 1981.

Ross, Laura. *Holiday Puppets.* New York: Lothrop, Lee and Shepard Company, 1974.

Sawyer, Ruth. *The Long Christmas.* New York: The Viking Press, 1941.

Sechrist, Elizabeth Hough. *Christmas Everywhere.* Philadelphia: Macrae Smith Company, 1962.

Smith, Elva, and Alice Hazeltine. *The Christmas Book of Legends and Stories.* New York: Lothrop, Lee and Shepard, 1944.

Stevens, Patricia Bunning. *Merry Christmas! A History of the Holiday.* New York: Macmillan Publishing Company, Inc., 1979.

Weiser, Francis X. *The Easter Book.* New York: Harcourt, Brace and Company, 1954.

Wernecke, Herbert. *Christmas Customs Around the World.* Philadelphia: The Westminster Press, 1959.

9

"Children in Crisis":

Books Can Help

Bibliotherapy: What Is It?

Bibliotherapy is the term for using books to help students solve their personal problems and to assist them in meeting the basic needs of growth and development. "Biblio," of course, refers to books, and "therapy" means to heal. A precise description of bibliotherapy was put forth more than a quarter of a century ago as "a process of dynamic interaction between the personality of the reader and literature."[1] The principles of bibliotherapy, however, go much farther back in history. Ancient Greek libraries were known to have borne the inscriptions "The Healing Place of the Soul" and "The Medicine Chest for the Soul."[2]

Interpreted in its broadest sense, bibliotherapy is based on the belief that through empathy with characters met in books, a reader is better able to understand self. When boys and girls read about a book character whose behavior has brought about failure or success, they recognize their own personality characteristics and are in a better position to make necessary adjustments. It is possible for young readers to be much more analytical about the book character's problems than about their own. Ego damage is not so threatening in the vicarious experience as in the real one.

---

1. David Russell and Caroline Shrodes, "Contributions of Research in Bibliotherapy to the Language Arts Program," *School Review,* Vol. 68 (Sept. 1950), pp. 335–342.

2. Mildred T. Moody and Hilda L. Limper, *Bibliotherapy: Methods and Materials* (Chicago: American Library Association, 1971), p. 3.

Another thing to be said for the vicarious nature of reading is that it is reversible. Readers can decide that they do *not* want to follow the book character's course of action, and no third person will be able to sit in judgment on that decision.[3]

A belief in the value of bibliotherapy is a belief that quality literature has the power to change behavior, to improve attitudes, and to aid in self-awareness and understanding. According to Charlotte Huck, "A book may be considered as suitable for bibliotherapy if it tells an interesting story and yet has the power to help a reader (1) acquire information and knowledge about the psychology and physiology of human behavior, (2) learn what it means to "know thyself," (3) find an interest outside himself, (4) relieve conscious problems in a controlled manner, (5) utilize an opportunity for identification and compensation, and (6) illuminate difficulties and acquire insight into his own behavior."[4]

In considering the use of bibliotherapy to help meet needs of young children, the classroom teacher is the most logical person to bring literature and children together. The teacher can observe each child to recognize unique needs and interests. It is also the classroom teacher who is most able to work closely with the school librarian to make available to children on a day-to-day basis the kind of humanistic literature they need.

To some, this may all sound as though a book is meant to be a "treatment instead of a treat." On the contrary, books are simply made available and the children are left to choose those that best fit their individual needs and interests at the moment. It is a low-key, unobtrusive plan that offends no one. Dedicated teachers and librarians have always practiced bibliotherapy whether or not they called it by that name. If they directed a child toward a particular book or purchased a book with a certain child's needs in mind, they were using bibliotherapy. Anytime they read aloud a sensitive story to improve the attitude or behavior of a group of students, bibliotherapy was being practiced.

Certainly we all agree that books do make a difference, but they have the power to make a positive difference only if we understand children and are keenly aware of their basic needs. We must also become familiar with many books that are so well written and illustrated that they seem inherently to meet the basic needs of early childhood.

---

3. Tony Shepherd and Lynn B. Iles, "What is Bibliotherapy?", *Language Arts* 53 (May, 1976), p. 569.

4. Charlotte S. Huck, *Children's Literature in the Elementary School,* 4th ed. (New York: Holt, Rinehart & Winston, 1987), p. 264.

Even if the book had no text, this
illustration alone would reveal a child who
is a failure in school, a fearful boy who
cannot make friends with other children.
(Illustration from *Crow Boy* by Mitsu and
Taro Yashima. Copyright © 1955 by Mitsu
and Taro Yashima. Reprinted by permission
of Viking Penguin Inc.)

The Basic Needs of Children

Every normal child has certain basic needs in life—needs that indicate that something vital must be supplied if he or she is to be a functional, well-adjusted, and happy individual. Each person spends a lifetime
striving to satisfy needs, and the state of his or her mental health depends
on how successfully the task is accomplished.

The classroom teacher sensitive to "need theory" recognizes that the
behavior of children does not just happen. It is caused. Maslow's theory
of motivation holds that all human behavior can be explained in terms
of the activity generated in satisfying the basic needs. He organizes these
needs into five fundamental groups: (1) physiological needs, (2) safety
needs, (3) love and belonging needs, (4) esteem needs, and (5) self-
actualization needs.[5]

---

5. Abraham H. Maslow, *Toward a Psychology of Being* (Princeton, N.J.: D. Van Nostrand
Co., Inc., 1968), p. 240.

This painting shows children frightened by a raging
storm, but being protected by a father who chinks the
cracks, and comforted by a mother who leads them in
song. (Illustration from *Time of Wonder* by Robert
McCloskey. Copyright © 1957 by Robert McCloskey.
Reprinted by permission of Viking Penguin Inc.)

Physiological Needs

Most people spend their waking moments in the struggle to meet the
overwhelming desire for food, drink, and shelter—the creature comforts
of life. To the teacher of young children, this means that "the basic needs
of food, clothing, rest and affection must be met before efficient school
learning can take place. The effective school curriculum will contain
provisions for these necessary ingredients."[6]

Some children spend their entire childhood outside the warm world
of security. "These are the children who cannot be sure of the basic ne-
cessities. Will there be enough food? Is there someone to take care of
you? There is uncertainty in their lives about whom they really belong
to. Who is the father? And is the mother available to the child in important mothering ways? In fact, is there anybody who really cares about this
child in a deep and important way?"[7] After painting a large bowl of fruit
on her art paper, a second-grade girl wrote at the bottom: "Happiness is
when my daddy has a job."

---

6. Joe L. Frost and Glenn R. Hawkes, eds., *The Disadvantaged Child, Issues and Innovations* (Boston: Houghton Mifflin Co., 1966), p. 248.

7. Barbara Biber, *Young Deprived Children and Their Educational Needs* (Washington,
D.C.: Association for Childhood Education International, 1967), p. 11.

It would be ludicrous, of course, to imply that books can relieve the suffering of a child who is hungry and fraught with anxiety. Obviously, other measures are needed in such cases. Books can, however, help a child to understand that the struggle for security is universal and timeless. And book characters can provide examples of what people have been able to accomplish in the mundane and often weary process of earning a living.

In Ellis Credle's book, *Down, Down the Mountain,* two children of the Blue Ridge Mountains raise and sell turnips to buy new shoes for themselves, and in the process find adventure and self-reliance. From ancient folktales to modern stories, this struggle for material security is a popular theme. It is a theme that is particularly appealing to children because of its infinite reality in their lives.

Safety Needs

Children's feelings of safety may be threatened by any situation that jeopardizes their well-being. They are easily frightened by strange people, surroundings, and activities. Such dangers to safety may be real or imagined; it makes little difference to children. They instinctively try to protect themselves from the hazards as best they can.

Maintaining an environment where the safety needs of young children can be gratified is an ethical responsibility of the classroom teacher. By adhering to a certain amount of routine in the daily program and by being a predictable person on whom the child can depend, it is quite possible for the teacher to shield a child from many of the threats to his or her safety. Keeping a delicate balance between the variety needed to create interest and the routine needed to provide security is one of the most important skills a teacher of early childhood can acquire.

The drawing of Sylvester's reunion with his parents, presents a reassuring portrait of a happy family. (Illustration reproduced with permission of Windmill Books/Simon and Schuster from *Sylvester and the Magic Pebble* by William Steig. Copyright © 1969 by William Steig.)

Children, as well as adults, fear crime, pollution, disease, poverty, drugs, and war as ominous threats to their well-being. Unfortunately, no teacher has the power to protect children from these harbingers of pain, but any teacher who cares can help a child to develop the inner strength to live courageously with elements of danger and not be devastated by them. Taro Yashima, author-illustrator of some of the finest books we have for helping children cope with their problems, said of his work:

> I would like to continue publishing picture books for children until my life ends. The theme for all those should be, needless to say, "Let children enjoy living on this earth, let children be strong enough not to be beaten or twisted by evil on this earth."[8]

Yashima's philosophy shines forth in all his writing and painting, and even the youngest children are able to sense the beauty and meaning in them. By endowing Crow Boy with the strength to rise above ridicule and prejudice, to find an honorable place for himself in the world, Yashima deliberately and consciously tries to give his readers the same inner strength to sustain them in times of crisis.

Love and Belonging Needs

Every child needs desperately to love someone and to have someone love him or her in return. The family unit is the first source of love and affection for most children, but unfortunately many children exist in a world where love is totally lacking. For such children the school of early childhood can become a refuge where affectionate relationships with adults and peers may compensate, to some extent, for the love that is lacking at home.

Adults who work with children must always be ready to give an extra measure of love and understanding to a child who needs it and should find ways to help him or her gain acceptance by his or her peers. To leave such matters to chance is to foreordain that some children will remain outsiders, perhaps for the rest of their lives. "In our society the thwarting of these love needs is the most commonly found core in cases of maladjustment and more severe psychopathology."[9]

Certainly a child's literature should reflect warm, affectionate, loving relationships between people. Such books can help more fortunate children to appreciate their circumstances and to be more sensitive to the love and belonging needs of others. The same books can help the deprived child to learn about giving and receiving love in generous and

8. Muriel Fuller, ed., *More Junior Authors* (New York: The H. W. Wilson Co., 1963), p. 231.

9. Raymond F. Gayle, *Developmental Behavior, A Humanistic Approach* (New York: The MacMillan Co., 1969), p. 105.

Shown here, trudging to school in his raincoat of dried zebra grass, is Crow Boy, an outsider without friends. This illustration points up to his loneliness. (Illustrations from *Crow Boy* by Mitsu and Taro Yashima. Copyright © 1955 by Mitsu and Taro Yashima. Reprinted by permission of Viking Penguin Inc.)

accepting ways, just as Wanda Petronski in *The Hundred Dresses* was able to bring a new awareness and compassion to the girls who taunted her about the faded cotton dress she wore to school every day. *Where the Wild Things Are, Apt. 3, Little Chief,* and *Ask Mr. Bear* are other examples of books that portray the struggle for love, and the ultimate achievement of acceptance.

Esteem Needs

Every child has a strong desire to feel worthy, to know that he or she has value, importance, and status, first in the immediate family, next in the extended family, and finally in groups outside the family. Children long to have their feelings, ideas, and opinions respected by others and often go to great lengths to prove to themselves that it is so.

A child's sense of esteem is closely linked to achievement and competency. To gain a sense of self-respect, a child needs to be successful in many of the ventures he or she undertakes, at least during the first few years of life. In *Oh, the Places You'll Go,* Dr. Seuss attempts to instill this sense of self-respect that every child wants by pointing optimistically to an unknown future. Children also require a reputation among others regarding their unique abilities to perform certain skills and tasks in an adequate, perhaps even superior manner. Crow Boy gained recognition and respect with his unusual ability to imitate the voices of crows. Helping a rejected child to acquire competency in some area is frequently all that is needed to gain him or her an entrée into peer groups.

The Little Engine that Could by Watty Piper is an inspirational book that focuses on the need to achieve. A mirror on this bulletin board encourages accomplishment. (Courtesy Barbara Ellis.)

As children mature, they learn from life how to control their behavior and, by doing so, to influence their environments. They also strengthen this understanding by associating with characters in literature who work to accomplish something worthy of respect, often in the face of many failures and setbacks. Such books as *The Little Engine That Could, Pelle's New Suit, Whistle for Willie, Yonie Wondernose,* and *Benjie on His Own* clearly depict heroes who achieve in spite of the odds against them. Children who come to know such characters in an intimate way are able to draw sustenance and inspiration from them over and over again. Many college students admit that they still say to themselves on occasion, "I think I can, I think I can." Georgiou describes the kind of books that have the power to move children in such deep and lasting ways:

> Books that reveal the skill and affection that have gone into their writing are books that speak to each individual in the personal, private voice of a friend. And it is with this friendship that a book, whether fact or fiction, establishes a world the child can join, learn from, and grow in; a world where he too can laugh, weep, rebel, and cherish.[10]

The Need for Self-Actualization

Closely akin to the need for esteem is the need to become a self-actualizing person. "Even when all other needs are reasonably well fulfilled, a person is discontented and restless unless he is doing that for

---

10. Constantine Georgiou, *Children and Their Literature* (Englewood Cliffs, N.J.: Prentice-Hall, Inc., 1969), p. 6.

As her grandmother lies dying, Lien watches new life spring forth from the earth, and she struggles to understand the mystery of life and death. (Illustration reproduced with permission of Random House, Inc., from *First Snow* by Helen Coutant, illustrated by Vo-Dinh. Copyright © 1974 by Vo-Dinh. Reprinted by permission of Alfred A. Knopf, Inc.)

which he is best fitted. This desire for self-fulfillment, in essence, is the need to become what one is capable of becoming."[11]

Children move in the direction of self-actualization as they set goals for themselves and then work toward those goals. Some goals they accomplish; others they fail to reach. Some goals are altered or abandoned along the way. The aims are the child's own, no matter what objectives others have in mind for him or her. "Each person illuminates and refines his goals as he works conscientiously and intelligently at a task, and one person's goals cannot be transferred to another."[12]

One significant way in which children seek to actualize themselves is by setting goals that align them with causes and issues that they consider important. "We have a deep capacity of caring for others, for protecting, encouraging, and for helping them grow and to find meaning and satisfaction in their lives. If we do not use this capacity we feel incomplete and unsatisfied."[13]

It is a mistake to assume that young children are not capable of thinking seriously about life or that they are unaware of the problems that exist in our society. Even young children are not exempt from personal conflicts. Neither are they oblivious to problems arising out of group relationships. They are more concerned about environmental problems

---

11. Kenneth H. Hoover and Paul M. Hollingsworth, *Learning and Teaching in the Elementary School* (Boston: Allyn & Bacon, Inc., 1970), p. 9.

12. Clyde Inez Martin, *An Elementary School Social Studies Program* (Austin: The University of Texas Press, 1963), p. 26.

13. Gale, op. cit., pp. 115–116.

than are most adults. Books have the power to direct their boundless creative energy into causes that lead to self-realization while helping other people. Mildred A. Dawson says of literature teachers:

> "We can build lifetime interests, provide future adults with a soul-satisfying means of recreation in the leisuretime hours ahead, build an inclination to find answers to personal problems by turning to the philosophers and perceptive expressers of wise action."[14]

A. A. Milne captured the essence of bibliotherapy long before the term was coined. Once Pooh Bear visited Rabbit and ate so much honey that he became wedged in the hole on his way out:

> Bear began to sigh, and then found he couldn't because he was so tightly stuck; and a tear rolled down his eye, as he said: "Then would you read a Sustaining Book, such as would help and comfort a Wedged Bear in Great Tightness?" So for a week Christopher Robin read that sort of book at the North end of Pooh. . . .[15]

All too often during life children find themselves "in a great tightness." It is a good friend who will hand them a sustaining book, or better yet, read one to them. Any teacher who recognizes a child's problems, pinpoints a book that might be helpful, and brings the two together in an unobtrusive manner is not only a good friend to the child, but is, at the same time, operating at a high level of professionalism.

Cushla and Her Books

Cushla and Her Books,[16] by Dorothy Butler of New Zealand, was first published in the United Kingdom in 1979. Published in this country in 1980 by The Horn Book, Inc., it has received wide acclaim for its scholarly approach to the role of literature in a child's development. It is a sensitive account of two parents who read aloud from children's books to placate their seriously ill and severely retarded daughter. The results were astounding.

Cushla was a restless and fretful baby and her mother began reading books as a way of soothing her to sleep. Since both her mother and grandmother were scholars and collectors of children's literature, Cushla was hearing the language and content of some of the finest books created for

---

14. Mildred A. Dawson, "Oral Interpretation," *Elementary English* 45 (1968):287.

15. A. Milne, *The World of Pooh* (New York: E. P. Dutton & Co., Inc., 1957), pp. 32–33.

16. Dorothy Butler, *Cushla and Her Books* (Boston: The Horn Book, Inc., 1980.)

For a young reader, a sensitive illustration of this type
helps to heighten the emotional appeal of the story.
(From *Annie and the Old One,* written by Miska Miles and
illustrated by Peter Parnall. Reproduced by permission of
Little, Brown, and Company in association with The
Atlantic Monthly Press. Illustration copyright © 1975 by
Peter Parnall.)

children. The almost constant reading began when Cushla was four
months old. The intent was to calm and quiet the infant rather than instruct her.

Book characters became Cushla's constant companions, bringing
warmth and color, security and stability into a young life that was plagued
by pain and frustration. Her book friends were able to go with her "into
the dark and lonely places where others could not follow."

At three years, eight months, Cushla's intelligence test scores ranked
her as well above average, but more important, she had turned out to be
a happy, well-adjusted child with many real-life friends. Parental love
and book experiences had been the key factors in her development.

Cushla and Her Books contains color illustrations from Cushla's favorite books and information about titles, authors, and publishers. Detailed charts of Cushla's interaction with individual books will be
extremely helpful to persons who are interested in child development
and children's literature.

A young boy attempts to understand the change his grandfather undergoes as a result of serious illness and lengthy hospitalization. From *First One Foot, Now the Other* by Tomie dePaola. (Reprinted by permission of G. P. Putnam's Sons from *Now One Foot, Now the Other* by Tomie dePaola. Copyright © 1981 by Tomie dePaola.)

The Personal Problems of Children

Many children in today's classrooms are burdened with personal problems brought on by pressures and circumstances over which they have no control. Some of them are ill. Others are plagued by failures at every turn. A number of children find it almost impossible to make friends. Some children have so little security that they seem to live in a constant state of fear and anxiety. With the prevalence of divorce in this country, more and more children live in single-parent homes. And, as has always been the case, some children must face the traumatic experience of death in the family. The problems go on and on. Most of today's teachers would agree that our rosy view of the happy, carefree world of childhood is largely a myth.

To ignore the problems of children we teach, to minimize and make light of them or, conversely, to be too hasty in turning them over to specialists is to shirk our responsibility as a child's most accessible and effective counselor.

Any teacher can be a good listener, a sounding board, a nonpunishing audience. The classroom teacher is always in a position to reassure, console, and encourage a troubled child. Books can also help. When good books are read and story characters are found to experience similar problems, the child may come to the realization that such problems are universal, and that people have always struggled and coped with them.

Obviously, there is not room here to discuss all problems and all books, but a few examples are given in order to introduce beginning teachers to the idea of bibliotherapy. A bibliography is provided at the end of the chapter for those who would like to probe the subject a bit more deeply.

CHILDREN'S BOOKS FOR BIBLIOTHERAPY

LONELINESS

Best Friends for Frances, written by Russell Hoban; illustrated by
Lillian Hoban. New York: Harper & Row, Publishers, 1969.

> When Albert forms a "no girls" baseball game, Frances counterattacks with
> a "no boys" picnic. Her plan works and Albert begs to come along, but Frances
> holds out for some commitments that definitely improve Albert's behavior.
> Little sister, Gloria, manages to get in on the fun every time she can.

Best Friends, written by Miriam Cohen; illustrated by Lillian Hoban.
New York: The Macmillan Company, 1971.

> A companion book to the one above. Of identical size and format, it features
> the same boy now comfortably situated in school and with a dependable best
> friend. Note: The fact that Jim decides against Anna-Maria as a best friend
> because she is a girl is a bit of bias that should be explored by the teacher
> and openly discussed with children.

Frog and Toad Are Friends, written and illustrated by Arnold Lobel.
New York: Harper & Row, 1970.

> A 1971 Caldecott runner-up that portrays the strength of the warm friend-
> ship between Frog and Toad. The text describes their friendship, and pastel
> shades of spring make a nice background for their activities.

Jafta—The Town, written by Hugh Lewin; illustrated by Lisa Kopper.
Minneapolis: Carolrhoda Books, Inc., 1984.

> Jafta is a young boy who leaves his rural home in South Africa to travel to a
> large city where his father works in a factory. His mother explains, "There
> are more people in town, you know, than ants in an anthill, all going hurry
> hurry and not talking to one another." Jafta is fascinated by his father's room,
> his workplace, and his friends. Best of all, he is permitted to attend a profes-
> sional soccer match with his father. A good story to help children understand
> that not all families can live together under the same roof.

My Friend John, written by Charlotte Zolotow; illustrated by Ben
Shecter. New York: Harper & Row, Publishers, 1968.

> John and his friend share everything with each other and know everything
> about each other. "John is my best friend and I'm his and everything that's
> important about each other we like."

Lonesome Little Colt, written and illustrated by C. W. Anderson. New
York: The Macmillan Company, 1961.

> Each pony on the farm is paired up with its own little colt and the colts are
> very happy, all except one. His mother has died and left him without anyone.
> He is very lonely until the day he is happily adopted by a pony who has lost
> her own colt.

Someone New, written by Charlotte Zolotow; illustrated by Erik
Blegvad. New York: Harper & Row, Publishers, 1978.

> The boy in this story is changing, growing up. He packs away his baby toys
> and takes a quiet walk with his friend, Jack. He finally realizes that he has
> packed his old self in with the toys. He is someone new.

The White Marble, written by Charlotte Zolotow; illustrated by Lilian Obligado. New York: Abelard-Schuman, 1962.

> An unusual story of friendship between a young boy and girl whose parents watch them run and play without realizing the intensity of their feelings for each other. A white marble is the treasured keepsake the boy gives to the girl at the end of the outing. A beautifully sensitive story of what adults mistakenly call "puppy love." Suitable for upper primary and above.

Will I Have a Friend?, written by Miriam Cohen; illustrated by Lillian Hoban. New York: The Macmillan Company, 1967.

> A simply told story of a boy's misgivings about the first day of school and whether or not he will have a friend. Excellent multiracial illustrations by a celebrated artist.

Youngest One, written and illustrated by Taro Yashima. New York: Viking Press, 1962.

> Step by step, Youngest One overcomes his shyness to begin a friendship with Momo. When he finds courage enough to keep his eyes open and to look at her, he finds, "Sure enough, right there, smiling eyes in Momo's face were looking straight at him! AND Bobby smiled right back."

DEATH OF FRIEND OR RELATIVE

Annie and the Old One, written by Miska Miles; illustrated by Peter Parnall. Boston: Little, Brown and Company, 1971.

> The best part of Annie's Navajo world were the evenings when she sat at her ancient grandmother's feet and listened to stories of long ago. When the grandmother prophesies that she will go to Mother Earth when the new rug is taken from the loom, Annie tries to delay the weaving. A young girl faces the death of a loved one and copes with her grief.

The Dead Bird, written by Margaret Wise Brown; illustrated by Remy Charlip. New York: Young Scott Books, 1965.

> A dead bird found by a group of sensitive children is given a proper funeral and burial with flowers, songs, kind words, and an inscribed headstone. The day comes when they forget the bird and go on about their play.

The Dead Tree, written by Alvin Tresselt; illustrated by Charles Robinson, New York: Parents' Magazine Press, 1972.

> Even as the old oak tree grew, death gnawed at its heart. A beautiful story that explains in a very natural way that all living things begin dying from the very beginning of life. Sensitively told and scientifically accurate. The conclusion offers a satisfying hope: "On the ground there remained only a brown ghost of richer loam where the proud tree had come to rest."

First Snow, written by Helen Coutant; illustrated by Vo-Dinh. New York: Alfred A. Knopf, 1974.

> Lien is a little Vietnamese girl who has moved with her family to New England where she anxiously awaits the first snow of the season. Lien's dying grandmother helps her to understand the Buddhist view of life and death, that they are but two parts of the same thing.

Growing Time, written by Sandol Stoddard Warburg; illustrated by Leonard Weisgard. Boston: Houghton Mifflin Company, 1969.

> Jamie goes through a long period of sadness and bitterness when his dog dies of old age—a dog that had been his lifelong companion. Granny explains that the spirit of something you love can never die. Jamie finally warms up to his new puppy and begins to accept the continuity of life.

The Happy Funeral, written by Eve Bunting; illustrated by Vo-Dinh Mai. New York: Harper & Row Publishers, Inc., 1982.

> A young Chinese-American girl fails to understand the concept of a "happy funeral." But her mother explains, "when someone is very old and has lived a good life, he is happy to go." Eve Bunting writes of the ancient grandfather's dying and death in a gentle, yet realistic way. She describes the funeral home visit, the funeral procession, and the funeral service in a kindly, illustrative manner. An excellent book to help children understand and cope with the sorrow of loss.

Life and Death, by Herbert S. Zim and Sonia Bleeker. New York: William Morrow and Company, 1970.

> A science–social studies book describing the aging and dying process of plants, animals, and human beings. It contains an interesting section on funeral and mourning customs in various cultures of the world. Zim's conclusion: Since death always comes, people have learned to expect it and accept it. Day by day, they try to add joy in living for themselves and for their relatives and friends. People who are loved and have useful, happy lives come to accept all of life, including its end.

Lifetimes, written by Bryan Mellonie; illustrated by Robert Ingpen. New York: Bantam Books, 1983.

> A book for parents and teachers to use in explaining death to young children—the death of a friend, a relative, or a pet. It explains that dying is a part of life and tells about beginnings and endings with living in between. Lovely paintings illustrate the lifetimes of plants, animals, and people. Written in a simple, poetic style easy enough for beginning readers.

The Magic Moth, by Virginia Lee. New York: The Seabury Press, 1972.

> A close, warm family helps six-year-old Mark-O to cope with his grief and to adjust to the death of his sister. On the night of the sister's death, a moth emerges from a cocoon she has kept by her bedside, and Mark-O believes that somehow her spirit lives on. The moth is a sign. He realizes that they are not saying good-bye to Maryanne, but beginning to remember her forever.

A Taste of Blackberries, written by Doris Buchanan Smith; illustrated by Charles Robinson. New York: Thomas Y. Crowell, 1973.

> The sensitive story of a young boy who faces grief and guilt at surviving the accidental death of his closest friend. One of the best books for children to show how the spirit and personality of a person lives on to provide companionship to loved ones after death.

Why Did He Die?, written by Audrey Harris; illustrated by Susan Dalke. Minneapolis: Lerner Publications Company, 1965.

> Jim's mother makes a heartfelt effort to explain to him why his grandfather died. She explains death as necessary in the natural order of things. Written in rhyming verse.

FEAR AND ANXIETY

Crow Boy, written and illustrated by Taro Yashima. New York: The Viking Press, 1955.

> Chibi is an "outsider" in his school and cannot make friends with the other children. An understanding teacher discovers a secret talent of Chibi's that wins him respect and banishes his loneliness.

Ira Sleeps Over, written and illustrated by Bernard Waber. New York: Scholastic Book Services, 1975.

> Ira has a big problem. He has never spent the night away from home or a night without his teddy bear. If he accepts Reggie's invitation to sleep over, will he be afraid? A humorous story that makes a security object acceptable.

The Monster That Grew Small, retold by Joan Grant and illustrated by Jill Karla Schwarz. New York: Lothrop, Lee & Shepard Books, 1987.

> This Egyptian folktale is the story of a young boy who is able to conquer his fear of the jungle by systematically facing each "monster" he fears most, one by one. A beautifully illustrated book that contains every classic element of a traditional folktale.

Nannabah's Friend, written by Marianne Perrine; illustrated by Leonard Weisgard. Boston: Houghton Mifflin Co., 1970.

> Nannabah dreads the day when she will be old enough to take the sheep into the canyon alone. Herding sheep is a lonely, frightening job for a small girl. Her grandfather says a Navajo prayer "to help you when you walk alone." Nannabah proves her courage and eventually makes friends with another young shepherdess in the canyon.

Oh, the Places You'll Go!, Dr. Seuss, Random House, 1990.

> Through his unique verse and pictures, Dr. Seuss points to the ups and downs of life and encourages us to find the success that lies within. He offers his own version of advice for succeeding in life; weathering fear, confusion and loneliness; and being in charge of our actions.

Swimmy, written and illustrated by Leo Leonni. New York: Pantheon Books, Inc., 1963.

> Swimmy, a frightened and lonely little black fish, explores the depths of the ocean to find a family he can adopt. When he finds a family of fish with whom he can swim, he uses his intelligence and creativity to teach his new brothers and sisters a way to protect themselves from larger fish. Lovely illustrations by a famous artist.

Sylvester and the Magic Pebble, written and illustrated by William Steig. New York: Simon & Schuster, 1969.

> Sylvester Duncan is a young donkey who lives with his parents at Acorn Road in Oatsdale. A mishap with a magic pebble causes him to become separated from his parents. The reunion is deeply satisfying.

Time of Wonder, written and illustrated by Robert McCloskey. New York: The Viking Press, 1957.

> This beautiful book of watercolor paintings tells the story of life on a Maine island before and after a hurricane. An excellent account is given of the way parents protect children during a frightening crisis.

Divorce

Breakfast with My Father, written by Ron Roy; illustrated by Troy Howard. New York: Houghton Mifflin, 1980.

> David's father leaves home and David is afraid he will never see him again. But the Saturday morning breakfast with his father becomes a happy ritual. The story shows an entire family in crisis, attempting to solve its problems together.

Emily and the Klunky Baby and the Next Door Dog, written by Joan Lexau; illustrated by Martha Alexander. New York: Dial Press, 1972.

> Emily, a victim of divorce, takes her baby brother and goes in search of their absent father; the mother is too busy to play with them. A story that shows the impact of divorce from a child's viewpoint.

A Friend Can Help, written by Terry Berger; illustrated by Heinz Kluetmeier. Milwaukee: Raintree Publishers, Ltd., 1974.

> Susan becomes a sympathetic listener for her friend whose parents have divorced. The story is told in the first person by Susan's friend.

Where Is Daddy? The Story of a Divorce, written and illustrated by Susan Perl. Boston: Beacon Press, 1969.

> A preschool child experiences the classic feelings of guilt that bother so many young children whose parents divorce. A grandmother becomes an important source of strength to the little girl.

Illness and Hospitalization

Curious George Goes to the Hospital, written and illustrated by Hans Augusto Rey. New York: Houghton Mifflin Co., 1966.

> Curious George, a favorite character from children's books, swallows a puzzle piece and has to have it surgically removed. Realistic, but humorous account of nurses, doctors, and other hospital personnel.

Love You Forever, written by Robert Munsch; illustrated by Sheila McGraw. Willowdale, Ontario, Canada: Firefly Books Ltd., 1986.

> This is a sensitive story of the relationship between a mother and her son. A little boy goes through all the stages of childhood while his mother takes care of him. As he grows to adulthood and his mother ages, their roles are

gradually reversed and he is shown gently caring for her. An excellent book to help children understand the process and problems of aging. Written by a popular, award-winning Canadian writer for children.

Madeline, written and illustrated by Ludwig Bemelmans. New York: The Viking Press, 1939.

Madeline lives in a Paris convent with eleven other girls. She becomes the envy of all others when an ambulance rushes her to the hospital for an appendectomy.

Now One Foot, Now the Other, written and illustrated by Tomie dePaola. New York: G. P. Putnam's Sons, 1981.

When Bobby's grandfather suffers a stroke, Bobby begins to help him with some of the things his grandfather had helped him learn—how to eat by himself, to talk, and to walk again.

A Visit from Dr. Katz, written by Ursula K. Le Guin; illustrated by Ann Barrow. New York: Atheneum, 1988.

Marianne is sick with the flu and has to stay in bed, but her mother sends in Marianne's two cats to make her feel better. They purr and walk around on the sickbed, entertaining her until she falls asleep. A soothing story to read aloud to a sick child, or to one who is not sick for that matter.

Overcoming Personal Failure

Alexander and the Terrible, Horrible, No Good, Very Bad Day, written by Judith Viorst; illustrated by Ray Cruz. New York: Atheneum, 1979.

Alexander knows it is going to be a terrible, horrible, no good, very bad day when he wakes up with gum in his hair. As the day progresses, things get worse. The best he can hope for is a better day tomorrow.

Benjie on His Own, written by Joan Lexau; illustrated by Don Bolognese. New York: The Dial Press, 1970.

Old enough to be in school for the first time, Benjie is faced with the problem of finding his way home in the large crowded city. He finds that independence can be both painful and pleasant.

The Country Artist: A Story about Beatrix Potter, written by David R. Collins; illustrated by Karen Ritz. Minneapolis: Carolrhoda Books, Inc., 1989.

For teachers seeking biographies easy enough for young readers, this series of books is a godsend. The print is large. The content is factual, interestingly written, and rich with dialogue—features preferred by children. Other books in the "Creative Minds" series are: *To the Point: A Story about E. B. White; Between Two Worlds: A Story about Pearl Buck; Good Morning, Mr. President: A Story about Carl Sandburg; What Do You Mean?: A Story about Noah Webster; What Are You Figuring Now?: A Story about Benjamin Banneker; Go Free or Die: A Story about Harriet Tubman; Walking the Road to Freedom: A Story about Sojourner Truth; America, I Hear You: A Story about George Gershwin; Raggin': A Story about Scott Joplin; Click!:*

A Story about George Eastman; We'll Race You, Henry: A Story about Henry Ford; A Pocketful of Goobers: A Story about George Washington Carver; and *Shoes for Everyone: A Story about Jan Matzeliger.*

Don't Feel Sorry for Paul, written and photographed by Bernard Wolf. New York: J. B. Lippincott Company, 1974.

> This real-life account of Paul Jockimo shows the challenges faced every day by a child who is orthopedically handicapped. Sometimes his classmates make unkind remarks, and sometimes people treat him with pity. Such reactions hurt Paul, but he is able to triumph over them when his mother says, "Don't feel sorry for Paul. He doesn't need it."

Hey, Al, written by Arthur Yorinks; illustrated by Richard Egielski. New York: Farrar, Straus and Giroux, 1986.

> Al and his dog Eddie struggle in poverty and misery until an act of magic transports them to a lush paradise. But even a life of ease and luxury has its pitfalls. The two make their way back home and find it the best place after all. The last illustration shows them painting and repairing their single room on the West Side: "Paradise lost is sometimes Heaven found." The exotic tropical flowers and foliage pictured could well be a point of departure for a frieze-making project (see chapter 6).

I Have a Sister My Sister Is Deaf, written by Jeanne Whitehouse Peterson; illustrated by Deborah Kogan Ray. New York: Harper & Row, Publishers, Inc., 1977.

> A young girl describes how her younger deaf sister copes with everyday life and how her deafness impacts on the entire family. (The author tells a true story of her relationship with a little sister who actually was totally deaf.) A gentle, poignant book simply written for young readers and excellent for use with both deaf and hearing children.

If I Were in Charge of the World and Other Worries, written by Judith Viorst; illustrated by Lynne Cherry. New York: Atheneum, 1981.

> This is a collection of lighthearted poems about the worries and concerns that plague us all at one time or another. The author calls it a book of "poems for children and their parents."

Mr. President: A Book of U.S. Presidents, written by George Sullivan; illustrated by individual photographers. New York: Scholastic Inc., 1989.

> Brief, lively biographical sketches introduce young readers to our forty-one presidents and the big events that took place during their terms of office. Also included are some of the funny things that made the presidents seem human. For example "Calvin Coolidge never wasted words. 'You must talk with me, Mr. Coolidge,' a woman once pleaded. 'I made a bet that I could get more than two words out of you.' President Coolidge looked straight at her. 'You lose,' he said." The book outlines the process of electing a president of the United States. Suitable for upper primary and above.

One Step Two, written by Charlotte Zolotow; illustrated by Cindy
Wheeler. New York: Lothrop, Lee & Shepard Books, 1981.

> A little girl and her mother share a medley of discoveries as they walk down
> the street from their house to the corner. It is early on a spring morning.
> "See that!" says the little girl. "What?" asks the mother. A yellow crocus
> appears in the grass. And then they take one step or two before the next
> discovery interrupts their walk. Anyone who has ever taken a walk with a
> young child will appreciate the realism of this Zolotow masterpiece.

Ragtime Tumpie, written by Alan Schroeder; illustrated by Bernie
Fuchs, Boston: Little, Brown and Company, 1989.

> A biographical picture book depicting the childhood of Josephine Baker, the
> legendary ragtime entertainer who began dancing on the streets of St. Louis
> at the turn of the century. "All summer long she danced barefoot up and
> down the hot St. Louis sidewalks." Luminous, full-page paintings capture
> the mood and rhythm of the young black girl's story.

Someday, written by Charlotte Zolotow; illustrated by Arnold Lobel.
New York: Harper & Row, Publishers, 1965.

> A little girl dreams of being successful: "Someday I'm going to be practicing
> the piano and the lady across the street will call and say, 'Please play that
> beautiful piece again.' " For the time being, however, it's fun to dream of
> being a hit. Zolotow has managed to capture the pipe dreams of both chil-
> dren and adults.

The Wednesday Surprise, written by Eve Bunting; illustrated by
Donald Carrick. New York: Houghton Mifflin Company, 1989.

> On Wednesday nights, Grandma rides the bus across town to sit with Anna.
> She always brings a bag of books to read to her granddaughter. The surprise
> is that Anna is teaching her grandmother to read. It is a happy day indeed
> for both Anna and her grandmother when Grandma reads aloud and acts out
> *The Velveteen Rabbit* for the rest of the family. The problem of illiteracy is
> told in a child's language and from a child's point of view.

Whistle for Willie, written and illustrated by Ezra Jack Keats. New
York: The Viking Press, 1964.

> Peter, a small black boy, accomplishes the important task of learning to
> whistle. Now he will be able to call his dog, Willie. A realistic story of pa-
> tient effort and achievement.

Yonie Wondernose, written and illustrated by Marguerite de Angeli.
Garden City, N.Y.: Doubleday and Company, Inc., 1944.

> Circumstances cause Yonie, a seven-year-old Pennsylvania Dutch boy, to
> assume responsibility for taking care of his grandmother, his mother, and
> sisters. His problems are compounded when lightning strikes the barn and
> the animals have to be evacuated. An exciting story of an Amish boy's growing
> maturity.

BIBLIOGRAPHY

Ashley, L. F. "Bibliotherapy, etc." *Language Arts,* April 1978.

Bernstein, Joanne E. *Loss and How to Cope with It.* New York: Houghton Mifflin/ Clarion, 1977.

Biber, Barbara. *Young Deprived Children and Their Educational Needs.* Washington, D.C.: Association for Childhood Education International, 1967.

Bixby, William. *A World You Can Live In: Our Ecological Past, Present, and Future.* New York: David McKay Co., Inc., 1971.

Butler, Dorothy. *Cushla and Her Books.* Boston: The Horn Book, Inc., 1980.

Cullinan, Bernice E. *Literature and the Child.* New York: Harcourt Brace Jovanovich, 1981.

Dawson, Mildred A. "Oral Interpretation." *Elementary English* 45 (1968):287–288.

Dreyer, Sharon Spredemann. *The Book Finder.* Circle Pines, Minn.: American Guidance Service, 1977.

Epstein, Sherrie L., Elliott D. Landau, and Ann Plaat Stone. *Child Development Through Literature.* Englewood Cliffs, N.J.: Prentice-Hall, Inc., 1972.

Fraenkel, Jack R. *How to Teach About Values: An Analytic Approach.* Englewood Cliffs, N.J.: Prentice-Hall, Inc., 1977.

Frost, Joe L., and Glenn R. Hawkes, ed. *The Disadvantaged Child, Issues and Innovations.* Boston: Houghton Mifflin Co., 1966.

Fuller, Muriel, ed. *More Junior Authors.* New York: The H. W. Wilson Co., 1963.

Gale, Raymond F. *Developmental Behavior, A Humanistic Approach.* New York: The Macmillan Co., 1969.

Georgiou, Constantine. *Children and Their Literature.* Englewood Cliffs, N.J.: Prentice-Hall, Inc., 1969.

Hoagland, Joan. "Bibliotherapy: Aiding Children in Personality Development." *Elementary English,* July 1972.

Hoover, Kenneth H., and Paul M. Hollingsworth. *Learning and Teaching in the Elementary School.* Boston: Allyn & Bacon, Inc., 1970.

Martin, Clyde Inez. *An Elementary School Social Studies Program.* Austin: The University of Texas Press, 1963.

Maslow, Abraham H. *Toward a Psychology of Being.* Princeton, N.J.: D. Van Nostrand Co., Inc., 1968.

Milne, A. A. *The World of Pooh.* New York: E. P. Dutton & Co., 1957.

Moody, Mildred T., and Hilda K. Limper, *Bibliotherapy: Methods and Materials.* Chicago: American Library Association, 1971.

Norton, Donna. *Through the Eyes of a Child: An Introduction to Children's Literature.* 2d ed. Columbus, Ohio: Merrill Publishing Co., 1987.

Russell, David, and Caroline Shrodes. "Contributions of Research in Bibliotherapy to the Language Arts Program." *School Review* 68 (1950).

Shepherd, Tony, and Lynn B. Iles. "What is Bibliotherapy?" *Language Arts* 53 (1976).

10

"Can You Suggest a Book?":

Helping Parents in the Selection and Use of Children's Books

Long before children reach school age, their attitudes and aptitudes for reading have been formulated. If they have been fortunate enough to flourish and thrive in an atmosphere of language where songs, rhymes, conversations, stories, and books were daily fare, their chances of success in the formal reading program are very good. To such children, books have already brought pleasure, information, and solace; they see them as a necessary and important part of life.

Practically speaking, children who have grown up with books know how to hold a book, how to turn its pages, and how to read left to right and top to bottom. They have a sense of the relationship between text and pictures. They can point out small details in illustrations, repeat a rhythmic refrain, and recognize the sequential development of a story. More important, such children are usually able to reason, deduct, and express thoughts in a fluent, efficient manner. In essence, they are ready to read.

A readiness to enter the school's reading program eagerly and confidently is not born out of a heavy-handed effort on the part of parents, but out of the mutual enjoyment of reading material—spontaneous, informal experiences with literature that were begun in infancy and continued throughout early childhood.

Well before children celebrate the first birthday, they should be introduced to Mother Goose rhymes and to other nursery rhythms and songs by parents and other members of the family who care for them. As soon as children begin to talk, they will repeat the sounds they have come to recognize. At first the sounds are unintelligible, but with time and practice they become more and more distinct. "The child seems to be playing with the sounds. And all the time he is learning to distinguish between sounds that are very much alike or easily confused. He is developing a sharp ear for differences. All of this will help him with his talking and later, with his reading."[1]

Once children have matured to the point that they are willing to sit still for several minutes at a time looking at the illustrations in books, they are ready for listening to simple, brief, uncomplicated stories of the type found in picture books. *Goodnight Moon, Little Hippo, All Falling Down, Make Way for Ducklings, Play with Me, Two Lonely Ducks,* and *How, Hippo!* are examples of the kind of books that might be used as "baby's first books," and they are all excellent for reading aloud as part of the bedtime ritual.

When reading aloud to a young child, the adult should make certain that the child is in a position not only to see the pictures but also to have full access to the book. He or she should be allowed to help turn the pages of the book and to point out items of interest along the way. The reading should be done at a leisurely pace, with the child setting the tone, and it should be continued only so long as the child remains interested and attentive. Above all, the experience ought to bring pleasure to both the reader and the listener; if it fails to do so, the book should be put aside until a later date. Perhaps a different book might be needed to set matters aright.

As the reading-aloud practice continues, the child enjoys having new books introduced but also likes to request old favorites. Some books are heard so often that a child commits them to memory and is able to quote them almost verbatim. The nearer a child approaches the ability to read on his or her own, the more interested he or she becomes in the language of the book, and the more curious about the printed symbols. But because children do not proceed through the developmental stages of reading readiness at the same pace, it is risky business to generalize about them. On the other hand, if we recognize them as approximations only, some generalizations can be helpful in the study of reading readiness. The accompanying chart shows an outline of concepts that are likely to have developed when books have been used routinely with young children.[2]

1. Nancy Larrick. *A Parent's Guide to Children's Reading,* 5th ed. (New York: Pocket Books, 1983), p. 11.

2. Chart based on information from *Foundations for Reading: Informal Pre-Reading Procedures,* by Marion Monroe and Bernice Rogers. (Glenview, Ill.: Scott, Foresman & Co., 1964), pp. 2–23. Copyright © 1964 by Scott, Foresman & Co. Reprinted by permission of the publisher.

Books and Concept Development

The First Year

Book as an Object	Books are made of interesting material. Books can be tasted, torn, manipulated.
Content of Book	Books contain brightly colored patterns. Twelve-month-old may appear to recognize realistic pictures of familiar objects.
Printed Symbols	No notice is given of printing.

From Twelve to Fifteen Months

Book as an Object	Books contain pages to be turned. Books that survive destruction may become well-loved objects.
Content of Book	Pictures resemble familiar objects. Pictures are identified in response to adult naming.
Printed Symbols	No notice is given of printing.

From Fifteen to Eighteen Months

Book as an Object	Books are to be taken care of. Tearing is usually due to lack of motor control.
Content of Book	Pictures represent objects both familiar and unfamiliar. Pictures of unfamiliar objects arouse curiosity. A few children begin to notice that pictures have a top and bottom. Pictures of familiar objects are named spontaneously. Pictures of unfamiliar objects are noticed to serve as a means of vocabulary building. Pictures are interpreted in a very simple way in terms of action or in terms of the sound the object makes.
Printed Symbols	Very rarely is notice given to printing.

From Eighteen to Twenty-four Months

Book as an Object	The child continues to develop concepts of good care of books (if care of books is taught). Turns pages carefully and does not tear them. Realizes that the book has a front and back.
Content of Book	Pictures have a top and a bottom. Pictures do more than represent objects; they suggest action and events taking place in sequence—they tell a story. Adults tell stories about the pictures. The same language is used with reference to each picture. The events portrayed by pictures are continuous from one picture to the next. The process of looking at books is called "reading."
Printed Symbols	Two-year-olds begin to show an awareness of print— they notice that there is something else on the page besides the pictures.

From Two to Three Years

Book as an Object	Books are to be put away after use. Books are decorated with color.
Content of Book	Pictured characters often seem as real as actual people. The events pictured or told about can make one feel happy or sad or angry. Books give information one needs to know about things like trains and airplanes. The language adults use in reading books is constant for each page or picture. This language can be remembered and retold to one's self, especially if the language contains catchy sounds and jingles and is very simple and repetitive.
Printed Symbols	Some children may notice the capital letters in alphabet books, but they rarely attempt to name them.

From Three to Six Years

Book as an Object	Concepts of book care are extended. The tendency to mark in books is decreasing.
Content of Book	The language value of books now comes to the foreground and begins to rival the picture to some extent, especially if the child has good verbal ability. Pictures and stories stimulate an abundant flow of ideas and expression from the child, usually of the "why" or explanatory type. The child likes to have a clear distinction made between fantasy and reality, since he or she is still not too sure of the difference. Language used in books is often memorized and repeated.
Printed Symbols	The child begins to recognize that the printed text tells the reader what to say. Print is differentiated roughly from writing. Little notice is taken of the orientation of a letter. Letters are frequently drawn or copied in reverse as well as in correct orientation.

Once parents recognize that their child's success in reading is greatly influenced by preschool experiences with literature, the problem becomes one of bringing parent and child and book together often enough to make a difference. In most modern households, this is no easy matter. Urie Bronfenbrenner writes:

> In today's world, parents find themselves at the mercy of a society which imposes pressures and priorities that allow neither time nor place for meaningful activities and relations between children and adults, which downgrade the role of parents and the functions of parenthood, and which prevent the parent from doing the things he wants to do as a guide, friend and companion to his children.[3]

Regardless of the pressures and demands of daily living, adults have a continuing responsibility to each generation of children for providing them with the many kinds of experiences necessary for normal growth and development. At the same time, they are also obligated to protect

---

3. Urie Bronfenbrenner, "Who Cares for America's Children?" *Young Children* (1971) vol. 15:158.

them, as much as possible, from harsh experiences that are limiting, negative, and damaging. Rudolph and Cohen point out that in spite of the busy, rushed lives of parents, various home operations and activities that take place naturally during the course of a day can enrich a child's background of experiences:

> These could include errands to repair shops, really helping once in a while with cooking and cleaning or animal feeding, taking part in shopping for food, clothes and housewares, or taking a trip to the father's place of work. The mother, having the intimate relation with the child and being herself really involved in all these activities, exerts greater influence than she realizes on the preschool child's attitudes toward responsibility and toward work and workers in ethical as well as material standards.[4]

It takes an understanding teacher to assure parents of the influence that everyday home experiences exert on the lives of their children. They can be of greater value when parents no longer take these experiences for granted but recognize them as the most powerful force in shaping the personality of a child. "Thus, during daily activities and companionship a mother is the greatest teacher to a kindergartener; she can bring much stimulation to her child if she can be helped to see where the possibilities are."[5]

Teachers must begin to look on parents as the child's first and most important teachers, and moreover, parents must begin to see themselves in this light. Certainly, there can be no justification for the wall of separation that has long existed between home and school. What young children need most are parents, teachers, and other supportive adults who will plan together, work together, and coordinate their energies into one great effort on their behalf. The following suggestions are offered as ways parents and teachers can reinforce and complement each other in providing a foundation of language and literature for young children.

How Parents Can Help

1. Create a home library for each child in the family. Enlarge the collection as he or she grows by adding the best books available for his or her age level. House books in wide shelves face out with the colorful jackets showing. Because children like owning their own titles, and are known to read more in books they own, it is well to separate their books from those belonging to older members of the family (figs. 10.1 and 10.2).

---

4. Marguerita Rudolph and Dorothy H. Cohen, *Kindergarten, A Year of Learning* (New York: Appleton-Century-Crofts, 1964), pp. 370–371.

5. Ibid., p. 371.

Figure 10.1.   Large soap boxes, cut as shown, make sturdy containers for books and magazines. Types of books may be grouped together to help teach classification of literature.

Figure 10.2.   Books should be placed at the eye level of the children no matter how young they are. There are countless books suitable for infants and toddlers to be found in bookstores and libraries. (Photography by Pete Churton of *The Beaumont Enterprise.*)

2. Read aloud and tell stories to young children on a day-to-day basis. If the books are carefully chosen, story time can be enjoyable for all members of the family. The mark of a good book for young children is that it also contains characteristics appealing to older children and adults (fig. 10.3).

3. Provide a time and place for each child in the family to look at books or read in quietness and privacy. Many failures in reading have been traced to a shortage of time available in which to practice the skills of reading in self-selected materials.

Figure 10.3.   A preschool child listens to a cassette of the familiar voice of one of her parents reading a picture book. (Courtesy of Michael Coody.)

4. As soon as children are old enough to enjoy picture books, take them to the library and acquire a card. Help them select books to be checked out. Make each excursion to the library a pleasant experience and allow plenty of time for browsing. Lifelong attitudes toward books and reading are being formed.

5. Take advantage of bookmobile services in your community. Just going inside a bookmobile can be a memorable experience for a child. In *Tough Enough,* Ruth and Latrobe Carroll describe the bookmobile's arrival at the Tatum farm.

Once every three weeks, the bookmobile would go pushing up the road toward the Tatum farm. The Tatums and other mountain people would borrow books and keep them till the next time the bookmobile came. So it was really a little library on wheels.

A librarian drove it and she also kept track of the books. The mountain people called her the book lady. She always brought her lunch in a cardboard box.[6]

6. Allow your child to accompany you to a bookstore well stocked with children's books. Children may develop misconceptions if they always see books as a sideline in a pharmacy or supermarket and never enter a store whose sole interest is bookselling.

6. Ruth and Latrobe Carroll, *Tough Enough* (New York: Henry Z. Walck, Inc., 1954), p. 5.

Figure 10.4. A child's home library need not cost a fortune. Shown here is a bookcase built from scrap lumber with shelves deep enough to hold oversized books. The bookends are bricks covered with contact paper, and the reading lamp is made of a pharmacy bottle. (Courtesy of Pat Russell.)

7. Make a study of children's books by reading as many of them as possible, and by reading the reviews of contemporary books in newspapers and magazines. Children's literature can be a fascinating hobby for adults, especially if old books and foreign books are included.

8. Consider supplementing your child's library of hardback books with the less expensive paperbacks (fig. 10.4). Excellent books of all kinds are now being reproduced in paperback, and they are proving extremely popular with children. Write Scholastic Book Services, 904 Sylvan Ave., Englewood Cliffs, New Jersey, 07632 for information on the hundreds of paperbacks they publish for children.

9. Serve as an example for your child by reading newspapers, magazines, and books in his or her presence, and by pointing out items of interest from time to time. Most parents pay lip service to the value of reading, but needless to say, their actions make a greater impression.

10. Work with school officials to provide excellent central libraries for all elementary schools in your community. A statement of standards for school libraries is available from the American Library Association, 50 E. Huron St., Chicago, Illinois, 60611.

Parents as Storytellers

Informal storytelling is an effective and pleasurable way to enrich a young child's vocabulary while simultaneously building a substantial body of concepts. Tales handed down from generation to generation become a family's folklore, and the word-of-mouth quality ascribed to such stories turns them into legends. These tales are not only fascinating to children but also develop in them a sense of story in the oral tradition. Successful reading and a lasting interest in literature depend largely on such a sense of story.

One family's collection of antique Christmas balls became the point of departure for a series of stories told to a three-year-old boy. Some of the balls were more than a hundred years old, and each one represented a small piece of the family's history. One bottle-green glass ornament had been brought from Scotland to the Hill Country of Texas. It had once belonged to the child's great-great-grandmother. He was intrigued by the story of the ornament and promptly labeled it "The Grandmother Ball."

Every family has its own unique body of folktales. At every opportunity they should be carefully and deliberately transmitted to the youngest members of the family who eventually, in turn, will hand them down to their own children. Such oral, informal storytelling sets the stage for the more formal literature recorded on the printed pages of a book (fig. 10.5).

The Role of Grandparents

A ten-year-old boy recently made the evening news by advertising for a grandfather. He explained that he had no natural grandparents, that both of his parents worked long hours and he found himself with too much spare time on his hands. The new grandfather must agree to meet just two requirements: to take him fishing and to tell him stories. The piece had a happy ending; the boy found a foster grandfather who would do both. The last scene showed them together in a boat in the middle of the lake, lines in the water, and with the grandfather spinning a yarn.

Grandparents have the reputation of being the best storytellers to be found anywhere. They deserve it. After all, they know stories of all kinds; they have lived them. They know their grandchildren's history from the beginning, they are practiced storytellers, and best of all, many have the time and patience to tell stories.

Figure 10.5.   Heirloom Christmas ornaments provide the opportunity for informal storytelling and serve to transmit family folklore from one generation to the next. (Courtesy of Sarah Matheny, Bray photo.)

Charlie and Martha Shedd have created a storybook just for grandparents and their grandchildren. *Tell Me a Story* includes Bible stories, fairy tales, poems, proverbs, folktales and ministories—all streamlined for ease in telling. There is a chapter on the art of storytelling, the how to's and how not to's of "once upon a time." It is the best example of the many books now being published on "grandparenting."

How Teachers Can Help

1. Provide parents with book lists that briefly review books of various types. The lists should include titles, authors, publishers, publication dates, and prices if they are available.

2. Instruct parents in ways to take an interest inventory in order to determine their child's preferences in reading material. Show them an informal method of ascertaining the approximate readability level of a book.

3. Make the school's professional library available to parents and encourage them to take out books on child development, reading readiness, and children's literature. Provide a simple, easy-to-use check-out system for children's books. Encourage children to take home many books that portray diverse cultures and ways of life that are different from their own. Reading such books together can broaden the horizons of a family and further the cause of world understanding.

4. Subscribe to *Hornbook Magazine,* published six times a year by The Horn Book, 31 St. James Ave., Park Square Bldg., Boston, MA 02108. It reviews current books for children and contains articles on children's literature. Share the magazine with interested parents.

5. Devise a record system in which each student keeps a personal account of self-selected reading. At the semester's end, send the list or card pack home to give parents an indication of the child's achievement.

6. Under the direction of a librarian or other literature specialist, conduct a "read-in" to better acquaint parents and teachers with children's books, their authors, and illustrators.

7. Draw on local college classes of speech, drama, literature, and education for storytellers, puppeteers, actors, literature specialists, and others who are able to aid in the promotion of books and reading.

8. Assist parents in surveying book club possibilities for their children. Provide names and addresses of suitable book clubs. For information on book clubs, write the Children's Book Council, 175 Fifth Avenue, New York, New York 10010. If the school purchases books for students through book clubs, explain the program to parents and enlist their cooperation.

9. Recruit parents as volunteer storytellers and library helpers. Suggest that at least one PTA program each year be devoted to children's literature and reading. Enlist the help of parents in conducting a book fair. It is an excellent means of getting additional good books into the homes and classrooms of children. The Children's Book Council will provide information on book fairs.

10. Plan school-sponsored programs on children's literature for newspapers, radio, and television. Throughout such programs, continue to emphasize the role of parents in reading readiness.

11. Conduct a sidewalk art show of children's painting and sculpture inspired by their literature. Label each piece and display the book alongside.

12. Urge factories and companies to establish lending libraries of children's books for their employees to take home for reading aloud. (Most public relations individuals have yet to recognize this practice as a great morale booster for the entire family.)

One of the most important educational endeavors of the nineties will be the formation of parent-teacher partnerships in which young children have the security of knowing, "My parents are concerned about my education and well-being; my teachers are concerned about my education and well-being, and they are all in agreement about what is best for me." The most natural means of creating this bond of cooperation and esprit between home and school is a dynamic program of children's literature, with good books circulating among children, their parents, and teachers. "Books that will become tattered and grimy from use, not books too handsome to grovel with. Books that will make them weep, books that will rack them with hearty laughter. Books that absorb them so that they have to be shaken loose from them. Books that they will put under the pillows at night. Books that give them gooseflesh and glimpses of glory"[7] (fig. 10.6).

Figure 10.6. With a Caldecott Award book as a catalyst, two kindergarten girls experience both the form and function of language. The book they are studying is *Ox-Cart Man* by Donal Hall, illustrated by Barbara Cooney. (Courtesy of Michael Coody and David Nelson.)

---

7. Robert Lawson, "The Caldecott Medal Acceptance," *The Hornbook Magazine* 17 (1941):284.

The following self-rating instrument was designed to give a teacher an informal method of ranking the classroom literature program by using a set of recommended criteria:

Developing Appreciation for Literature Inventory (DALI)

For Primary Teachers

Circle the numeral on each five-point scale below that best describes the teaching practices under consideration. One (1) is the lowest rating and five (5) is the highest. Add total points and refer to key.

1. Do you provide a wide collection of books in the classroom that range from easy to difficult? 1 2 3 4 5

2. Do you schedule a period each day for independent reading? 1 2 3 4 5

3. Do you conduct private conferences with students in regard to self-selected reading? 1 2 3 4 5

4. Do you provide students with an efficient record system for keeping a personal account of self-selected reading? 1 2 3 4 5

5. Are your students given an opportunity for creative "reporting" on favorite books? 1 2 3 4 5

6. Do you invite resource persons to your classroom to discuss literature? 1 2 3 4 5

7. Do your students make use of puppetry to enhance literature? 1 2 3 4 5

8. Do you read aloud to students on a regular basis? 1 2 3 4 5

9. Do you use the procedure of storytelling on a regular basis? 1 2 3 4 5

10. Do you study children's books and reviews of children's books on a regular basis? 1 2 3 4 5

11. Do your students frequently write and illustrate their own books? 1 2 3 4 5

12. Do you discuss with students the parts of a book and the people who work to make a book? 1 2 3 4 5

13. Do you have an organized plan of parent involvement in the literature program? 1 2 3 4 5

14. Do you help select books for the school library and do you have a voice in determining library policy? 1 2 3 4 5

15. Do your students read widely and do they appear to enjoy the literature program? 1 2 3 4 5

Total _____

Interpret your total score as follows:

Below 50	You definitely need to enrich your literature program.
From 50 to 65	Your literature program is about average.
From 65 to 75	You have an excellent literature program.

CHILDREN'S BOOKS FOR FAMILY ENJOYMENT

All Falling Down, written by Gene Zion; illustrated by Margaret Bloy Graham. New York: Harper & Row, Publishers, 1951.

> A picture book that teaches the concept of "falling down." Snow falls down, rains falls down, leaves fall down, and so do apples. An excellent book for the youngest child who will want to add many other things that fall down.

All My Little Ducklings, written and illustrated by Monica Wellington. New York: E. P. Dutton, 1989.

> Seven yellow ducklings waddle in a line from nest to pond. In between they explore barnyard and orchard. When the day ends, they return to the familiar nest and snuggle under mother for another night. An appropriate bedtime story for the very young child.

The Alphabet Tree, written and illustrated by Leo Lionni. New York: Pantheon Books, Inc., 1968.

> The letters of the alphabet cling to the leaves of the alphabet tree without purpose until a word bug comes along and teaches them to group themselves together into words. The purple caterpillar teaches them to group the words together into an important message for all humankind.

Another Day, written and illustrated by Marie Hall Ets. New York: The Viking Press, 1953.

> All the animals in the forest perform for the little boy so that he can decide which trick is best. The most unique talent of all turns out to be the little boy's ability to laugh. Excellent for the very young child.

Beanie, written and illustrated by Ruth and Latrobe Carroll. New York: Oxford University Press, 1953.

> Beanie is the youngest member of a large mountain-farm family of Appalachia, and the only one who does not own a pet of some kind until a birthday puppy called "Tough Enough" changes all that. The story shows warm, affectionate family relationships.

Bedtime for Frances, written by Russell Hoban; illustrated by Garth Williams. New York: Harper & Row, Publishers, 1960.

> Small children will recognize themselves at bedtime as Mother and Father Badger struggle to get Frances settled down to sleep on time. Beautiful, soft drawings. The badgers appear to have a furry texture.

Better Not Get Wet, Jesse Bear, written by Nancy White Carlstrom; illustrated by Bruce Degen. New York: Macmillan Publishing Company, 1988.

> In spite of his parents' daily warning, "Better not get wet, Jesse Bear," Jesse wants more than anything to do just that. He helps a goldfish flap about, a worm squirm in a puddle, and a blackbird splash in the birdbath. Finally, on a warm summer day, Jesse is rewarded with his own wading pool. His parents say, "Better get all wet, Jesse Bear." A good choice for reading aloud at the preschool level.

The Big World and the Little House, written by Ruth Krauss; illustrated by Marc Simont. New York: Henry Schuman, Inc., 1949.

> A beautifully illustrated story of an abandoned house being transformed into a real home by a family that moves in and restores it. Throughout the book, emphasis is placed on the little house's relationship to the rest of the world, and in turn, the world's influence on the little house.

The Camel Who Took a Walk, written by Jack Tworkov; illustrated by Roger Duvoisin. New York: E. P. Dutton & Co., Inc., 1951.

> A brief, lively animal story filled with humor and suspense. Reminiscent of an old folktale. Very large print.

Danny and the Dinosaur, written and illustrated by Syd Hoff. New York: Harper & Row, Publishers, 1958.

> An easy-to-read book about a dinosaur who leaves the museum to become Danny's friend and pet. All the children are given a ride on his back, and he learns to play hide and seek with them. At the end of a wonderful day of play he goes back to the museum, leaving Danny with memories of the fun.

Death of the Iron Horse, written and illustrated by Paul Goble. New York: Bradbury Press, 1987.

> Paul Goble's words and pictures tell the story of an event in Cheyenne history in which the Indians were successful in their struggle to halt the progress of white settlers who seemed determined to take their land. The date was August 7, 1867—the only time on record that an iron horse was destroyed by Indians.

Do Not Open, written and illustrated by Brinton Turkle. New York: E. P. Dutton, 1981.

> Miss Moody, an elderly, reclusive woman, and her cat find a small dark bottle nearly hidden in the sand. It is clearly marked: DO NOT OPEN. A voice from the bottle asks, "What do you want more than anything in the world?" Should she answer the voice? Should she open the bottle? Her cat hides under the wheelbarrow. Children will be reminded of the popular Greek myth of Pandora's Box.

Ellie's Doorstep, written and illustrated by Alison Catley. New York: Barron's Educational Series, Inc., 1988.

> The story of a young girl's world of make-believe in which her imaginary playmate is a spider named Sidney. He helps his small friend cast a spell that brings her toys to life for the day. Excellent for reading aloud as a bedtime story since the book ends with the girl's father reading her a favorite story as she falls asleep. Written in verse form.

Fly Homer Fly, written and illustrated by Bill Peet. Boston: Houghton Mifflin Co., 1969.

> A farm pigeon named Homer is lured to the big city by a sparrow named Sparky. City life is not all Homer expected it to be, and he eventually makes his way back to the farm. Sparky and the other sparrows decide Homer's is a better way of life and take up residence on the farm.

Frederick, written and illustrated by Leo Lionni. New York: Pantheon Books, Inc., 1967.

> While the other field mice are working to store up nuts and grain for the long hard winter, Frederick is storing up words and colors to warm them during the cold days ahead. He is such a good storyteller they are able to see the colors "as clearly as if they had them painted in their minds."

Give a Guess, written by Mary Britton Miller; illustrated by Juliet Kepes. New York: Pantheon Books, Inc., 1957.

> A book of riddle-poems about animals, designed to be read aloud and discussed with young children. The book presents an unusual combination of art and science.

Goodnight Moon, written by Margaret Wise Brown; illustrated by Clement Hurd. New York: Harper & Row, Publishers, 1947.

> A good-night rhyme that names familiar objects found in a small child's room. The pages grow darker and darker toward the end of the book. Excellent as a bedtime story for infants and toddlers, and very good to foster oral language development.

A Gopher in the Garden and Other Animal Poems, written by Jack Prelutsky; illustrated by Robert Leydenfrost. New York: The Macmillan Co., 1967.

> Rollicking, tongue-twisting rhymes about animals of all kinds. Illustrated with humorous drawings that provide perfect accompaniment to the verses.

Grandaddy's Place, written by Helen V. Griffith; illustrated by James Stevenson. New York: Greenwillow books, 1987.

> Janetta's mother takes her to the country for a visit with Grandaddy. Gradually she becomes acquainted with him and also with the farm animals. As they begin to talk with each other, Grandaddy tells her about the mule, "You don't have to give it anything. That mule just likes you for your own self." Since the book is divided into chapters, it is an excellent one to read aloud and discuss by episodes.

Hi, Mister Robin!, written by Alvin Tresselt; illustrated by Roger
Duvoisin. New York: Lothrop, Lee & Shepard, Co., Inc., 1950.

> A red-breasted robin shows a little boy how to look and listen for the un-
> mistakable signs of spring. Very large print accompanied by beautiful paint-
> ings of spring landscapes.

I Want to Go to School Too, written by Astrid Lindgren; illustrated by
Ilon Wikland. New York: Farrar, Straus and Giroux, 1987.

> Lena is five years old and curious about school. At home she plays school
> every day. Then one morning Peter takes her to visit his class. Lena is finally
> accepted by the older children when, during nature study, she is the only
> one able to identify a small stuffed bird held by the teacher. Excellent for
> reading aloud during the first days of the school year.

Little Hippo, written by Frances Charlotte Allen; illustrated by Laura
Jean Allen. New York: G. P. Putnam's Sons, 1971.

> After Little Hippo's mother surprises him with a baby sister, he is never lonely
> again. A simple and short animal story that appeals to children as young as
> two years of age.

Lovable Lyle, written and illustrated by Bernard Waber. Boston:
Houghton Mifflin Co., 1969.

> Lyle the Crocodile is a favorite character of children, but in this book he
> finds he has an enemy. "Someone out there hates me." A mystery story with
> suspense and excitement for young children.

Mirandy and Brother Wind, written by Patricia C. McKissack;
illustrated by Jerry Pinkney. New York: Alfred A. Knopf, 1988.

> The author bases her story on an old photograph of her grandparents dated
> 1906. Teenagers at the time, her grandparents had just won a cakewalk (first
> introduced in America by slaves, the cakewalk is a dance rooted in Afro-
> American culture). Mirandy and Ezel are the teenage couple determined to
> win their first cakewalk and its prize of an elaborately decorated cake. As the
> author writes the story she imagines her grandparents "strutting around a
> square with their backs arched, toes pointed, and their heads held high."

Miss Rumphius, written and illustrated by Barbara Cooney. New York:
The Viking Press, 1982.

> As a young girl Alice has three goals in mind for herself. She wants to travel
> the world over and then she wants to come home and live by the sea. The
> third desire she has is to find a way to make the world a bit more beautiful.
> Alice grows up to be Miss Rumphius and accomplishes all three wishes. This
> sensitive story describes the legacy of an artist and the process of graceful,
> productive aging.

One Wide River to Cross, adapted by Barbara Emberley and illustrated
by Ed Emberley. Englewood Cliffs, N.J.: Prentice-Hall, 1966.

> A famous writing-illustrating team has made use of wood block prints to il-
> lustrate this popular old folk song. The story gives children counting prac-
> tice as Noah's animals come two by two, three by three, and ten by ten.

Sparky, The Story of a Little Trolley Car, written and illustrated by Hardie Gramatky. New York: G. P. Putnam's Sons, 1952.

> Sparky the Trolley Car's wonderful imagination livens up his routine job of running back and forth on the same track. Hardie Gramatky's stories about machines personified are always extremely popular with children.

Tell Me a Story, Mama, written by Angela Johnson; illustrated by David Soman. New York: Franklin Watts, Inc., 1989.

> A subtle, humorous book about a young girl who requests a bedtime story. As it turns out she does all the telling while her mother simply confirms each fact with "uh-huh", "yes", "no sir!", and other appropriate comments. Children and parents who share the experience of storytelling will be familiar with the interaction between mother and daughter.

Tom and Pippo and the Washing Machine, written and illustrated by Helen Oxenbury. New York: Macmillan Publishing Company, 1988.

> Tom's toy monkey, Pippo, is due for a tumble in the washing machine. Tom watches and worries through each cycle of the washing and then talks to Pippo as he dries on the clothesline. Bold illustrations, large print, and easy-to-read text.

Two Lonely Ducks, written and illustrated by Roger Duvoisin. New York: Alfred A. Knopf, Inc., 1955.

> Children are given three separate counting situations in this book. They count the eggs laid by the mother duck, they count the days she sits on them, and finally they count the ducklings that hatch out.

Umbrella, written and illustrated by Taro Yashima. New York: The Viking Press, 1958.

> Momo's third birthday brings a new umbrella and red rubber boots, but it is many days before the rain comes. Something special happens to Momo when she carries the umbrella. Beautiful Japanese art. Excellent for reading to very young children.

Uncle Elephant, written and illustrated by Arnold Lobel. New York: Harper & Row, Publishers, 1981.

> When Mother and Father Elephant are lost at sea, their young son is cared for by Uncle Elephant, an old, old uncle who says, "My back creaks, my knees creak, my feet creak, even my trunk creaks." In the days to follow, the young elephant and the old one learn to know and appreciate each other. Arnold Lobel has drawn a picture of an elderly family member who contributes to the welfare of the young, just the way it might happen in any family. One in a long list of "I Can Read" books.

A Week of Lullabies, compiled and edited by Helen Plotz; illustrated by Marisabina Russo. New York: Greenwillow Books, 1988.

> A collection of fourteen good-night poems, two for each night of the week. Excellent as a bedtime companion. It contains poems by such favorites as Robert Louis Stevenson, Alfred Lord Tennyson, Aileen Fisher, and Karla Kuskin. Bold, colorful illustrations contain fascinating details for discussion between adult and child.

What Happened Today, Freddy Groundhog?, written and illustrated by Marvin Glass. New York: Crown Publishers, Inc., 1989.

> Freddy suffers from low self-esteem after days of criticism and ridicule by the other groundhogs. He is determined to become a star on February 2, Groundhog Day. On the dot, Freddy's mother wakes him from hibernation, brushes his fur, and sends him to the surface. Farmer Brown shouts, "This here groundhog can't find his shadow. That means we're going to have an early spring." That evening the entire groundhog family comes out to see Freddy on TV.

Where's Julius?, written and illustrated by John Burningham. New York: Crown Publishers, Inc., 1986.

> Julius is simply too busy exploring the Lombo Bombo River and cooling the hippopotamuses with pails of water to come to lunch. He's also too busy crossing the Novosti Kroski ice field by sleigh in Russia to come to supper. Julius is a boy prone to high adventure, but his parents are patient and understanding and eventually Julius favors them with his presence at the table. John Burningham has won many awards, including two Kate Greenaway Medals, for his children's books.

• BIBLIOGRAPHY

Applebee, Arthur N. *The Child's Concept of Story.* Chicago: The University of Chicago Press, 1978.

Bronfenbrenner, Urie. "Who Cares for America's Children?" *Young Children* 26 (1971):157–63.

Carroll, Ruth, and Latrobe Carroll. *Tough Enough.* New York: Henry Z. Walck, Inc., 1954.

The Children's Book Council, Inc., 67 Irving Place, P.O. Box 706, New York, N.Y. 10276.

Croft, Doreen J. *Parents and Teachers: A Resource Book for Home, School, and Community Relations.* Belmont, Calif.: Wadsworth Publishing Company, Inc., 1979.

Larrick, Nancy. *A Parent's Guide to Children's Reading.* 4th ed. New York: Pocket Books, 1975.

———. *Encourage Your Child to Read.* New York: Dell Publishing Company, Inc., 1980.

Lawson, Robert. "The Caldecott Medal Acceptance." *The Hornbook Magazine* 17 (1941):273–8.

Lipson, Eden Ross. *The New York Times Parent's Guide to the Best Books for Children.* New York: Random House, Inc., 1988.

Monroe, Marion, and Bernice Rogers. *Foundations for Reading, Informal Pre-Reading Procedures.* Glenview, Ill.: Scott, Foresman & Co., 1964.

Oxley, Mary. *An Illustrated Guide to Individual Kindergarten Instruction.* New York: Parker Publishing Co., 1977.

Rudolph, Marguerita, and Dorothy H. Cohen. *Kindergarten, A Year of Learning.* New York: Appleton-Century-Crofts, 1964.

Shedd, Charlie, and Martha Shedd. *Tell Me a Story, Stories for Your Grandchildren and the Art of Telling Them.* Garden City, N.Y.: Doubleday & Company, 1984.

11

"What's Black and White and Read All Over?":

The Newspaper as Literature

The main purpose of a free press is to provide citizens with vital information they need to help them survive and succeed in society. By the same token, the primary function of early childhood education is to aid in the development of competent, skillful citizens who will be able to make worthy contributions to the world in which they live. When we consider two such similar goals, the role of the newspaper in kindergarten and primary classrooms becomes much more than just another instructional tool.

If we acknowledge that newspapers serve to ensure our freedom and independence, then we must also view newspapers as suitable literature for young children. Even the youngest pupils in school can be led to discover that the daily newspaper holds important messages for them and will continue to do so throughout their lives.

Although most young children have yet to accomplish the specific reading skills necessary for critical, analytical reading, creative teaching of the newspaper can help them synthesize the main functions of a newspaper: to give information, to offer opinions, to provide service, and to entertain. When newspapers are used routinely as part of the daily curriculum, students will find themselves studying them for a variety of reasons, such as locating news stories for class discussion, seeking out the viewpoint of a school board member, scanning the television guide for reviews of a favorite program, or laughing at the actions of a popular comic strip character. There is definitely something in the newspaper for every classroom and every child in a classroom.

Teachers who are, with good cause, interested in the cost and practicality of any material selected for classroom use would be hard-pressed to find a more economical or practical teaching tool than the daily paper. The newspaper is accessible and inexpensive. Most households subscribe to at least one paper and are usually more than willing to donate it to a classroom. (A day-old paper is as effective as a current one where young children are concerned.)

The newspaper is expendable. Because it is so transient, it provides an appealing change for teachers and children alike. Textbooks can be pretty formidable at times. The newspaper is varied. Each issue brings interesting surprises and helps to dispel the monotony that plagues much of education. The newspaper is relevant and popular, and every issue contains articles of keen interest and significance to children, running the gamut from human interest stories to animal and sports stories. Motivation is seldom a problem when newspapers are literally spread all over the classroom.

Suggested Activities _____

Reading

- Plan an exercise in which children search for familiar logos and brand names. Ask them to cut out the logos and paste them on poster board for rereading (fig. 11.1).

Figure 11.1.   Two kindergarten boys are searching the newspaper for letters and logos they recognize. (Courtesy Helena Park Elementary School, Nederland, Texas.)

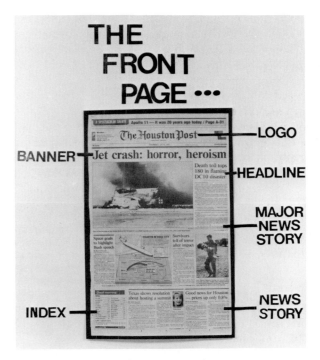

Figure 11.2.   A front page with important parts
labeled forms an instructional bulletin board.

- Assign groups of students to compile alphabet books by cutting
  large letters from headlines. Each letter may be illustrated with
  newspaper or magazine pictures.

- Mount a front page on the bulletin board and label the main
  parts (see fig. 11.2). Teach the main parts of the paper by
  name.

- Collect favorite comic strips for a class scrapbook. Place it in
  the reading or library center for independent use.

- Teach the main features of newspaper articles by name using
  the inverted pyramid as a guide (see fig. 11.3). Note: Not all
  elements are found in every article.

- Assist more advanced readers to locate Who? What? When?
  Where? Why? and How? in newspaper articles. For emphasis,
  these features may be underlined with colored markers.

- Make a set of flash cards containing comic strip characters. Ask
  children to identify characters by name and strip title, such as
  Charlie Brown from *Peanuts*.

**NEWS STORY
THE INVERTED PYRAMID**

LEAD

MOST IMPORTANT DETAILS

MAIN BODY

LESS
IMPORTANT
DETAILS

LEAST
IMPORTANT
DETAILS

Figure 11.3.   The traditional inverted pyramid with labels helps to teach the main features found in most newspaper articles. (Courtesy of Barbara Ellis.)

- Plan newspaper activities that "walk" readers through the various levels of reading comprehension—literal, interpretive, critical, and creative.

Speaking and Listening

- Mount popular comic strips on construction paper. Cut the frames apart. Keep an unmutilated copy of each strip for self-checking. As children work in pairs let one tell the story while the other listens. The listener then arranges the strip in proper sequence based on the storyteller's effectiveness in presenting details. Pairs may then repeat the process with other strips.

- Collect animal stories from the newspaper over several days. Ask students to present the stories to the class in the form of oral summaries.

- Ask students to study the action in a favorite comic strip. Encourage them to describe the action orally. Check for accuracy of comprehension and observe descriptive terms used.

- Select newspaper articles that have child appeal and tape-record them. As children listen to the teacher, they are able to read the same article at a more rapid rate and with better comprehension.

- Arrange for older students to read newspaper articles aloud to young children in a cross-age grouping procedure.

WRITE YOUR OWN NEWS STORY

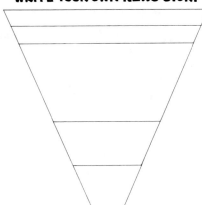

Figure 11.4.   Provide blank inverted pyramids on which children may write the main features as they find them in reading an article or in writing their own. (Enlarge diagram to 8¼″ × 11″.)

Writing

- Provide blank inverted pyramids and help children write their own articles inside them (fig. 11.4).

- Duplicate copies of student writing to compose a classroom newspaper (fig. 11.5).

- Use paper folding as a technique for recording Who? What? When? Where? Why? and How? as they are gleaned from newspaper articles (fig. 11.6).

- Duplicate copies of a "comprehension herringbone" and ask students to write the five Ws and H on the diagram as they locate them in an article. The article may then be cut out and clipped to the drawing for later checking (fig. 11.7).

Social Studies

- Discuss the part a free press plays in our democracy and the obligation of the press to report accurately.

- Relate the idea of a free press to freedom of speech guaranteed in the Bill of Rights.

- Classify newspaper stories into local, state, national, and international news. Use large maps to locate the origin of news stories.

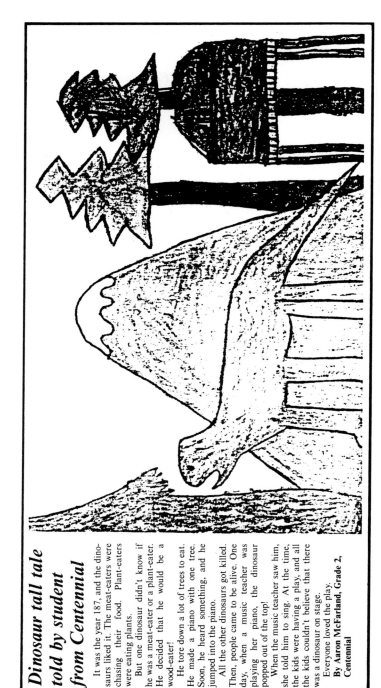

Dinosaur tall tale told by student from Centennial

It was the year 187, and the dinosaurs liked it. The meat-eaters were chasing their food. Plant-eaters were eating plants.

But one dinosaur didn't know if he was a meat-eater or a plant-eater. He decided that he would be a wood-eater!

He tore down a lot of trees to eat. He made a piano with one tree. Soon, he heard something, and he jumped into the piano.

All the other dinosaurs got killed. Then, people came to be alive. One day, when a music teacher was playing her piano, the dinosaur popped out of the top!

When the music teacher saw him, she told him to sing. At the time, the kids were having a play, and all the kids couldn't believe that there was a dinosaur on stage.

Everyone loved the play.
By Aaron McFarland, Grade 2, Centennial

Figure 11.5. This second grade boy's story, which was selected for the school paper, has captured the essence of a tall tale. (Courtesy Janean B. Davis and Centennial Elementary School, Nampa, Idaho.)

PAPER FOLDING

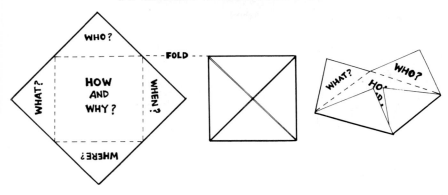

Figure 11.6.   On squares of folded paper, children write the "five W's and an H" as they locate them in a news story. They then cut out the newspaper article and fold it inside for others to read.

COMPREHENSION HERRINGBONE

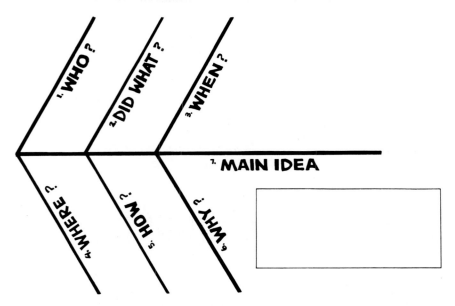

Figure 11.7.   Copies of the "comprehension herringbone" placed in the reading or writing center help children locate and list the main features of a newspaper article. (Courtesy of Barbara Ellis.)

- Compile a topical scrapbook of newspaper clippings over a period of days. Select an appropriate social studies topic such as "Our President Visits Europe."
- Invite a local reporter to your class to discuss how the news is covered. Help students prepare pertinent questions to ask your resource person.

Science

- Collect clippings pertaining to conservation and the environment. Discuss the concepts inherent in such stories. Compile a list of words connected with environmental issues; write them on the chalkboard.
- Make a monthly weather calendar and record the daily weather as reported by the paper. Help children become efficient in interpreting weather maps.
- Study the farm and gardening section of the paper. Discuss the purposes of this section and the people who rely on the information it provides.
- Use a collection of newspaper clippings to illustrate an instructional unit on health and safety.
- Ask students to identify various sources of energy alluded to in different newspaper articles. List them on a vocabulary chart.

Mathematics

- Ask students to collect examples of the use of fractions, decimals, percentage, and so on from the paper. File them in a "numbers" box for future reference.
- Compare different types of graphs found in the newspaper (bar, line, circle, pictograph, etc.). Discuss the reasons why different types of graphs are used.
- Survey the class to determine the most popular comic strip. Plot the results on a large bar graph for the bulletin board. Compare results with other classes in the school.
- Read the maximum temperature each day in the paper for one month and plot the numbers on a large line graph.
- Compile grocery lists from food advertisements and calculate the sum of each list. (Limit each student to a set number of items.)

Art

- Make a layout of a newspaper page by pasting headlines, articles, stories and other features on a large poster board. Use only student work and illustrate how all pieces must fit together just right. This is a good way to point out that art is order.

- Recycle newspapers by using them for a variety of painting and crafts projects in the classroom. Newsprint makes an excellent "canvas" for tempera, watercolors, pastels, felt point pens, crayons, and paste. Children can relax and paint to their heart's content without the usual admonition to save paper. The familiar papier-mâché technique we grew up with is as effective as ever and provides creative and challenging enjoyment to each new generation of children.

This chapter has illustrated only a small sample of the many activities available to teachers who wish to guide children toward becoming discerning consumers of the daily newspaper. If the newspaper needs justification as literature, teachers should remind themselves that newspapers are read more systematically and over more years in a person's lifetime than either books or magazines. Our primary concern as teachers of literature is to develop efficient readers who will read and understand *all* kinds of reading material.

For information on the newspaper's role in education, write your local newspaper's headquarters. Be specific in your requests as to grade level and subject area. Two other excellent sources for teachers are:

Newspaper in Education Manager
American Newspaper Publishers' Foundation
P.O. Box 17407
Dulles International Airport
Washington, DC 20041

and

International Reading Association
800 Barksdale Road, P.O. Box 8139
Newark, Delaware 19714–8139 USA

CHILDREN'S BOOKS RELATED TO WRITING

A German Printer, written by Giovanni Caselli; illustrated by N. J. Heweston. New York: Peter Bedrick Books, 1987.

> The story of a young boy living around A.D. 1485 who serves as an apprentice in his father's printing plant. The story begins with the invention of a system of printing by Johannes Gutenberg. For the first time, thousands of books and papers could be printed easily and quickly. An excellent source to use with a "Newspaper in the Classroom" unit.

How Paper Is Made, written by Lesley Perrins; designed by Arthur Lockwood. New York: Facts on File, Inc., 1985.

> The process of papermaking is explained by means of color photography supplemented by art work and text. Introduces children to the idea of recycling paper and carefully explains the need for a "waste not, want not" philosophy.

If You Were a Writer, written by Joan Lowery Nixon; illustrated by Bruce Degen. New York: Four Winds Press, 1988.

> Melia's mother is a writer who gradually and subtly introduces Melia to the craft of creative writing. In the process, readers are led to discover all the elements needed in creating a story. Children are encouraged to find stories of their own to be recorded in written form. An excellent companion book to *How a Book Is Made.*

If the Dinosaurs Came Back, written and illustrated by Bernard Most. New York: Harcourt Brace Jovanovich, 1978.

> A picture book depicting a child's fantasy game, "What if the dinosaurs came back?" The author was inspired to write the book by his eight-year-old son, who loved the dinosaurs so much he wished they would come back. A classroom writing project might be initiated with the book as children write their own "what ifs?"

Paper, written and illustrated by Elizabeth Simpson Smith. New York: Walker and Company, 1984.

> This book maintains that most individuals use close to one-thousand pounds of paper each year without realizing it. It looks into the history and evolution of papermaking and includes a chapter entitled "Papermaking and You." It offers teachers a list of paper companies to write to for information on careers in papermaking—manufacturing, engineering, research, sales, and management.

The Secret Life of School Supplies, by Vicki Cobb; illustrated by Bill Morrison. New York: J. B. Lippincott, 1981.

> Discusses the scientific and technological processes used in manufacturing paper, ink, pens, chalk, pencils, carbon paper, paste, glue, and erasers. Includes experiments and formulas for making school supplies at home and in the classroom. Illustrated with humorous, cartoonlike drawings.

appendix a

Caldecott Award Books

The Caldecott Medal is awarded annually by the Association for Library Services to Children, a Division of the American Library Association. It is awarded to the artist of the most distinguished picture book for children published in the United States during the preceding year. The Caldecott Medal has been awarded for the following books:

1990 — *Lon Po Po: A Red Riding Hood Story from China* by Ed Young. (Philomel Books)

1989 — *Song and Dance Man* by Stephen Gammell. Text by Karen Ackerman. (Knopf)

1988 — *Owl Moon* by Jane Yolen. Text by John Schoenherr. (Putnam's)

1987 — *Hey, Al* by Richard Egielski. Text by Arthur Yorinks. (Farrar)

1986 — *The Polar Express* by Chris Van Allsburg. (Houghton Mifflin)

1985 — *Saint George and the Dragon* by Trina Schart Hyman. Text by Margaret Hodges. (Little)

1984 — *The Glorious Flight: Across the Channel with Lois Bleriot July 25, 1909* by Alice and Martin Provensen. (Viking)

1983 — *Shadow* by Marcia Brown. Text by Blaise Cendrars. (Scribner's)

1982 — *Jumanji* by Chris Van Allsburg. (Houghton Mifflin)

1981 — *Fables* by Arnold Lobel. (Harper & Row)

1980 — *Ox-Cart Man* by Barbara Cooney. Text by Donald Hall. (Viking)

1979 — *The Girl Who Loved Wild Horses* by Paul Goble. (Bradbury)

1978 — *Noah's Ark* by Peter Spier. (Doubleday)
1977 — *Ashanti to Zulu: African Traditions* by Leo and Diane Dillon. Text by Margaret Musgrove. (Dial)
1976 — *Why Mosquitos Buzz in People's Ears* by Leo and Diane Dillon. Text by Verna Aardema. (Dial)
1975 — *Arrow to the Sun* by Gerald McDermott. (Viking)
1974 — *Duffy and the Devil* by Margot Zemach. Text by Harve Zemach. (Farrar)
1973 — *The Funny Little Woman* by Blair Lent. Text by Arlene Mosel. (Dutton)
1972 — *One Fine Day* by Nonny Hogrogian. (Macmillan)
1971 — *A Story, A Story* by Gail E. Haley. (Atheneum)
1970 — *Sylvester and the Magic Pebble* by William Steig. (Simon & Schuster)
1969 — *The Fool of the World and the Flying Ship* by Uri Shulevitz. Text by Arthur Ransome. (Farrar)
1968 — *Drummer Hoff* by Ed Emberley. Text by Barbara Emberley. (Prentice-Hall)
1967 — *Sam, Bangs, and Moonshine* by Evaline Ness. (Holt)
1966 — *Always Room for One More* by Nonny Hogrogian. Text by Sorche Nic Leodhas. (Holt)
1965 — *May I Bring a Friend?* by Beni Montresor. Text by Beatrice Schenk de Regniers. (Atheneum)
1964 — *Where the Wild Things Are* by Maurice Sendak. (Harper)
1963 — *The Snowy Day* by Ezra Jack Keats. (Viking)
1962 — *Once a Mouse . . .* by Marcia Brown. (Scribner's)
1961 — *Baboushka and the Three Kings* by Nicolas Sidjakov. Text by Ruth Robbins. (Parnassus)
1960 — *Nine Days to Christmas* by Marie Hall Ets. Text by Marie Hall Ets and Aurora Labastida. (Viking)
1959 — *Chanticleer and the Fox* by Barbara Cooney. (Crowell)
1958 — *Time of Wonder* by Robert McCloskey. (Viking)
1957 — *A Tree Is Nice* by Marc Simont. Text by Janice May Udry. (Harper)
1956 — *Frog Went A-Courtin'* by Fedor Rojankovsky. Text by John Langstaff. (Harcourt)
1955 — *Cinderella, or the Little Glass Slipper* by Marcia Brown. Text by Charles Perrault. (Scribner's)
1954 — *Madeline's Rescue* by Ludwig Bemelmans. (Viking)
1953 — *The Biggest Bear* by Lynd Ward. (Houghton)
1952 — *Finders Keepers* by Nicholas Mordvinoff. Text by William Lipkind and Nicholas Mordvinoff. (Harcourt)

1951 — *The Egg Tree* by Katherine Milhous. (Scribner's)

1950 — *Song of the Swallows* by Leo Politi. (Scribner's)

1949 — *The Big Snow* by Berta and Elmer Hader. (Macmillan)

1948 — *White Snow, Bright Snow* by Roger Duvoisin. Text by Alvin Tresselt (Lothrop)

1947 — *The Little Island* by Leonard Weisgard. Text by Golden MacDonald. (Doubleday)

1946 — *The Rooster Crows: A Book of American Rhymes and Jingles* by Maud and Miska Petersham. (Macmillan)

1945 — *A Prayer for a Child* by Elizabeth Orton Jones. Text by Rachel Lyman Field. (Macmillan)

1944 — *Many Moons* by Louis Slobodkin. Text by James Thurber. (Harcourt)

1943 — *The Little House* by Virginia Lee Burton. (Houghton)

1942 — *Make Way for Ducklings* by Robert McCloskey. (Viking)

1941 — *They Were Strong and Good* by Robert Lawson. (Viking)

1940 — *Abraham Lincoln* by Ingri and Edgar Parin d'Aulaire. (Doubleday)

1939 — *Mei Li* by Thomas Handforth. (Doubleday)

1938 — *Animals of the Bible: A Picture Book* by Dorothy P. Lathrop. Text selected from the King James Bible by Helen Dean Fish. (Lippincott)

appendix b

Publisher Index ▽

Abelard-Schuman, Ltd., 6 W. 57th St., New York, NY 10019.
Abingdon Press, 201 8th Ave., S., Nashville, TN 37202.
Allyn & Bacon, Inc., 470 Atlantic Ave., Boston, MA 02110.
American Heritage Press, 551 5th Ave., New York, NY 10017.
Appleton-Century-Crofts, 440 Park Ave., S., New York, NY 10016.
Association for Childhood Education, International, 3615 Wisconsin Ave., N.W., Washington, DC 20016.
Barron's Educational Series, Inc., 250 Wireless Boulevard, Hauppauge, NY 11788.
Blaisdell Publishing Co., Inc., 255 Wyman St., Waltham, MA 02154.
Brown, Wm. C. Publishers, 2460 Kerper Blvd., Dubuque, IA 52001.
Carolrhoda Books, Inc., 241 First Ave., North, Minneapolis, MN 55401.
Children First Press, Box 8008, Ann Arbor, MI 48107.
Columbia University Press, 440 W. 110th St., New York, NY 10026.
Coward-McCann, Inc., 200 Madison Ave., New York, NY 10016.
Crowell, Thomas Y., 10 East 53rd St., New York, NY 10022.
Crown Publishers, Inc., 225 Park Ave., South, New York, NY 10003.
Day, The John Co., 62 West 45th St., New York, NY 10036.
Denison, T. S. & Co., Inc., 315 5th Ave., S., Minneapolis, MN 55415.
Dial Press, 750 3rd Ave., New York, NY 10017.
Dodd, Mead & Co., 79 Madison Ave., New York, NY 10016.
Doubleday & Co., Inc., 277 Park Ave., New York, NY 10017.
Dover Publications, Inc., 180 Varick St., New York, NY 10014.
Dutton, E. P. & Co., Inc., 201 Park Ave., S., New York, NY 10003.
Facts on File, Inc., 460 Park Avenue South, New York, NY 10016.
Farrar, Straus & Giroux, Inc., 19 Union Square West, New York, NY 10003.
Fearon Pitman Publishers, Inc., 6 Davis Drive, Belmont, CA 94002.

Firefly Books Ltd., 250 Sparks Avenue, Willowdale, Ontario, Canada.

Follett Publishing Co., 1010 W. Washington Blvd., Chicago, IL 60607.

Golden Press, Inc., 850 Third Ave., New York, NY 10022.

Greenwillow Books, 105 Madison Ave., New York, NY 10016.

Harcourt Brace Jovanovich, 757 Third Ave., New York, NY 10017.

Harper & Row, Publishers, 49 E. 33rd St., New York, NY 10016.

Heath, D. C. & Co., 285 Columbus Ave., Boston, MA 02116.

Holiday House, 18 E. 53rd St., New York, NY 10022.

Holt, Rinehart & Winston, Inc., 282 Madison Ave., New York, NY 10017.

Horn Book, Inc., 585 Boylston St., Boston, MA 02116.

Houghton Mifflin Co., 53 We. 43rd St., New York, NY 10036.

Indiana University Press, 10th & Morton Sts., Bloomington, IN 47401.

Kendall/Hunt Publishing Co., 2460 Kerper Blvd., Dubuque, IA 52001.

Knopf, Alfred A., Inc., 501 Madison Ave., New York, NY 10022.

KTAV Publishing House, Inc., Box 6249, Hoboken, NJ 07030.

Lane Magazine and Book Co., Menlo Park, CA 94205.

Lippincott, J. B. Co., E. Washington Sq., Philadelphia, PA 19105.

Little, Brown & Co., 34 Beacon St., Boston, MA 02106.

Longmeadow Press, 201 High Ridge Road, P.O. Box 10218, Stamford, CT 06904.

Lothrop, Lee & Shepard Co., 419 Park Ave., S., New York, NY 10016.

Macmillan Co., The, 866 Third Ave., New York, NY 10022.

McKay, David Co., Inc., 750 Third Ave., New York, NY 10017.

McGraw-Hill Book Co., 330 W. 42nd St., New York, NY 10036.

Merrill, Charles E. Books, Inc., College Div., 1300 Alum Creek Dr., Columbus, OH 43216.

Morrow, William and Co., 425 Park Ave., S., New York, NY 10016.

National Council of Teachers of English, 508 S. Sixth St., Champaign, IL 61820.

New American Library, Inc., 1301 Ave. of the Americas, New York, NY 10019.

Odyssey Press, Inc., 55 5th Ave., New York, NY 10003.

Oxford University Press, Inc., 200 Madison Ave., New York, NY 10016. Orders to 1600 Pollitte Drive, Fair Lawn, NJ 07410.

Pantheon Books, Inc., 22 E. 51st St., New York, NY 10022.

Parents Magazine Press, 52 Vanderbilt Ave., New York, NY 10017.

Philomel Books, 51 Madison Ave., New York, NY 10010.

Pocket Books, 1 W. 39th St., New York, NY 10018.

Prentice-Hall, Inc., 70 5th Ave., New York, NY 10011.

Putnam's, G. P. Sons, 200 Madison Ave., New York, NY 10016.

Scarecrow Press, Inc., 52 Liberty St., Box 656, Metuchen, NJ 08840.

Scholastic Book Services, 50 W. 44th St., New York, NY 10036.

Scott, Foresman and Co., 1900 E. Lake Ave., Glenview, IL 60025.

Scott, William R., Inc., 333 Avenue of the Americas, New York, NY 10014.

Scribner's, Charles Sons, 597 Fifth Ave., New York, NY 10017.

Steck-Vaughn Co., Box 2028, Austin, TX 78761.

Tuttle, Charles E. Co., 28 S. Main St., Rutland, VT 05701.

University of Texas Press, Austin, TX 78712.

Vanguard Press, 424 Madison Ave., New York, NY 10017.

Von Nostrand Co., Inc., Princeton, NJ 08540.

Viking Press, Inc., 625 Madison Ave., New York, NY 10022.

Walck, Henry Z. Inc., 19 Union Square, W. New York, NY 10003.

Warne, Frederick & Co., Inc., 40 W. 23rd St., New York, NY 10010.

Warner Books, Inc., 666 Fifth Ave., New York, NY 10103.

Watts, Franklin, Inc., 575 Lexington Ave., New York, NY 10022.

Wilson, H. W. Co., 950 University Ave., Bronx, NY 10452.

index